Celebrations Italian Style

OTHER BOOKS BY MARY ANN ESPOSITO

*Ciao Italia: Traditional Italian
Recipes from Family Kitchens*

*Nella Cucina: More Italian Cooking
from the Host of* Ciao Italia

Celebrations Italian Style

Recipes

and

Menus

for

Special

Occasions

and

Seasons

of the

Year

Mary Ann Esposito

Illustrations by Tomie dePaola

Hearst Books   *New York*

It is the policy of William Morrow and Company, Inc., and
its imprints and affiliates, recognizing the importance of preserving
what has been written, to print the books we publish on acid-free
paper, and we exert our best efforts to that end.

Library of Congress Cataloging-in-Publication Data

Esposito, Mary Ann.
    Celebrations Italian style: recipes and menus for special
occasions and seasons of the year / Mary Ann Esposito.
        p.   cm.
    Includes index.
    ISBN 0-688-13038-0
    1. Cookery, Italian. 2. Holiday cookery. 3. Menus.
I. Title.
TX723.E85 1995
641.5945—dc20   95-3055
                                                        CIP

Printed in the United States of America

First Edition

1 2 3 4 5 6 7 8 9 10

BOOK DESIGN BY RICHARD ORIOLO

For Guy

My wonderful husband

and best friend,

who loves Italy as

much as I do

*S*ono fortunata. I am fortunate to have had the help of many wonderful people, whose extraordinary talents have made this book possible. *Mille grazie* to Harriet Bell, executive editor at William Morrow, my publisher, who has been my guide since the very first book; my admiration and respect for her run very deep. To my good friend Tomie dePaola, world-renowned children's author and artist, whose engaging illustrations have brought my folk stories to life; his work is a treasure, and for him, there is no end to the *baci*. To photographer Bill Truslow and food stylist Trish Dahl, for their energy, attention to detail, and ability to translate my recipes into photographs worth thousands of words. To Glenn Gerace and John Seath of City and Country, for loaning their beautiful kitchenware and props for the photographs. To my mother, Louise Saporito, who diligently helped with the testing of the recipes, as did meticulous cooks and friends Ruth Moore and Jan Enzmann. To Louis Terramagra and his staff, for their generous time and talent. To Christine Hoppe of the Italian Department of the University of New Hampshire. To copy editor Judith Sutton, and to Kathleen Hackett for their valuable suggestions.

Sincere thanks and gratitude to NYNEX, Joe Pace and Son Grocer of Boston, and Kitchen Etc., whose generous financial support has made possible the production of my television series, *Ciao Italia*.

To Guy, Beth, and Chris, for their constant support; I love you all. And to my agent, Michael Jones, for his professional guidance.

Acknowledgments

Special Acknowledgment

*T*o Joan Norris, Marketing Director of the Isabella Stewart Gardner Museum in Boston, Massachusetts, for graciously allowing us to photograph the book cover in the courtyard of Fenway Court, a Venetian-style palazzo housing an exquisite collection of European and American art.

Contents

This book offers Italian recipes with menu suggestions for holidays, seasons of the year, and special occasions. It contains traditional and nontraditional (*cucina nuova*) recipes for entertaining at home.

With this book, I occasionally step over tradition's line, creating contemporary recipes based on classic Italian cooking techniques. You will find versions of traditional stuffed pasta dishes, such as *caramelle di pasta*, twisted wrappers of beet-flavored pasta filled with a fresh Gorgonzola cheese filling, and eye-appealing vegetable combinations, such as individual Swiss chard molds encasing a delicate potato filling. But you will also find an unusual, tasty, and thrifty soup made with cheese rinds and something old, but also new, a spectacular Italian wedding cookie cake, which always gets more attention than the wedding cake itself.

These recipes have been served time and again to guests who have come to my kitchen for an informal supper by the fireplace as well as to those who have been guests at larger celebrations like Christmas and Easter.

In addition there are foods for gift giving, with a chapter devoted to making fruit vinegars, flavored olive oils, spicy mustard, almond candy, zucchini chips, two-colored biscotti, and more.

When it comes to holidays and special occasions, I am a hopeless sentimentalist, regarding these occasions as unique links in our lives that reaffirm our feelings about those we care about. For me, the preparing and sharing of food is one of the best expressions of those feelings. When I am working in the kitchen for long hours, I recall the wise words of my father, who never wavered in his belief that "the best place to eat is always at home," no matter what the occasion. The recipes in this book reaffirm that belief.

If you are familiar with my previous cookbooks, you know how much I value the traditions surrounding Italian food. Much of what is known about these traditions can be found in culinary manuscripts, books, and other historical documents or has been handed down orally, often through folktales. I have added to that tradition by including my own stories about how such regional classic dishes as *maccheroni alla chitarra* (pasta cut on a musical instrument), from Abruzzo, and *colomba*, Easter bread shaped like a dove, found all over Italy, came to be.

Today, more and more people are entertaining at home not only because of the expense of eating out but because cooking for,

Introduction

and eating with, friends is a simple, honest pleasure—not merely pleasure for our senses but also the pleasure of being with others.

In Santa Caterina Villarmosa in Sicily, the home of my Grandfather Saporito, I inquired at the town office about some land our family once owned. One of the town office workers, Antonio Fiaccato, spent several hours with me, answering my inquiries, and when we were through, insisted that I have dinner at his home, with his mother and grandmother! I was welcomed as a member of the family, and treated to a wonderful *cenone*, just because my grandfather came from Antonio's town! This openness and generosity of spirit reminded me that the camaraderie of the table, sharing a meal with family and friends, knows no equal and knows no boundaries, and that as the Italians say, *A tavola non si invecchia mai*: "No one grows old at the table."

Buon appetito!

Antipasti

Appetizers

Pomodori Ripieni da Viterbo

Stuffed Tomatoes from Viterbo

🐗

Viterbo is about two hours north of Rome, a city rich with medieval architecture, ancient towers, splendid fountains, and friendly piazzas. But of all of its treasures, the most memorable to me are Viterbo's tomatoes stuffed with rice and peas. Eaten at room temperature as a merenda, or snack, they are also delicious served hot as an accompaniment to meat, poultry, or fish. I love them so much that they are a must for company when tomatoes are in season. Leftovers are good the next day.

🐗

Serves 8

8 medium tomatoes

2 tablespoons olive oil

1 small white onion, finely diced

$^{1}/_{2}$ cup long-grain rice

1 cup hot Homemade Chicken Broth (page 14)

$^{1}/_{2}$ cup fresh or frozen peas

$^{1}/_{3}$ cup fresh bread crumbs

$^{1}/_{4}$ cup diced mozzarella or caciocavallo cheese

1 tablespoon minced fresh basil

Fine sea salt and freshly ground black pepper to taste

1. Cut off the tops of the tomatoes and reserve. With a spoon, scoop the flesh and seeds from each tomato into a bowl, leaving about a $^{1}/_{4}$-inch-thick shell. If the tomatoes do not stand erect, cut a small slice off the bottom of each one. Drain the tomatoes upside down on paper towels. Strain the flesh and seeds through a sieve set over a bowl, pressing on the pulp to extract the juice, and reserve the juice. Discard the pulp and seeds.

2. In a large skillet, heat the olive oil. Add the onion and cook over medium heat until it begins to wilt. Add the rice and stir to coat it well.

3. Add the reserved tomato juice and the chicken broth, stir once, cover, and cook over low heat for 15 minutes. Add the peas and cook for 5 minutes more, or until the rice has absorbed all the liquid.

4. Transfer the rice mixture to a bowl and stir in the bread crumbs, cheese, basil, and salt and pepper.

5. Preheat the oven to 350°F. Lightly grease a baking dish with olive oil.

6. With a spoon, fill the tomato cavities with the rice mixture. Replace the tomato tops and place the tomatoes in the baking dish. Cover the dish with foil and bake the tomatoes for 30 minutes. Uncover the dish and bake for an additional 15 minutes, or until golden brown on top. Serve the tomatoes hot or at room temperature.

4 red bell peppers (about 2 pounds)

2 pounds thin asparagus, stalks trimmed

1/4 cup plus 3 tablespoons extra-virgin olive oil

1/4 cup balsamic vinegar

Fine sea salt to taste

1. Preheat the broiler. Place the peppers on a broiler pan and broil, turning, until blackened all over. Remove the peppers to a dish and let cool. Peel, core, and seed the peppers, and cut into 1/4-inch-wide strips. Set aside.

2. Preheat the oven to 350°F. Brush a cookie sheet with 1 1/2 tablespoons of the olive oil. Place the asparagus on the sheet and turn to coat with the oil. Roast for 20 to 30 minutes, until a knife is easily inserted in the stalk.

3. Remove the asparagus to a cutting board, and cut in half. Place on a platter and add the pepper strips. Add the remaining 1/4 cup plus 2 1/2 tablespoons olive oil, the balsamic vinegar, and salt, and toss gently. Cover and let marinate at room temperature for several hours before serving.

Insalata di Asparagi e Peperoni Rossi

Asparagus and Red Pepper Salad

Make this roasted asparagus and sweet red pepper salad early in the day to allow the flavors to mingle. This salad is very versatile: Serve as part of an antipasto table or instead of a mixed green salad.

Serves 8

Asparagi Fritti

Fried Asparagus

When I buy asparagus, I usually look for pencil-thin stalks, but for this dish, I prefer to use thicker stalks. The asparagus is cooked al dente, then cooled, breaded, and fried. The dish can be prepared in advance up to the frying step. After breading the asparagus, cover and refrigerate, and fry later. I serve this as a side dish or an antipasto dish.

Serves 4

1 pound thick asparagus, stalks trimmed

Fine sea salt to taste

2 large eggs

²/₃ cup toasted bread crumbs (see Note)

¹/₂ cup freshly grated Asiago or Parmigiano-Reggiano cheese

¹/₃ cup olive oil, or more as needed

1. With the tip of a knife, make a small slit in the base of each asparagus stalk.

2. Bring about 1½ cups of water to a boil in a skillet large enough to hold the asparagus in one layer. Add the asparagus and salt and cook, covered, just until a knife is easily inserted into the stalk, about 4 minutes. Carefully drain the asparagus and let cool.

3. In a shallow bowl, lightly beat the eggs. Combine the bread crumbs and cheese on a piece of wax paper.

4. Dip the asparagus spears in the eggs, then roll in the bread crumb mixture, making sure they are evenly coated, and place on a cookie sheet.

5. In a large skillet, heat the olive oil over medium-high heat. Fry the asparagus, in batches, until nicely browned, adding additional oil if needed. Drain the asparagus on brown paper, sprinkle with salt, and serve immediately.

Note: To toast the bread crumbs, preheat the oven to 300°F. Spread the crumbs on a cookie sheet and toast for about 8 to 10 minutes, until light golden brown. Remove the crumbs to a dish to cool. Or heat 2 tablespoons olive oil or butter in a skillet over medium heat. Add the crumbs and stir until well coated, then stir until the crumbs start to brown. Remove to a dish to cool.

1 bulb fennel

1 pound carrots, peeled and halved lengthwise

6 ribs celery, trimmed

1 bunch scallions

1 red bell pepper, cored, seeded, and cut into chunks

1 yellow bell pepper, cored, seeded, and cut into chunks

2 tiny artichokes, quartered (if available)

⅔ cup extra-virgin olive oil

Fine sea salt to taste

Freshly ground black pepper

1. Remove the feathery leaves from the fennel and separate the bulb into pieces, leaving the stalks attached.

2. Arrange the vegetables in a deep salad bowl: Stand the fennel, carrots, and celery on end. Place the pepper chunks and artichoke quarters, if using, in the center.

3. Pour the olive oil into a small serving bowl and add the salt and a dash of black pepper.

4. To eat, dip the vegetables in the olive oil.

Pinzimonio

Pinzimonio, an assortment of raw vegetables dipped in extra-virgin olive oil and eaten out of hand, can be served as antipasto or salad. The colorful array usually includes fennel, tiny artichokes tender enough to eat raw, sweet peppers, carrots, celery, and scallions. Leaving the vegetables in large pieces makes it easy to dip them in the olive oil.

Serves 4 to 6

Bruschetta alla Lorenza

Lorenza's Grilled Bread

❦

According to my Reggio Emilian friend Lorenza Iori, it is la madre, "the mother oil," that provides the flavorful taste to this bruschetta, which Lorenza serves as a quick antipasto. Extra-virgin olive oil is steeped with fragrant, woodsy-smelling juniper berries, hot red peppers, and bits of green bell peppers.

❦

Serves 6

2 cups extra-virgin olive oil

½ cup diced green bell pepper

1 teaspoon hot red pepper flakes or 2 small dried hot red peppers, slit

2 tablespoons juniper berries

6 slices Italian bread, cut ½ inch thick

2 to 3 cloves garlic, peeled

1. Place the oil, bell peppers, hot pepper, and juniper berries in a jar, and shake well. Let marinate in the refrigerator for at least 3 weeks. Bring to room temperature before using.

2. Toast or grill the bread slices. Place on individual serving plates, and rub the garlic over the slices. Drizzle about 2 tablespoons of the seasoned oil over each slice and serve immediately.

Note: Replenish the jar with as much oil as you used, and store for the next time.

1 clove garlic, minced, plus 5 whole cloves, unpeeled

2 ½ tablespoons olive oil

½ pound portobello mushrooms, trimmed and cleaned

Fine sea salt and freshly ground black pepper to taste

4 slices dense country bread, cut ½ inch thick

½ cup thin shavings Parmigiano-Reggiano cheese

1. Preheat the oven to 350°F. In a small baking dish, toss the garlic cloves with 1 teaspoon of the oil. Roast, turning occasionally, for about 30 minutes, or until the cloves are very soft when pierced with a knife.

2. Meanwhile, remove the mushroom stems, and slice the stems and caps into ¼-inch slices. Set aside.

3. In a large skillet, heat 1 tablespoon of the olive oil over medium heat. Add the minced garlic and sauté until it begins to soften. Do not let the garlic brown. Add the mushrooms and cook, stirring occasionally, until the mushrooms are soft and their liquid has evaporated. Season with salt and pepper and remove from the heat.

4. Place the bread slices on a baking sheet and bake for about 12 minutes, or until golden brown. Remove and set aside.

5. Peel the roasted garlic and place in a bowl with the remaining 1 tablespoon plus ½ teaspoon olive oil. Mash with a fork until smooth.

6. Spread the mashed garlic over the bread slices, and place on individual serving plates. Top with the mushrooms, sprinkle with the cheese, and serve immediately.

Bruschetta con Funghi

Portobello-Parmesan Bruschetta

Italian cooks have a wide variety of mouth-watering mushrooms to choose from. In this antipasto, sautéed slices of mild and meaty portobello mushrooms rest atop bruschetta, country bread that has been thinly spread with mashed roasted garlic and sprinkled with thin shavings of Parmigiano-Reggiano cheese.

Serves 4

Quaglie di Zucchini

Zucchini Quails

❧

This unusual method of cooking zucchini in a skillet under bricks makes a festive presentation either as an antipasto, served over crusty bread with an extra drizzle of olive oil and a few shavings of Pecorino cheese, or as an accompaniment to meat or fish. The zucchini are cut to resemble the fanned tail feathers of a bird. The success of this dish depends on using very thin, young zucchini. You will need two clean bricks or a heavy cast-iron skillet.

❧

Serves 6

3 small zucchini, about 8 inches long and 1 inch thick
3 tablespoons olive oil
2 cloves garlic, cut lengthwise in half
Fine sea salt and coarsely ground black pepper to taste
1 tablespoon chopped fresh oregano or 1 teaspoon dried

1. Cut off the stem ends of the zucchini, and cut each crosswise in half. Stand each half on one end and, with a sharp knife, cut lengthwise into ¼-inch-thick strips, cutting almost but not quite all the way through to the end (leave about ½ inch uncut at the base). Carefully fan the slices out, pressing on them lightly with your hand.

2. If you have them, wrap two clean bricks in aluminum foil.

3. In a skillet large enough to hold all the zucchini in one layer, heat the olive oil. Add the garlic and swirl it in the oil, pressing down on it with the back of a wooden spoon, until it starts to turn golden. Discard the garlic. Add the zucchini and gently place the bricks or a heavy cast-iron skillet on top of them to hold their fan shape. Cook over medium heat for about 5 minutes, or until the fans begin to brown on the underside. Remove the bricks or heavy skillet and turn the fans over. Replace the bricks or skillet and continue cooking until the fans are nicely browned on the other side.

4. Remove the zucchini fans to a serving dish, sprinkle with the salt and pepper and oregano, and serve immediately.

$^3/_4$ cup plus 1 tablespoon red wine vinegar

1 large white onion, thinly sliced

$^1/_2$ cup unbleached all-purpose flour

$1^1/_2$ teaspoons fine sea salt, or more to taste

2 pounds flounder fillets, cut into 3-inch pieces and patted dry

$^1/_2$ cup olive or vegetable oil

Freshly ground black pepper to taste

$2^1/_2$ tablespoons finely minced fresh mint

1. In a large skillet, heat $^1/_2$ cup of the vinegar. Add the onions and cook until they wilt, about 3 to 4 minutes. Remove the onions and vinegar to a shallow glass or ceramic serving dish. Wipe out the skillet and set aside.

2. Mix the flour and salt together on a plate. Dredge the fish on both sides in the flour mixture and shake off the excess.

3. Heat the oil in the skillet. Add the fish in a single layer and cook over medium heat until golden brown on both sides. (Cook in batches if necessary.) Carefully remove the fish with a slotted spatula and place on top of the onion and vinegar mixture. Pour the remaining $^1/_4$ cup plus 1 tablespoon vinegar over the fish. Season with pepper, and sprinkle on the mint.

4. Cover the dish with plastic wrap and refrigerate for at least several hours, or overnight. Occasionally tilt the dish to distribute the juices while the fish is marinating. Bring to room temperature and add salt to taste if necessary before serving.

$\mathscr{S}$capece

Marinated Fish

During long days at sea, sailors preserved their catch of fish in oil and vinegar. It is often called scapece. The best scapece, an antipasto of marinated fish, I have ever eaten was served at Ristorante Monte San Giuliano in Erice, Sicily, where fresh anchovies are marinated in vinegar and a few seasonings. Since fresh anchovies are rarely available here, this version is prepared with flounder. Fresh sardines are also a good choice.

Serves 10

Melone e Prosciutto

One of the classic antipasti is simply sweet melon accompanied by paper-thin slices of salmon-pink prosciutto. For an interesting holiday presentation, I like to cut the melon into Christmas or Easter shapes.

Serves 10

1 large cantaloupe, peeled, seeded, and cut lengthwise into
  ¼-inch slices
½ pound prosciutto, thinly sliced

1. If you like, using 1-inch cookie cutters, cut out stars, Christmas trees, angels, rabbits, eggs, or other desired shapes from the cantaloupe slices.

2. Cut the prosciutto slices crosswise in half and roll each half up like a jelly roll. Arrange the prosciutto around the outside edge of a large serving platter. Arrange the melon pieces in the center, and serve.

Variation: After cutting the melon into shapes, toss with a mixture of ½ cup fresh lemon juice, ¼ cup sugar, and 2 tablespoons minced fresh mint. Let marinate, covered, for several hours before arranging on a platter.

Zuppe

Soup

Brodo di Pollo

Homemade Chicken Broth

❦

Fresh chicken broth is easy to make and so much better than the heavily salted canned varieties. In the old days, a tough old bird was the essential ingredient for a rich-tasting broth, but I find that chicken wings produce a similarly rich flavor. I also save the bones when boning chicken breasts and freeze them until I have enough to make a big batch of broth. Freeze the broth in one- or two-cup containers, so it is always on hand.

❦

Makes 3½ to 4 quarts

4 pounds chicken parts (a combination of necks and wings and/or breast bones)

2 teaspoons coarse sea salt

2 cloves garlic, cut in half

2 large white onions, quartered

2 plum tomatoes, fresh or canned, quartered

1 bay leaf

2 sprigs each flat-leaf parsley and fresh basil, tied together with kitchen string

Juice of 1 lemon

2 ribs celery, cut into 4 pieces each

2 carrots, peeled and halved

5 black peppercorns

1. Put the chicken pieces in a large stockpot, and add the salt and cold water to cover. Cover the pot and bring to a boil. Skim off the foam with a slotted spoon. Add the remaining ingredients, reduce the heat, and simmer, covered, for 45 minutes to 1 hour. Skim off any additional foam that collects as the broth cooks.

2. Remove the chicken pieces with a slotted spoon and reserve for another use. Pour the broth and vegetables into a large strainer lined with damp cheesecloth set over another pot. With the back of a spoon, press on the vegetables to release all the juices. Discard the solids left in the strainer. Let cool, then cover the broth and refrigerate overnight.

3. With a spoon, remove the congealed fat from the top of the broth. The broth is ready to use. It can be refrigerated for up to 1 week or frozen for up to 3 months.

2 pounds veal bones

1 large carrot, peeled and quartered

1 large onion, unpeeled, quartered

2 large cloves garlic, peeled

1 teaspoon black peppercorns

1 large bay leaf

1 rib celery, cut in half

1 cup hot water

Fine sea salt and freshly ground black pepper to taste

1. Preheat the oven to 350°F. Generously oil a roasting pan. Add all the ingredients except the water and salt and pepper and roast for about 45 minutes, turning occasionally, until the veal bones are nicely browned. Transfer all of the ingredients to a large soup pot.

2. Pour the hot water into the roasting pan and, using a wooden spoon, scrape up any browned bits remaining in the pan. Add this liquid to the soup pot along with enough water to just cover the ingredients. Bring to a boil, lower the heat, and let simmer for 30 minutes.

3. Remove the bones and strain the stock through a cheese-cloth-lined colander set over a bowl. Press hard on the solids with a wooden spoon to extract all the juices. Discard the solids. Season the stock with salt and pepper. The stock is ready to use. It can be covered and refrigerated for up to 3 days or frozen for up to 3 months.

Brodo di Vitello
Veal Stock

❧

Homemade stocks can be the building blocks of flavor for so many dishes. For rich veal stock, keep a supply of inexpensive veal shoulder bones in the freezer. Veal stock provides a light flavor for mushroom- and pasta-based dishes such as the Pappardelle con Vitello on page 40.

❧

Makes 1½ quarts

Brodo di Manzo

Homemade Beef Broth

❧

I save meat bones to make beef broth, in the same way that I do for chicken broth (page 14). Beef shin is always a good choice and is readily available in supermarkets. In this recipe, I add chicken as well, an old habit from watching my Nonna Galasso do this at home. This full-bodied broth can be frozen in small containers, ready to use.

❧

Makes 2½ to 3 quarts

1 pound beef shin

1 pound beef brisket

2 to 3 beef neck bones

1½ pounds chicken parts

1 tablespoon fine sea salt

4 to 5 sprigs flat-leaf parsley

3 sprigs fresh thyme

1 bay leaf

2 red onions, cut in half

2 carrots, peeled and quartered

2 ribs celery with leaves, cut in half

2 plum tomatoes, coarsely chopped

5 black peppercorns

1. Put all the meat and the chicken in a large stockpot and cover with cold water. Add the salt and bring to a boil. Skim off the foam with a slotted spoon.

2. Tie the parsley, thyme, and bay leaf together with kitchen string and add to the pot. Lower the heat to medium, and add all the remaining ingredients, and stir with a wooden spoon. Let the broth simmer for 2½ to 3 hours. (The chicken will cook faster than the other meat; remove it when tender, after about 1 hour. Let cool, and remove the meat from the bones to use in another dish.) As the broth cooks, skim off the foam that collects on the top with a slotted spoon.

3. When the meat is tender, remove it along with the bones and reserve for another use. Pour the broth and vegetables into a colander lined with damp cheesecloth set over another pot. Press on the solids with the back of a wooden spoon to release all the juices. Discard the solids. The broth is ready to use. It can be refrigerated for up to 1 week or frozen for up to 3 months.

Note: If you want clear broth, mix 1 large egg white with a cup of the cooled broth and return this mixture to the pot of strained broth. Bring the broth to a boil and, using a wire whisk, whisk the mixture vigorously until the residue begins to float to the surface. Let simmer gently, without stirring, to allow the residue to accumulate on the surface; remove the residue with a slotted spoon.

3 pounds beef shin and neck bones

2 ribs celery, halved

2 carrots, peeled and halved

2 large onions, unpeeled, cut into quarters

1 large bay leaf

5 cloves garlic, unpeeled

8 cups water

Fine sea salt and coarsely ground black pepper to taste

1. Preheat the oven to 350°F. Lightly brush a roasting pan with olive oil. Place all the ingredients except the water and salt and pepper in the pan. Roast for 1 to 1½ hours, or until the bones and vegetables are browned.

2. Transfer all the ingredients to a large stockpot. Add the water and salt and pepper and bring to a boil. Cover, reduce the heat, and simmer for 30 to 35 minutes.

3. Remove the meat and bones from the pot with a slotted spoon and reserve for another use. Pour the vegetables and stock into a colander set over a large bowl. Press on the vegetables with the back of a spoon to extract all the juices. Discard the solids. Cover the stock and refrigerate overnight.

4. With a spoon, remove the layer of congealed fat from the top. The stock is ready to use. It can be refrigerated for up to 1 week or frozen for up to 3 months.

Consumato di Manzo

Beef Stock

❧

Beef stock lends a deeper flavor to stews, soups, and sauces than beef broth. It differs from the broth in that the meat, bones, and vegetables are roasted in the oven first to intensify their flavor, then added to the stockpot to simmer in water.

❧

Makes 2 quarts

Brodo Vegetale

Vegetable Broth

❧

This vegetable-based broth gives off the most welcoming aroma as it cooks. For a dinner party, it makes a delicious light first course. For a heartier lunch soup, add pastina, rice, or spinach. Use in any recipe that calls for clear broth.

❧

Makes 1½ quarts

2 white onions, quartered

2 leeks, white parts only, cut into quarters

2 carrots, peeled and cut into chunks

2 potatoes, peeled and quartered

1 cup sliced green beans (cut into thirds)

3 ribs celery, cut into chunks

4 ripe plum tomatoes, cut into chunks

1 large clove garlic, peeled

1 small bunch flat-leaf parsley

4 sprigs fresh thyme

1 bay leaf

1 teaspoon black peppercorns

Fine sea salt to taste

8 cups water

1. Put all the ingredients in a large stockpot and bring to a boil over high heat. Lower the heat to a simmer and cook, covered, for 2 hours.

2. Place a large colander lined with damp cheesecloth over a large bowl. Strain the broth through the colander, pressing on the vegetables with the back of a wooden spoon to release all the juices. Discard the solids in the colander. The broth is ready to use. It can be refrigerated for up to 1 week or frozen for up to 3 months.

1 pound very ripe plum tomatoes

1¼ pounds zucchini, sliced into thick rounds

¾ pound green beans

1 tablespoon butter

1 medium white onion, diced

¼ pound prosciutto, diced

1 tablespoon minced fresh basil

1 tablespoon minced flat-leaf parsley

1 teaspoon grated lemon zest

2 tablespoons fresh lemon juice

2 cups Homemade Chicken Broth (page 14)

Fine sea salt and coarsely ground black pepper to taste

1. In a large pot of boiling salted water, blanch the tomatoes for about 1 minute, just to loosen the skin. Using a slotted spoon, remove the tomatoes and let cool, then peel and dice them. Set aside.

2. Add the zucchini to the boiling water and cook until very soft, about 10 minutes. Using the slotted spoon, transfer the zucchini to a colander and drain well, then transfer to a food processor or blender.

3. Add the green beans to the boiling water and cook until tender, about 10 minutes. Drain well. Add half the beans to the food processor, and transfer the remaining beans to a bowl.

4. Process the vegetables in the processor until very smooth. Set aside. Cut the remaining beans into small pieces and set aside.

5. In a large soup pot, melt the butter over medium heat. Add the onion and prosciutto and cook until the onion is soft and the prosciutto is crisp, about 5 minutes. Add the basil and parsley and cook for 1 minute longer. Add the pureed vegetables, the remaining beans, the tomatoes, lemon zest, lemon juice, and chicken broth. Stir well. Reduce the heat to medium-low and bring just to a simmer. Season the soup with salt and pepper and ladle into bowls.

Zuppa di Estate

Summer Soup

❧

For this refreshing soup, made from fresh garden zucchini, tomatoes, green beans, and fragrant herbs, the vegetables are cooked separately to prevent overcooking, before being combined with the herbs and stock. Lemon juice and zest give the soup a refreshing clean taste.

❧

Serves 6

Zuppa di Zucchini e Menta

Zucchini-Mint Soup

This soup is a good starter for just about any occasion. To make quick work of this recipe, I keep bags of pureed zucchini and dried tomatoes in the freezer.

Serves 6

2 pounds small zucchini, cut into chunks

2 tablespoons butter

1 white onion, minced

$\frac{1}{2}$ cup finely diced Dried Tomatoes (page 310)

2 cups hot Homemade Chicken Broth (page 14)

Fine sea salt and freshly ground black pepper to taste

2 tablespoons finely minced fresh mint

Freshly grated Parmigiano-Reggiano cheese for sprinkling, optional

1. Bring a medium pot of water to a boil. Add the zucchini and cook until soft enough for a knife to penetrate the skin easily, about 10 minutes. Drain and place the chunks in a food processor or blender. Puree the zucchini until very smooth. Set aside.

2. In a soup pot, melt the butter over medium heat. Add the onion and cook until very soft but not browned. Add the tomatoes and cook for 1 minute. Stir in the zucchini, chicken broth, and salt and pepper, lower the heat, and simmer for 15 minutes. Add the mint and simmer for 5 minutes longer.

3. Ladle the soup into serving bowls and sprinkle with Parmigiano-Reggiano cheese if desired.

1½ tablespoons butter

1 teaspoon olive oil

1 medium onion, thinly sliced

3 ribs celery, thinly sliced

¼ cup minced flat-leaf parsley

1 large sprig fresh rosemary

3 cups thinly sliced zucchini

8 cups hot water

2 chicken bouillon cubes

One 3 by 3-inch piece Parmigiano-Reggiano cheese rind
(or more if you have it)

1 cup long-grain white rice

Fine sea salt and freshly ground black pepper to taste

1. In a soup pot, heat the butter and olive oil until hot. Add the onion, celery, parsley, and rosemary and cook over low heat until the vegetables soften. Add the zucchini and cook for 2 to 3 minutes. Add the water, bouillon cubes, and cheese rind and bring to a boil. Lower the heat and let simmer for 30 minutes.

2. Add the rice, raise the heat to medium-high, and cook until the rice is al dente, about 15 minutes. Season with salt and pepper.

3. Remove the cheese rind from the pot and, with a small knife, scrape off any remaining cheese. Add it to the soup and discard the rind. Serve.

Zuppa di Crosta di Formaggio

Cheese Rind Soup

This soup gets its flavor from the rinds of Parmigiano-Reggiano cheese, an ingenious Italian habit I learned from Nonna Galasso. When cheese ends can no longer be grated because they are too hard, toss them into the soup pot, where they soften and produce a wonderful, nourishing soup. Save your Parmigiano-Reggiano cheese ends and use them in vegetable, meat, and bean soups. Despite its simplicity, this first-course soup is well suited to any occasion.

Serves 6 to 8

Minestra di Fava e Anelletti

Fava Bean and Macaroni Soup

❧

When I am up to my elbows in biscotti dough during the holidays, I like to have supper ready and waiting. That's when I'm sure to have a large soup pot full of fava bean and macaroni soup on the back burner. Dried fava beans, which are available year-round, and anelletti, small ring-shaped pasta, make this a very satisfying soup. Beef bouillon cubes and water can be substituted for the stock.

❧

Serves 8 to 10

A Winter Meal in a Pot

......

Fava Bean and Macaroni Soup

Carmelo's Sicilian Bread
(page 99)

Pears with Mint
(page 204)

......

2 cups (10 ounces) dried split fava beans

1½ cups anelletti or other small macaroni

2 tablespoons olive oil

1 large onion, diced

2 cloves garlic, minced

3 tablespoons chopped flat-leaf parsley

One 16-ounce can plum tomatoes, diced, juice reserved

4 cups Beef Stock (page 17)

Fine sea salt to taste

1 cup fresh or frozen peas

Freshly grated Pecorino Romano cheese for sprinkling

1. Put the fava beans in a large pot, add 8 cups of water, and bring to a boil. Cook the beans, covered, for 12 minutes. Add the anelletti and cook, uncovered, for 10 minutes, or until the macaroni is al dente and the beans are tender but not mushy. Drain well.

2. While the beans and macaroni are cooking, heat the olive oil in a soup pot over medium heat. Add the onions, garlic, and parsley, and cook, stirring occasionally, for about 3 minutes, until the onions are wilted. Add the tomatoes, the reserved juice, and the beef stock, bring to a simmer, and cook for 3 minutes. Add the salt.

3. Stir the fava beans and macaroni into the soup. Add the peas and cook for 3 to 5 minutes longer. Ladle the soup into bowls and sprinkle with the cheese.

Note: The longer this soup sits, the thicker it gets. If you prefer, thin it with a little water or additional stock.

*Rosemary-Cranberry Sauce, Rhubarb and Fig Tart, Pumpkin Risotto,
Rolled Stuffed Veal Breast with Green Beans and Fontina*

Strawberry Tart, Oven-Fried Veal Chops, Leeks with Mustard Sauce

*R*ustic Bread, Pears with Mint, Fava Bean and Macaroni Soup

Mixed Green Salad, Ricotta Cheesecake with Pomegranate Sauce, Pork Loin with Rosemary and Wine, Ravioli Stuffed with Red Peppers and Ricotta

Zuccotto, Pasta Caramels, Poached Salmon with Herbs,
Rice and Eggplant Palermo Style

Panettone, Oven-Roasted Mixed Vegetables, Ricotta-Filled Pastry Cones, Sausage and Lentils

Wedding Cookie Cake

Nana's Easter "Dolls," Easter Dove Bread, Fried Dough Puffs,
Holiday Fruit Bread

Macaroni and Chicken in a Pastry Crust, Stuffed Shells,
Semolina Gnocchi with Red Pepper Sauce, Small Pasta Molds

Ricotta Tart, Carrot Salad, Spinach Tart

TOP ROW: *Two-Color Butterflies, Raspberry-Mint Vinegar, Cherries in Vodka, Orange Liqueur, Eggplant Preserved in Olive Oil* BOTTOM ROW: *Eggplant Salad, Prosciutto and Rosemary Breadsticks, Dried Fruit Sauce, Parsley Sauce, Basil Vinegar, Thyme-Peppercorn Oil*

Orange Cream Bavarian, Sicilian Salad, Stuffed Beef Rolls

1 large egg

½ pound ground veal

½ pound ground beef sirloin

⅓ cup fresh bread crumbs

2 tablespoons finely minced flat-leaf parsley

1½ teaspoons grated lemon zest

1 teaspoon grated nutmeg

Fine sea salt to taste

8 cups Homemade Beef Broth (page 16)

10 black peppercorns

3 cups escarole leaves, washed, drained, and torn into small pieces

Freshly grated Parmigiano-Reggiano cheese for sprinkling

1. Preheat the oven to 350°F. In a large bowl, lightly beat the egg. Add the veal, sirloin, bread crumbs, parsley, lemon zest, nutmeg, and salt and mix until well blended. Do not overmix. Form the mixture into small marble-size balls with your hands and place the meatballs on a rimmed baking sheet or in a shallow baking pan.

2. Bake for 30 minutes. Drain off the fat from the pan.

3. Meanwhile, in a large pot, combine the broth and peppercorns and bring to a boil.

4. Add the escarole to the broth, cover, and boil for 5 minutes. Add the meatballs and simmer for 5 minutes. Serve the soup in individual soup bowls and pass the cheese for sprinkling.

Zuppa di Nozze

Wedding Soup

❧

Escarole is a slightly bitter chicory that southern Italians are very fond of using in traditional wedding soup. The escarole is combined with marble-size veal and beef meatballs and simmered in a rich beef broth. The soup can be made ahead and reheated before serving.

❧

Serves 8

Do-Ahead Dinner

....

Wedding Soup

Rolled Stuffed Veal Breast
(page 156)

Polenta (page 72)

Baked Fennel (page 181)

Little Rolls (page 107)

Orange Cream Bavarian
(page 211)

....

Zuppa di Fagioli, Datteri di Mare, e Pasta

Beans, Mussels, and Pasta Soup

❧

A personal favorite for Christmas Eve is this mussel and pasta soup, thickened with two kinds of dried beans and potatoes. The original recipe comes from my friend Maria Castaldo Esposito's mother, who lives in Scisciano, near Mount Vesuvius.

❧

Serves 6 to 8

½ cup dried Great Northern or cannellini beans

½ cup dried red kidney or borlotti beans

¼ cup plus 2 tablespoons olive oil

3 cloves garlic, minced

¼ cup minced flat-leaf parsley

2 pounds mussels, scrubbed and debearded

½ cup dry white wine

1 teaspoon fine sea salt, or more to taste

Freshly ground black pepper to taste

1 large onion, chopped

2 tablespoons minced fresh basil

¼ cup chopped fennel leaves or flat-leaf parsley

2 cups diced peeled tomatoes or 2 cups Tomato-Basil Sauce (page 32)

2 medium all-purpose potatoes, peeled and cubed

2 cups cooked ditalini or elbow macaroni

1. Place the beans in a pot, cover with 5 cups of water, and bring to a boil. Cover and simmer over medium heat for 40 to 50 minutes, or until the beans are al dente. Drain, reserving 2 cups of the cooking liquid.

2. Meanwhile, heat 3 tablespoons of the olive oil in a large skillet. Add half the garlic and sauté until it softens. Add the parsley, mussels, wine, salt, and pepper, cover, and simmer until the mussels open, about 6 to 8 minutes. Scoop the mussels out of the pan with a slotted spoon and let them cool. Strain the cooking liquid into a bowl.

3. When cool enough to handle, shell the mussels, discarding any that are cracked or did not open. Add the mussels to the reserved cooking liquid, cover, and refrigerate.

4. Return the skillet to the stove and heat the remaining 3 tablespoons olive oil over medium heat. Add the remaining garlic, the onion, basil, and fennel leaves. Sauté until the onion is wilted.

Add the diced tomatoes or tomato sauce, stir well, cover, and simmer for 5 minutes. Add the beans, the reserved bean cooking liquid, and the potatoes and mix well. Cover and simmer for 25 minutes.

5. Add the mussels and their reserved liquid and cook, covered, for 5 minutes. Add the ditalini or elbow macaroni and cook for 2 to 3 minutes, until heated through. Serve immediately.

Note: If you prefer a thinner soup, add additional bean water.

Giorno dello Sposalizio

Wedding Day

❧

On the day before my wedding, a dangerous winter storm worked its way toward my home town. Even with all the last-minute details to attend to, I was concerned that many guests would not be able to get there. My mother calmed me with Italian "magic" and said that if I put a rosary on a bush outside, my wedding day would be sunny and beautiful. Done. On my wedding day, a blizzard raged. Looking outdoors early that morning, I could see neither the rosary nor the road, and I wondered how I would even get to the church!

I remember every detail about my wedding. It was no ordinary affair; an Italian wedding never is. It was the talk of the town, not because I was anyone important, but because five hundred people, from the grocer to the florist, were invited. The guests knew the food would be exceptional, prepared weeks and months ahead by a team of hardworking women, presided over by my mother, grandmothers, aunts, and all the ladies of the church kitchen at Our Lady of Pompeii. I was happy to leave the preparations to them while I concentrated on buying china and lamps.

Cookies of every description were baked for the wedding cookie cake, a pyramid of sweets, decorated with white and green confetti and trailing ribbons, which had a place of honor on the table with the wedding cake itself. Guests plucked off what they wanted. Small amounts of cookies were packaged in white netting as well, for each guest to take home.

Other family members made trays of antipasti, pasta, Italian sausage, tiny veal meatballs for the wedding soup, roasted chicken, garlic-and-rosemary-flavored oven-roasted potatoes, bitter green salads, and breads of all kinds. There were two meals for the wedding guests. The main meal was served after the one o'clock service. Then we rested and ate a "lighter" meal in the evening.

My Grandmother Saporito had the honor of tending the *busta*, a large white box in which guests deposited gifts of money, which, in Italy, are used to defray the costs of the wedding. Her other job was to roast peanuts for all the guests.

After the meal, more wine was poured, and the band played Italian music, which made the wedding guests from the old country very happy; the younger generation wanted to hear Beatles' songs.

Since half of my family is Neapolitan, we danced the tarantella. Folklore has it that the tarantella was named after the tarantola, a spider with a poisonous bite. It was associated with the city of Taranto in the region of Puglia, where the disease of tarantism was said to have originated. The only cure for the dreaded bite was to dance in a frenzy, exhausting oneself and, in effect, shaking off the bite. From the sixteenth to the nineteenth centuries, bands of traveling musicians went from place to place providing the music for the dance that would destroy the poison of the tarantola. At my wedding, the guests formed a large circle, then held their arms up and danced in a circle around the wedding cookie cake.

After the dance, I was presented with a dish, which I raised above my head and promptly smashed on the floor. The shattered pieces were carefully counted, and their total represented the number of years my husband, Guy, and I would spend together.

Pasta e Riso

Pasta and Rice

Pasta Casalinga

Homemade Pasta

Pasta casalinga *(homemade pasta)* will never go out of style, even though there are many good brands of commercially prepared dried pasta (pasta secca) one can buy. For me, making pasta is a personal expression of accomplishment. I like working the dough to achieve just the right elastic texture, I enjoy making different shapes, and I love the light taste and delicate texture of fresh pasta, and the fact that it cooks in just a few minutes. Combining unbleached all-purpose flour with semolina flour produces a golden-yellow pasta. If semolina flour is unavailable, simply use unbleached flour. This dough can be used to make fettuccine, vermicelli, lasagne, ravioli, tortellini, cappelletti, and farfalle.

Makes about ³/₄ pound, enough for 3 to 4 servings

About 2¹/₂ cups unbleached all-purpose flour
¹/₂ cup fine semolina flour
¹/₂ teaspoon fine sea salt
4 large eggs

1. Combine the flours and salt and mound on a work surface. Make a well in the center of the flour and break the eggs into the well. Beat the eggs with a fork, then gradually incorporate the flour from the inside walls of the well. When the dough becomes too firm to mix with the fork, knead it with your hands, incorporating just enough of the flour to make a soft but not sticky dough. You may not need all the flour.

2. Brush the excess flour aside and knead the dough for about 10 minutes, adding additional flour as needed, until the dough is smooth. Cover with a bowl and allow to rest on a floured surface for 10 minutes.

3. Cut the dough into 4 pieces. Work with one piece at a time, keeping the remaining dough covered. Roll the dough out as thin as possible on a floured surface, or use a pasta machine to roll the dough out through the thinnest setting. Drape the sheets of pasta over dowel rods suspended between two chairs to dry slightly, about 5 minutes.

4. Cut the pasta into the desired width with the pasta machine. Hang the pasta strips over the dowel rods as they are cut, or spread them on floured towels. Or cut the pasta by hand: Lightly flour the rolled-out dough, then roll up each sheet loosely like a jelly roll, and cut into the desired shape, with a sharp knife. Cook the pasta immediately, or let dry completely, draped over the dowel rods or spread on floured towels, for long storage.

About 3 cups fine semolina flour

½ teaspoon fine sea salt

8 medium egg whites

2 tablespoons white wine or water

1. Mound the flour on a work surface and sprinkle it with the salt. Make a well in the center of the flour and add the egg whites and wine or water. Beat the egg whites with a fork, then gradually incorporate the flour from the inside walls of the well. When the dough becomes too firm to mix with the fork, knead it with your hands, incorporating just enough of the flour to make a soft ball of dough.

2. Push the excess flour aside and knead the dough until smooth and no longer sticky, adding additional flour as needed. Cover with a bowl and allow to rest for 10 minutes.

3. Roll and cut the dough following the directions on page 30.

Pappardelle Senza Tourli

WIDE NOODLES WITHOUT EGG YOLKS

❦

This version of pappardelle is for people who are watching their egg intake. Egg whites replace whole eggs, a common practice in some places in northern Italy and around Genoa. Sometimes a little dry white wine is added to the egg whites. Instead of unbleached all-purpose flour, I use durum wheat flour, which is very finely ground semolina. It compensates for the absence of the yolks by giving the dough a yellow hue. If you cannot find durum wheat flour, use unbleached all-purpose flour; you may need a bit less.

❦

Makes 1 pound, enough for 4 servings

Salsa di Pomodoro e Basilico

Tomato-Basil Sauce

❧

It is a myth to think that making tomato sauce takes hours. With a few good-quality ingredients, tomato sauce can be ready in less than thirty minutes.

❧

Makes about 2½ quarts

8 pounds peeled and coarsely chopped ripe plum tomatoes, or three 28-ounce cans crushed Italian plum tomatoes

½ cup extra-virgin olive oil

3 cloves garlic, minced

1½ cups dry red wine

4 to 5 sprigs fresh basil, tied together with kitchen string

Coarse salt and freshly ground black pepper to taste

1. If using fresh tomatoes, puree them in a food processor until smooth. Strain through a fine sieve to remove the seeds.

2. In a deep heavy pot, heat the olive oil. Add the garlic and sauté until soft. Add the tomatoes and stir to blend. Add the wine, basil, and salt and pepper and stir well. Bring to a boil, lower the heat, and simmer for 25 minutes. The sauce is ready to use. The sauce keeps for up to a week in the refrigerator or up to 3 months in the freezer.

3 cups pureed ripe cherry or plum tomatoes (about 1½ pounds)

3 tablespoons extra-virgin olive oil

1 onion, diced

3 cloves garlic, minced

1 small hot red pepper, diced

Fine sea salt to taste

1 pound orecchiette

1 cup shredded arugula leaves

Freshly grated Pecorino Romano cheese for sprinkling

1. Place a fine-mesh sieve over a bowl. Pour the tomatoes into the colander and press the puree through the colander with a spoon to remove the seeds. Set aside.

2. In a large saucepan, heat the olive oil over medium heat. Add the onions and cook until soft. Add the garlic and red pepper and cook until the garlic is golden. Slowly stir in the tomatoes, lower the heat, and cook, covered, for about 10 minutes. Season with salt, and keep warm over very low heat.

3. Meanwhile, bring 4 quarts of salted water to a boil in a large pot. Add the orecchiette and cook for 10 to 12 minutes, or until al dente. Drain well and place on a large serving platter. Toss with 2 cups of the sauce, sprinkle the arugula over the top, and toss gently. Serve immediately. Pass the cheese and remaining sauce on the side.

Orecchiette con Salsa di Pomodorini ed Arugola

Orecchiette with Tomato and Arugula Sauce

❧

Puglia, the region at the heel of the Italian peninsula, is the home to a unique type of pasta called orecchiette (little ears). It is tossed with sauces made from bitter chicories (cima di rape) to classic tomato sauce topped with vibrant green and pungent-tasting arugula leaves. I have taken my inspiration for this sauce from three basic ingredients in Pugliese cuisine: densely flavored olive oil from ancient trees, pomodorini (tiny cherry tomatoes) that grow prolifically and are strung up everywhere like household decorations, and peperoncini (hot red peppers).

❧

Serves 4

Una Chitarra per Natale

A Chitarra for Christmas

Cristoforo lived with his mother, Anna, near Chieti, in the mountainous region of Abruzzo, Italy. Most of the people in the town were sheep farmers and each day, Cristoforo helped his old friend Carmelo, a gentle and quiet old man, lead his sheep—called *testa rossa*, because of their red heads—to pasture. While the sheep grazed in the fields, Cristoforo and Carmelo would sit on a large rock. At midday, they ate lunch, which was usually *pane di casa*, a golden bread with a hard crust, and some fresh sheep's milk cheese. Sometimes there were grapes or figs.

When not tending his sheep, Carmelo loved to carve small figures or animals from wood, using cedar and Judas tree branches. Cristoforo loved to watch the old man work. With Christmas coming, Carmelo started to make the *presepio*, nativity figures, which he would sell on market day in Piazza San Giovanni, the town square.

Cristoforo wanted to ask Carmelo to make a special Christmas gift for his mother, who made maccheroni all day at home to sell to people in the piazza. Each night, his mother collected eggs from the few hens she had and mixed them with flour to make a dough. Then she rolled the dough out on her table with a broom handle and cut the dough into long strands with a knife. The maccheroni was hung on old olive branches and left to dry near the fire. If only it did not take so much time to make the maccheroni, mamma would not have to work so hard, thought Cristoforo.

When he asked Carmelo to make something for his mother, "*Ma certo* (certainly)" came the reply. "*Che vuole* (what do you want)?" Cristoforo was not sure and said he would think about it. On the way home, he heard music coming from the Piazza San Giovanni. A band of traveling gypsies had gathered among the townspeople to play their instruments. Cristoforo stopped to watch and listen.

"Bravo!" the people yelled. "*Cantate, cantate più* (sing more)," they begged. Music filled the piazza and one of the gypsies began to dance as the crowd clapped its hands. Cristoforo moved closer to the mandolin player, who was playing his instrument so hard the strings broke. "Basta!" shouted the mandolin player as he motioned to the gypsies to gather up their things and move on. Cristoforo watched as they walked away, leaving behind on the ground the tangle of broken strings that had produced such wonderful sounds. Cristoforo had an idea. He gathered up the strings and the next day took them to Carmelo.

"Here," he said, "these strings once made beautiful music. Can you make music with them?" He tried to explain the shape of the instrument to Carmelo, and the old man said that he would try to make one. But Carmelo did not really understand, and when Cristoforo came to see him a few days later, he brought out a strange-looking wooden frame with the wires stretched across it, held tightly in place with little nails. It did not look at all like the mandolin Cristoforo had seen.

"Ascolti (listen)," said Carmelo, as he moved his fingers across the strings to create a wonderful sound. Carmelo called it a chitarra, or guitar. He gave it to Cristoforo, who could not resist plucking the strings. Tucking the chitarra under his arm, he hurried home, thinking about how wonderful it would be for him to play music for his mother while she worked making the maccheroni.

When he arrived home, he saw a large sheet of partially rolled-out maccheroni dough on the table, with the broom handle resting on top. Anna was outside gathering eggs, and he could hear her footsteps coming closer. He wanted to surprise her, but there was no time to hide the chitarra, so he quickly lifted up the large sheet of pasta and slipped the chitarra underneath it. Then he placed the broom handle back on top, just as she came through the door. Cristoforo stood in front of the table, half hiding the maccheroni.

"Mamma," he shouted, "sorpresa (surprise)!" Anna was puzzled. Everything was just as she left it. What surprise? she wondered. She walked over to the table and instead of lifting up the dough to see what was underneath, as Cristoforo thought she would do, she picked up her broom handle and rolled over the dough to continue her work. Suddenly, the dough separated into long thin strands and fell into a golden pile beneath the chitarra, while musical sounds were heard as the broom handle cut the dough.

"*Che cos' è* (what is this)*?*" she whispered in surprise. Cristoforo had tears in his eyes. He wanted to tell her that Carmelo had made *him* a chitarra so he could play music for her while she worked, but instead he said that this special instrument, the only one of its kind, was made for her to cut maccheroni. Together Anna and Cristoforo took turns rolling and cutting the dough over the strings, while the beautiful sounds of the chitarra filled their little house. In no time, they had a large mound of maccheroni, much more than Anna could ever have turned out in a day cutting it with a knife. Anna and Cristoforo took the maccheroni to the piazza to sell, and Cristoforo brought along the chitarra. He played on the strings, filling the piazza with beautiful sounds. To him, a chitarra for Christmas was the best present that he could have given his mother... and himself.

¼ cup plus 1 tablespoon olive oil

1 small hot red pepper, slit

1 large clove garlic, minced

One 2-ounce tin anchovies, drained and chopped

1 pound ripe plum tomatoes, peeled, seeded, and chopped

¼ cup capers, rinsed, dried, and chopped

½ cup chopped pitted oil-cured black olives

¼ cup Dried Tomatoes in Olive Oil (page 312)

1 pound spaghetti

1. In a large skillet, heat ¼ cup of the olive oil over medium heat. Add the pepper and garlic and cook, pressing on the pepper with a wooden spoon, until the garlic begins to color. Remove the pepper and discard. Add the anchovies and swirl them in the oil until they begin to dissolve. Add the tomatoes, capers, and olives, and cook, covered, for 5 minutes more.

2. While the sauce cooks, puree the dried tomatoes with the remaining 1 tablespoon olive oil in a blender or food processor.

3. Add the tomatoes to the sauce and cook, covered, for 5 minutes. Turn the heat to very low to keep the sauce warm.

4. Meanwhile, bring 6 quarts of salted water to a boil in a large pot. Add the spaghetti and cook until al dente. Drain well and add to the sauce. Toss the spaghetti in the sauce and turn out onto a platter. Serve immediately.

Note: To peel tomatoes, drop them into a pot of boiling water for 2 minutes. Drain, cool, and slip off the skins.

Spaghetti alla Puttanesca

Harlot-Style Spaghetti

❧

Every Italian cook has a recipe for "harlot-style spaghetti," named for the hot red pepper that gives it quite a kick. Assuming you have the staples on hand, including oil-cured black olives, anchovies, capers, and dried tomatoes, this colorful and spicy dish can be put together in twenty minutes.

❧

Serves 4

Penne, Pistacchio, ed Asparagi

Penne, Pistachio Nuts, and Asparagus

❧

The inspiration for this velvety-smooth pasta dish comes from memories of eating the pencil-thin wild asparagus of Umbria. I combine the tender stalks with penne, a slant-cut short macaroni, and pistachio nuts, in a creamy cheese sauce. For a thinner sauce, add a few tablespoons of the pasta water to the sauce.

❧

Serves 8

4 tablespoons butter

3 tablespoons extra-virgin olive oil

2 cloves garlic, minced

$1/4$ pound prosciutto, diced

2 pounds thin asparagus, trimmed, halved crosswise and then lengthwise

Fine sea salt to taste

2 cups good-quality whipped cream cheese, at room temperature

1 cup light cream or half-and-half

1 cup diced Emmentaler cheese

$1/4$ cup freshly grated Parmigiano-Reggiano cheese

2 pounds penne

1 cup finely chopped pistachio nuts

1. In a large skillet, heat the butter and olive oil over medium heat. Add the garlic and cook until it begins to soften. Add the prosciutto and cook until the prosciutto begins to brown and render some of its fat. Add the asparagus, sprinkle with a little salt, and cook, stirring gently, for 2 to 3 minutes. Cover, reduce the heat to low, and cook for about 3 minutes, or until a knife easily pierces the asparagus. Reduce the heat to very low.

2. In a medium bowl, whisk together the cream cheese and light cream until smooth. Season with salt. Add the cream cheese mixture to the asparagus and gently stir to blend. Set aside, uncovered, and keep warm.

3. Meanwhile, bring 8 quarts of salted water to a boil in a large pot. Add the penne and cook until al dente. Drain well.

4. Spread the Emmentaler and Parmigiano cheeses on a large deep platter. Place the penne on top of the cheese, then pour the asparagus sauce over the top. Gently mix the ingredients until the penne is well coated. Sprinkle the pistachio nuts over the top and serve immediately.

2 large red bell peppers

1 pound Fresh Sausage (page 151)

¹/₄ cup olive oil

1 large onion, diced

1 small hot red pepper, diced

3 cloves garlic, minced

¹/₄ cup chopped flat-leaf parsley

*Two 9-ounce packages frozen artichoke hearts, thawed and cut
into thin wedges*

¹/₂ cup dry red wine

3 tablespoons chopped fresh basil

Fine sea salt and coarsely ground black pepper to taste

1 pound fettuccine

Freshly grated Pecorino Romano cheese for sprinkling

1. Roast the bell peppers on a grill or under a preheated
broiler, turning, until blackened all over. Let the peppers cool, then
core, peel, and seed them. Cut into thin strips and set aside.

2. Place the sausage in a skillet, add about 1 inch of water, and
cook the sausage over medium heat, uncovered, until it is no longer
pink. Drain off the water and let the sausage cook in its own juices
until nicely browned on all sides. Transfer the sausage to a cutting
board and let cool slightly. Cut into ¹/₄-inch slices and set aside.

3. In a large skillet, heat the olive oil. Add the onions and
cook, stirring, until golden brown. Add the hot pepper, garlic, and
parsley and cook until the garlic is soft, about 5 minutes. Add the
sausage, artichokes, and bell peppers and cook for about 5 minutes.
Add the wine, basil, and salt and pepper and simmer, covered, for
5 minutes. Set aside, covered to keep warm.

4. Meanwhile, bring 6 quarts of salted water to a boil in a large
pot. Add the fettuccine and cook until al dente. Drain well and
place on a large serving platter. Pour the sausage mixture over the
fettuccine and toss gently. Sprinkle on the cheese and serve immediately.

Fettuccine e Salsiccia Fresca

Fettuccine and Fresh Sausage

*All of the time-consuming steps in
this dish can be done ahead. Make
the fennel-flavored pork sausage
the day ahead and refrigerate
overnight. Likewise, the red
peppers can be roasted a day in
advance. To save even more time,
use frozen or water-packed
artichoke hearts.*

Serves 6

Informal Supper

Little Olive Pizzas (page 76)

Fettuccine and Fresh Sausage

Green Bean, Chickpea, and
Tomato Salad (page 202)

Small Country Chocolate Cake
(page 286)

Pappardelle con Vitello

Pappardelle with Veal

❧

Pappardelle are wide noodles that, in Tuscany, are usually teamed with a hare sauce. In this country version, I use veal shoulder slowly simmered in red wine. Use the veal bones to make veal stock, which gives an added layer of flavor to the sauce. The pasta can be made one day in advance, and placed on kitchen towels.

❧

Serves 4

PASTA

About 2 cups unbleached all-purpose flour

⅛ teaspoon fine sea salt

3 large eggs

1 teaspoon extra-virgin olive oil

VEAL SAUCE

½ cup (about ½ ounce) dried porcini mushrooms

1 cup hot water

¼ cup plus 2 tablespoons olive oil

1 large onion, thinly sliced

1 medium red bell pepper, cored, seeded, and cut into thin strips

1 large clove garlic, minced

2 cups sliced button mushrooms

2 tablespoons unbleached all-purpose flour

1½ teaspoons fine sea salt

½ teaspoon coarsely ground black pepper

3½ pounds veal shoulder blade, boned, trimmed of excess fat and sinew, and cut into 1-inch pieces

2 tablespoons minced fresh sage

1 cup Veal Stock (page 15)

1 cup dry red wine

1. Mound the flour on a work surface and sprinkle it with the salt. Make a well in the center of the flour and add the eggs and olive oil. Beat the eggs and oil with a fork until smooth, then gradually incorporate the flour from the inside walls of the well. When the dough becomes too firm to mix with the fork, knead it with your hands, incorporating just enough of the flour to make a smooth ball of dough. You may not need all the flour.

2. Push the excess flour aside and knead the dough for about 5 minutes, adding flour as needed. Place the dough on a floured surface, cover with a bowl, and let rest for 10 minutes.

3. Cut the dough into 2 pieces. Keeping the second piece covered, roll one piece with a rolling pin to flatten it slightly. Roll out the dough through the rollers of a pasta machine on the thinnest setting. Cut the strip into 9-inch lengths, then cut each piece lengthwise into 1½-inch-wide strips. Spread the pasta on floured towels while you roll out the remaining dough.

To make the pappardelle by hand, roll each piece of dough into a 20 by 14-inch rectangle. Cut lengthwise into 1½-inch-wide strips, then cut the strips in half crosswise.

4. Place the porcini mushrooms in a bowl, cover with the water, and let soak for 30 minutes. Drain the mushrooms, reserving the liquid. Cut the porcini into small pieces and set aside. Strain the soaking liquid, and reserve half.

5. In a large skillet, heat 2 tablespoons of the oil. Add the onion and bell pepper and cook over low heat until the onion has softened. Add the garlic and cook for about 2 minutes. Remove the mixture to a medium bowl. Add the sliced mushrooms to the skillet and cook, stirring, until they begin to brown. Add them to the onions and peppers.

6. In a medium bowl, combine the flour, salt, and pepper. Add the veal pieces and toss well. Shake off the excess flour and set the veal aside.

7. Heat the remaining ¼ cup olive oil in the skillet. Add the veal and cook until browned on all sides. Add the onion and pepper mixture, the porcini, the reserved soaking liquid, and the sage. Add the veal stock and wine and bring to a boil. Lower the heat, cover, and simmer until the meat is tender, about 50 minutes.

8. Meanwhile, bring 6 quarts of salted water to a boil in a large pot. Add the pappardelle and cook until al dente. Drain the noodles and place on a large serving platter.

9. Spoon the veal and sauce over the noodles and toss gently. Serve immediately.

Do-Ahead Tuscan Supper

Pappardelle with Veal

Prosciutto and Rosemary Breadsticks (page 317)

Mixed Green Salad (page 192)

Pomegranate Gelatin (page 209)

Caramelle di Pasta

Pasta "Caramels"

❧

In addition to pasta all'uovo, pasta made from just eggs and unbleached flour, traditional pastas are also made from purees of fresh spinach, carrots, tomatoes, and beets. In this unusual recipe, strips of beet pasta are twisted around a filling of Gorgonzola cheese, prosciutto, and pine nuts and transformed into caramelle, pasta resembling paper-wrapped candies.

Serve this as a first course.

❧

Makes about 10 dozen pasta twists; serves 12

DOUGH

1 small beet, stem trimmed to 2 inches
2 1/2 to 3 cups unbleached all-purpose flour
1/2 cup fine semolina flour
1/8 teaspoon fine sea salt
4 large eggs

FILLING

3 tablespoons butter
3 tablespoons minced flat-leaf parsley
1/4 pound prosciutto, minced
1/3 cup pine nuts
1/2 pound Gorgonzola cheese, chopped

SAUCE

1/2 pound (2 sticks) unsalted butter, at room temperature
3 cloves garlic, peeled
1 1/4 cups packed flat-leaf parsley leaves
Fine sea salt to taste
1 to 2 tablespoons extra-virgin olive oil

1. Preheat the oven to 350°F. Wrap the beet in foil and bake for 20 minutes, or until a fork pierces the flesh easily. Let cool, then peel and puree in a food processor. Set aside.

2. Meanwhile, make the filling: In a medium skillet, melt the butter. Add the parsley and prosciutto and cook until the prosciutto begins to crisp. Add the pine nuts and cook, stirring, until golden, about 3 minutes. Remove the mixture to a bowl and add the cheese, mashing it with a fork until the mixture is smooth and well blended. Cover and refrigerate until ready to use.

3. To make the pasta, combine 2 cups of the unbleached flour, the semolina flour, and salt and mound on a work surface. Make a well in the center of the flour and add the beet and eggs. Mix the beet and eggs together with a fork until well blended, then gradually incorporate the flour from the inside walls of the well. When the dough becomes too firm to mix with the fork, knead it with your hands until a ball of dough forms that is soft but no longer sticky.

4. Push aside the excess flour. Knead the dough for about 5 minutes, adding additional flour as needed. Cover the dough with a bowl and let rest for 10 minutes.

5. Divide the dough into 5 pieces. Work with one piece at a time, keeping the rest covered. Flatten each piece with a rolling pin, then roll the dough out through a pasta machine into $1/8$-inch-thick strips 40 inches long and 4 inches wide. Cut twenty 2-inch-wide strips from each piece. Or roll the dough out by hand.

6. Spread a scant $1/2$ teaspoon of the filling over each strip, leaving a $1/2$-inch border all around. Fold each strip lengthwise in half and pinch the edges to seal. Twist the ends to resemble a candy wrapper. Place the caramelle on clean kitchen towels in a single layer.

7. To make the sauce, place all the ingredients except the olive oil in a food processor or blender and pulse until blended. With the motor running, drizzle in the olive oil. Pulse until a smooth paste is obtained. Transfer to a small saucepan and set aside until ready to use. (The sauce can be made ahead and refrigerated for up to 4 days.)

8. Bring 8 quarts of salted water to a boil in a large pot. Carefully add the caramelle and cook until al dente, about 4 minutes. Carefully remove the caramelle with a slotted spoon and place them on a warm serving platter.

9. Meanwhile, heat the parsley sauce. Pour the sauce over the caramelle, toss gently, and serve immediately.

Note: To make ahead and freeze: Place the caramelle in single layers on a floured cookie sheet between sheets of plastic wrap. Cover with foil and freeze until hard. Transfer to plastic bags, seal tightly, and freeze for up to 2 months. Cook without thawing, until al dente, about 6 minutes.

Tonno, Uove di Tonno, e Spaghetti

Tuna, Tuna Roe, and Spaghetti

❧

I cannot praise this dish enough; for me it is a satisfying reminder of wonderful days spent in Sicily. I preserve fresh tuna in olive oil and keep it in the refrigerator for up to two months to quickly satisfy my craving for it. Salted tuna roe, available in seafood stores, makes the flavors even more intense. Use salted anchovies if tuna roe is not available.

❧

Serves 4

PRESERVED TUNA

1/2 pound fresh tuna

2 bay leaves

1 lemon, sliced

3/4 teaspoon fine sea salt

Freshly ground black pepper to taste

About 3/4 cup extra-virgin olive oil

SAUCE

1/2 cup olive oil (from the tuna)

1 medium white onion, diced

2 cloves garlic, minced

1/3 cup minced flat-leaf parsley

1 teaspoon hot red pepper flakes, or more to taste

Fine sea salt and coarsely ground black pepper to taste

1 pound spaghetti

2 tablespoons grated tuna roe (bottarga)

1. Place the tuna, 1 bay leaf, and the lemon slices in a nonreactive pot. Cover with salted water, bring to a simmer, and cook for 25 to 30 minutes, or until the tuna flakes easily with a fork. Drain the tuna and let it cool.

2. Cut the tuna into chunks and place in a sterilized 1-pint jar. Add the remaining bay leaf and salt and pepper. Cover with the olive oil, making sure that the tuna is totally covered. Cap the jar and let marinate overnight at room temperature.

3. The following day, check the level of the oil. Add more if needed to cover the tuna completely. Cap the jar and store it in the refrigerator until needed. (Use within 2 months.) Bring to room temperature before serving.

4. To make the sauce, heat the oil in a medium skillet. Add the onion, garlic, parsley, and red pepper and sauté until the garlic starts to soften. Add the tuna, breaking it up with a fork. Season with salt and pepper. Remove from the heat and keep warm.

5. Meanwhile, bring 6 quarts of salted water to a boil in a large pot. Add the spaghetti and cook until al dente. Drain well. Place the spaghetti on a warm serving platter.

6. Pour the sauce over the spaghetti and toss well. Sprinkle the tuna roe over the top and serve immediately.

Pasta e Salmone

Pasta and Salmon

❧

Poached salmon combined with spinach and a shallot-flavored cream provides the sauce for this exquisite dish. To ensure that the salmon remains moist, I use a fish poacher and a cooking thermometer to gauge when the fish is cooked. A large deep skillet or pot with a rack can be used in place of a fish poacher.

❧

Serves 6

1 ³/₄ *pounds salmon fillet, in one piece*

1 *large bay leaf*

2 *teaspoons fine sea salt*

4 *tablespoons butter*

4 *large shallots, minced*

One 10-ounce bag fresh spinach, cooked, squeezed dry, and finely chopped

1 ¹/₂ *cups heavy cream*

1 *tablespoon grated lemon zest*

1 *pound fettuccine*

1. Place the salmon fillet skin side down on the rack of a fish poacher and set aside. Fill the poacher with enough water to come halfway up the sides, add the bay leaf and 1 teaspoon of the salt, and bring to a simmer. Lower the rack into the poacher, submerging the salmon. Cover and poach the salmon until the fish easily flakes with a fork and registers 175° to 185°F on an instant-read thermometer, 8 to 10 minutes.

2. Carefully lift the poaching rack out of the poacher, draining the salmon well. When the salmon is cool enough to handle, remove and discard the skin. Cut the salmon into 1-inch chunks.

3. In a large skillet, melt the butter. Add the shallots and cook until they are very soft. Add the spinach and cook for 2 minutes. Stir in the heavy cream, lemon zest, and the remaining 1 teaspoon salt, and bring to a simmer. Add the salmon, mixing carefully. Remove from the heat and cover to keep warm.

4. Meanwhile, bring 6 quarts of salted water to a boil in a large pot. Add the fettuccine and cook until al dente. Drain and place on a large platter.

5. Pour the salmon sauce over the fettuccine and gently toss. Serve immediately.

1½ pounds littleneck clams

1½ pounds mussels, scrubbed and debearded

1 cup water

¼ cup olive oil

1 to 2 small dried hot red peppers

2 cloves garlic, chopped

⅔ pound cleaned octopus or squid, cut into ¼-inch rings (see Note)

½ pound cooked medium shrimp

¼ cup minced flat-leaf parsley

1 cup dry white wine

1½ pounds spaghetti

1½ teaspoons fine sea salt

3 tablespoons minced fresh thyme

1. Discard any clams or mussels with cracked shells. Place the clams and mussels in a large skillet, add the water, cover, and bring to a boil. Boil until the clams and mussels open. Remove the clams and mussels from their shells and set aside. Strain the cooking liquid and reserve ¼ cup.

2. In another skillet, heat the oil over medium heat. Add the hot pepper(s) and garlic and sauté until the garlic is soft but not browned. Add the octopus or squid and gently cook over low heat until the octopus turns opaque or the squid begins to curl and brown. Stir in the shrimp, mussels, clams, and 2 tablespoons of the parsley. Add the reserved shellfish cooking water, the wine, and salt, cover the pan, and cook until heated through, about 3 minutes.

3. Meanwhile, bring 6 quarts of salted water to a boil in a large pot. Add the spaghetti and cook until al dente. Drain well. Place the spaghetti on a large platter.

4. Pour the seafood mixture over the spaghetti. Sprinkle with the thyme and remaining 2 tablespoons parsley, mix well, and serve immediately.

Note: If using octopus or squid, precook it in boiling water until tender, about 5 to 10 minutes, depending on size.

Spaghetti alla Pescatore

Spaghetti with Seafood

Usually I eat bistecca *(steak) when I'm in Florence, but I forgo the Florentine specialty when I eat at a small trattoria called Pierot on the Piazza T. Gaddi. They serve a wonderful* spaghetti alla pescatore *that would make a wonderful meal on Christmas Eve. It is chock-full of mussels, clams, and octopus; if octopus is unavailable, use squid.*

Serves 6

Vongole al Pomodoro

Pasta with Red Clam Sauce

❧

On Christmas Eve (la vigilia), it is traditional to serve seven fish courses. Some say the number represents the seven sacraments of the Catholic Church, while others claim it is a practice reserved for Advent, the last full week before Christmas Eve. Plenty of these traditional fish dishes were part of my childhood Christmases, including this one of clams and linguine in tomato sauce. Other fish dishes on the Christmas Eve table included salt cod in tomatoes and wine, haddock cooked in olive oil and marinated in lemon juice, garlic, salt and pepper, and squid, both with spaghetti and broccoli, and stuffed with bread crumbs and stewed.

❧

Serves 4

$^1/_4$ cup plus 1 tablespoon olive oil

3 cloves garlic, minced

$^1/_3$ cup minced flat-leaf parsley

1 teaspoon hot red pepper flakes

2 cups fresh minced clams, with their juice

$1^1/_2$ cups Tomato-Basil Sauce (page 32) or prepared tomato sauce

$^1/_3$ cup dry red wine

Fine sea salt and freshly ground black pepper to taste

1 pound linguine

1. In a large skillet, heat the olive oil over medium heat. Add the garlic and cook until it softens but does not color. Add the parsley and red pepper flakes and cook, stirring, for 1 to 2 minutes. Add the clams and their juice, cover, and cook for 1 minute. Add the tomato sauce, wine, and salt and pepper, stir well, cover, and simmer for 5 minutes.

2. Meanwhile, bring 6 quarts of salted water to a boil in a large pot. Add the linguine and cook until al dente. Drain well, and place on a large serving platter.

3. Pour the sauce over the linguine. Toss and serve immediately.

Se è giovedì, ci vogliono gnocchi

If It's Thursday, It Must Be Gnocchi

〰

My sixteenth birthday party stands out as one of my fondest memories—and as one of my most embarrassing moments. I desperately wanted to be like my friends and have American food served at my Sweet Sixteen party.

For weeks before the party, I argued with my mother and Grandma Galasso about the menu. Pizza or hamburgers gushing with melted cheese would be just fine, I insisted, and chocolate cake for dessert. No cannoli! They promised me that no chickpeas would appear in the salad, and no one would be forced to eat fennel. But there would be a surprise on the menu. After all, how often was I going to turn sixteen, they cried with their hands raised toward heaven. How could I say no to two women whose whole lives centered around making food for others to enjoy? On the morning of my birthday, I left for school, worrying about the "surprise." I prayed that they would be reasonable.

Finally, the hour of my party arrived. My girlfriends filled our living room and took turns placing brightly wrapped boxes over my head, daring me to guess the contents. I didn't even think about the food until Grandma appeared, raised her arms, and said, *"Marianna, venga, venga, siamo pronte."* I took a deep breath and motioned everyone into the dining room.

Grandma stood at the head of the table, her once-white apron looking like an impressionist painting of tomato sauce. In front of her waited a steaming platter of small dumplings under a blanket of brilliant red sauce, *gnocchi patan*. I loved potato gnocchi, delicate dumplings made from potatoes and flour, but I didn't want my enthusiasm to show. Couldn't they get anything right? I said I wanted pizza! All my friends gathered around my grandmother for a closer look. I hoped no one would go home or say that they were not hungry.

"Gee, Mrs. Galasso," piped up my friend Barbara, "what are those?" I could sense the long, slowly delivered English answer coming, and I quickly intercepted the reply, describing them as macaroni, only a little chewier. Grandma dished them out, all the while telling everyone to "mangia, mangia." To my surprise, they were a big hit, and everyone wanted to know how to make them.

I could hear my mother shuffling pots and pans in the basement kitchen, and I wondered what would be next. Oh please, I prayed, don't let it be tripe! This time, it was another version of gnocchi, made with spinach and ricotta cheese. I knew I was in trouble now. No one in their right mind ate anything with spinach in it. My friend Christine picked all the spinach out of her gnocchi and left it in a pile on the edge of her plate. Annie, my best friend, chewed hers a long time before swallowing. And Wendy wanted more of "the other kind" of gnocchi. Now the fear of what was next started to create beads of sweat under my birthday hat. *Allora*, didn't they do it again! This time it was pumpkin gnocchi, perfumed with sage leaves from Grandma's garden. I slid lower in my chair as she dished them out and blessed each plate with a quizzical "basta?"

I excused myself from the table and went straight to the steamy kitchen. I could dimly perceive the figure of my mother, putting the last touches on a pizza. When she saw me, she knew that I was annoyed.

"I wanted an American birthday," I snapped. I suppose I had her reply coming.

"We wanted your friends to eat something traditional and special too," she said, opening the oven door to reveal a large baking pan full of hamburgers. She handed them to me and said, "*Buon compleanno.*"

I took the platter upstairs and she carried the pizza. When we got to the dining room, everyone clapped, acknowledging my mother and grandmother's handiwork. The eating resumed in earnest, as my friends polished off the pizza and all the hamburgers.

When the birthday cake arrived with sixteen dancing candles, it was just what I had requested, a fudgy, moist chocolate cake, stylishly swirled in thick chocolate frosting. After the cake was eaten, the games played, and the favors given out, I said my good-byes to my friends. Grandma and my mother were already at work cleaning up. I gave them each a big hug, but I could not resist asking, "Why did you serve three different kinds of gnocchi?"

"*Guardi*," said Grandma, "*è giovedi* (it's Thursday)." Of course! In all my excitement I had forgotten that for my Grandmother Galasso, gnocchi was always eaten on Thursdays in her native province of Avellino. And today, for my Thursday birthday, they were a must, and the surprise was making three kinds! I looked at the calendar again and calculated when my birthday would again fall on Thursday... I had a long reprieve! But now, with many more years behind me, it is always tradition to serve gnocchi on my birthday, whether it's Thursday or not.

Gnocchi di Pane

Bread Gnocchi

❧

Good chewy country bread, soaked in milk and then combined with egg, flour, and cheese, is the basis for these unusual gnocchi, served with a butter, garlic, and parsley sauce. The success of this dish depends on the quality of the bread and the judicious use of flour.

❧

Makes about 5 dozen gnocchi; serves 6 to 8

GNOCCHI

2 cups finely crumbled crustless fresh bread

1¼ cups milk

1 large egg

½ cup freshly grated Asiago or Parmigiano-Reggiano cheese

1 to 1½ teaspoons fine sea salt (to taste)

1¾ to 2 cups unbleached all-purpose flour

SAUCE

8 tablespoons (1 stick) butter

1 large clove garlic, thinly sliced

½ cup finely minced flat-leaf parsley

1. Place the bread in a bowl, add the milk, egg, cheese, and salt, and mix well. Add just enough flour to make a thick dough, and knead until it is the consistency of mashed potatoes. Cover the bowl with plastic wrap and refrigerate for 1 hour.

2. Bring 3 quarts of salted water to a boil in a large pot. Preheat the oven to 200°F. Butter a large ovenproof casserole dish with 1 tablespoon of the butter.

3. Meanwhile, in a medium saucepan, melt the remaining 7 tablespoons butter. Add the garlic and cook, pressing on it with a wooden spoon to flavor the butter, for about 1 minute. Discard the garlic, add the parsley, and cook until the butter browns slightly. Keep the sauce warm over very low heat.

4. Using 2 teaspoons dipped in ice water, drop small spoonfuls of the dough into the boiling water, about 2 dozen at a time. Once the gnocchi bob to the top, cook until just tender, about 5 minutes longer. Remove with a slotted spoon, draining well, and place in the casserole dish. Keep warm in the oven while you cook the remaining gnocchi.

5. Pour the butter sauce over the gnocchi, toss gently with a spoon to coat them evenly, and serve immediately.

Note: To make this ahead, prepare and boil the gnocchi as directed. Place them in the buttered dish, cover with aluminum foil, and refrigerate. To serve, heat the gnocchi for 20 minutes in a preheated 350°F oven. Prepare the sauce while they are warming.

1½ cups finely grated ricotta salata cheese (about 3 ounces)

2 cups skim-milk ricotta cheese

1 large egg

About 1½ cups fine durum flour or unbleached all-purpose flour

⅛ teaspoon salt

1. In a large bowl, mix the cheeses and egg together until well combined.

2. Mound the flour on a work surface and sprinkle with the salt. Make a well in the center of the flour and add the cheese mixture. Using your hands, gradually incorporate just enough of the flour into the cheese mixture to form a soft ball of dough. To check for the right consistency, shape a piece of dough the size of a grape into a ball, and put it into a small pot of boiling water. If it falls apart, add a little more flour to the dough and test again.

3. Divide the dough into 8 pieces. Work with one piece at a time, keeping the rest of the dough covered. On a lightly floured surface, roll each piece into a rope the width of a finger. Cut the rope into 1-inch pieces. Roll each piece down and off the tines of a fork to create ridges. Place the gnocchi in a single layer on kitchen towels as you form them.

4. Bring 6 quarts of salted water to a boil in a large pot. Cook 3 to 4 dozen gnocchi at a time, just until they rise to the surface. Use a slotted spoon to transfer to a serving platter or bowl, draining them well. Serve with Tomato-Basil Sauce (page 32) or melted butter and Pecorino cheese, and serve immediately.

Note: To freeze, cook the gnocchi as directed, place them in a casserole dish, and toss with the desired sauce. Cover well with plastic wrap and foil and freeze. When ready to use, let the gnocchi defrost in the refrigerator, then reheat in a moderate oven.

Gnocchi di Due Formaggi

Two-Cheese Gnocchi

To achieve the taste of traditional Italian sheep's-milk ricotta gnocchi, I use two types of cheese: skim-milk ricotta and ricotta salata, a dried salted ricotta cheese, sold by the wedge, that can be grated. I use finely ground durum wheat flour to give a golden hue to the gnocchi, but all-purpose flour is fine too. Lightly spoon the flour into your measuring cup, rather than firmly packing it in.

Makes about 14 dozen

Gnocchi di Semolina con Salsa di Peperoni Rossi

Semolina Gnocchi with Red Pepper Sauce

🦅

Tradition and experimentation meet in this recipe. Gnocchi, made from semolina flour and milk, are cut into disks and sauced with a puree of sweet red peppers, instead of the classic butter and cheese sauce. This is a good choice for a buffet because the gnocchi can be made ahead and held in the refrigerator for up to eight hours before baking, or frozen for up to a month. The pepper sauce can be made three days ahead (thin with a little water if it thickens while refrigerated).

🦅

Makes about 6 dozen gnocchi; serves 20 as part of a buffet, 6 to 8 as a pasta course

GNOCCHI

4 cups low-fat milk

7 tablespoons butter, at room temperature

1 tablespoon grated nutmeg

¹/₂ teaspoon fine sea salt

1 teaspoon white pepper

1 cup plus 2 tablespoons fine semolina flour (durum flour)

1 large egg

³/₄ cup freshly grated Parmigiano-Reggiano cheese

SAUCE

5 large red bell peppers

3 tablespoons butter

2 tablespoons minced fresh sage

1 teaspoon fresh lemon juice

Fine sea salt to taste

1. Lightly grease a marble slab or rimless cookie sheet with olive oil. In a large nonstick saucepan, combine the milk, 3 tablespoons of the butter, the nutmeg, salt, and pepper, and bring to just under a boil. Add the semolina in a steady stream, stirring constantly with a wooden spoon so no lumps form. Cook, stirring, until the mixture looks like thick Cream of Wheat and begins to leave the sides of the pan, about 6 minutes.

2. Remove the pan from the heat and add the remaining 4 tablespoons butter, the egg, and cheese. Stir well to blend. Spread the mixture out on the oiled slab and let cool for 20 minutes.

3. Preheat the broiler. Place the peppers on the broiler rack and broil, turning, until charred and blackened all over. Remove the peppers to a dish and let cool. Peel, core, and seed the peppers and place in a food processor or blender. Pulse until a smooth puree.

4. In a medium saucepan, melt the butter. Add the sage and cook over low heat for about 5 minutes, pressing on the leaves to extract their oil. Add the pepper puree, lemon juice, and salt, stir well, and cook for about 5 minutes. Remove from the heat and cover to keep warm.

5. Preheat the oven to 350°F. Lightly grease a 14 by 9½-inch baking pan with olive oil. Place a sheet of oiled wax paper over the gnocchi dough and roll out the dough ½ inch thick. Use a round 1-inch cookie cutter to cut disks from the dough, and arrange the disks slightly overlapping in the baking pan, making six rows of ten disks in all. Reroll the dough scraps to form more disks.

6. Spoon the red pepper sauce over the gnocchi and bake, uncovered, for 10 to 12 minutes, or until heated through. Serve immediately.

Note: To freeze, place the unbaked gnocchi in a freezer-to-oven baking dish or disposable aluminum baking pan. Cover with plastic wrap, then with foil, and freeze. Defrost in the refrigerator, top with the sauce, and bake as directed.

Gnocchetti di Pesce

Little Fish Dumplings

❧

The tiny dumplings called gnocchetti vary in shape and ingredients from region to region in Italy. The more common are made with potatoes and cheese or with pumpkin, spinach, ricotta, or semolina. I find that fish and potatoes in a tomato-anchovy sauce works well too. Prepare this dish as the opener to a complete fish meal, using sole, haddock, or flounder. These delicate gnocchetti achieve their lightness from a minimal amount of flour. After making the dough, test one dumpling in boiling water; if it disintegrates, add a little more flour and test again.

❧

Makes about 20 dozen gnocchetti (serves 15 to 20); makes about 2 cups sauce, enough to dress 10 dozen gnocchetti

SAUCE

2 tablespoons olive oil

2 large shallots, finely diced

3 anchovy fillets

1 tablespoon prepared olive paste

2 pounds large plum tomatoes, peeled, cored, seeded, and pureed in a food processor

2 teaspoons minced fresh sage

2 teaspoons minced fresh thyme

2 teaspoons minced fresh rosemary

Fine sea salt and freshly ground black pepper to taste

GNOCCHETTI

1½ pounds baking potatoes (5 medium)

1 tablespoon olive oil

1 clove garlic, minced

1 onion, diced

¾ pound sole fillet, cut into chunks

¼ cup dry wine

1 large egg, lightly beaten

1 to 1½ cups unbleached all-purpose flour

Fine sea salt and freshly ground black pepper to taste

1. Preheat the oven to 400°F. Bake the potatoes until tender, about 1 hour. Let cool slightly. Peel the potatoes and mash them with a potato masher or a ricer. Set aside.

2. Meanwhile, in a large saucepan, heat the olive oil over medium heat. Add the shallots and cook until soft. Add the anchovy fillets, breaking them up with a fork. Add the olive paste, tomatoes, herbs, and salt and pepper and bring to a simmer over high heat. Cook for 6 to 7 minutes longer. Remove from the heat and set aside.

3. In a medium skillet, heat the olive oil. Add the onion and garlic and cook until soft. Add the fish and sauté for 2 to 3 minutes. Sprinkle on the wine and let it evaporate. Sprinkle the fish with salt and pepper and cook until opaque, about 5 minutes. Remove from the heat and let cool.

4. Transfer the fish, onions, and garlic to a bowl and mash with a fork until the fish is in small shreds. Blend in the egg, then add the mashed potatoes and mix well.

5. Place 1 cup flour on a work surface. Place the potato and fish mixture on top and work the flour in with your hands until a ball of dough is formed, adding additional flour only if the dough is very sticky. Too much flour will make the gnocchetti heavy.

6. Divide the dough into 6 pieces. Work with one piece at a time, keeping the rest covered. On a lightly floured surface, roll each piece into a 24-inch-long rope. Cut into $^1/_2$-inch pieces and roll each piece down and off the tines of a floured fork to create ridges. Place the gnocchetti in a single layer on clean towels as you form them.

7. Bring 6 quarts of salted water to a boil in a large pot. Add the dumplings about 50 at a time and cook just until they rise to the surface. Using a slotted spoon, transfer half the cooked gnocchetti to a lightly oiled platter and keep warm. Place the remaining gnocchetti in a disposable aluminum baking dish, cover with plastic wrap, then with foil, and freeze for future use.

8. Meanwhile, reheat the sauce over low heat. Pour the sauce over the gnocchetti, toss gently, and serve immediately.

Note: Frozen gnocchetti should be defrosted in the refrigerator, tossed with sauce, and reheated in a preheated 350°F oven until hot.

Ravioli ai Funghi con Salsa all Aglio, Panna, e Fontina

Mushroom Ravioli with Garlic, Cream, and Fontina Sauce

❧

Portobello mushrooms can be as large as dinner plates. They are exquisite when simply grilled, with a brushing of olive oil. Creating more elaborate recipes with them is fun too. I developed this mushroom-stuffed ravioli dish when a crate of the brown beauties arrived at my door. To complement rather than overpower the woodsy taste of the filling, I teamed the ravioli with a cream and Italian Fontina cheese sauce. I knew my efforts had paid off when I took the first bite. If you cannot find portobello mushrooms, use cremini (smaller versions of portobellos) or shiitake mushrooms. This dish makes an elegant first course for a bridal luncheon.

❧

Makes 7 dozen ravioli; serves 8 to 10

FILLING

6 tablespoons butter

1 small hot red pepper, diced

1 pound portobello mushrooms, stemmed, cleaned, and diced

Fine sea salt to taste

$1/3$ cup dry red wine

DOUGH

$2 1/2$ cups unbleached all-purpose flour

3 large eggs

$1/8$ teaspoon fine sea salt

SAUCE

3 tablespoons butter

3 large cloves garlic, cut lengthwise in half

1 cup heavy cream

$1/3$ pound Italian Fontina cheese, diced

$1/2$ teaspoon peppercorns, preferably Tellichery, crushed

Fine sea salt to taste

1. In a large skillet, melt the butter over medium heat. Add the chili pepper and cook for about 5 minutes, pressing on the pieces and swirling them in the butter with a wooden spoon. Add the mushrooms and cook, stirring occasionally, until soft and lightly browned, about 8 minutes. Sprinkle the salt over the mushrooms and raise the heat to high. Add the wine and let it evaporate. Transfer the mushrooms to a blender or food processor and process to a paste. Transfer to a bowl and set aside.

2. Mound the flour on a work surface. Make a well in the center and crack the eggs into the well. Sprinkle the salt over the eggs and beat with a fork until blended. Pushing the flour from the inside of the well into the center with your hands, gradually incorporate enough flour into the eggs to make a soft dough.

3. Push any excess flour aside, and knead the dough for 5 minutes, or until it is smooth. Cover the dough with a bowl and let it rest for 10 minutes.

4. Divide the dough into 4 pieces. To make the ravioli using a ravioli form, roll each piece out through a pasta machine set to the next-to-the-last-setting. Cut the pasta into 13-inch lengths. Place one sheet of dough over the bottom part of a ravioli form, and make impressions with the top piece of the form. Fill each cavity with about ½ teaspoon of the mushroom filling. Place a second sheet of dough over the top and roll over the dough with a rolling pin to create the ravioli. Shake the ravioli out onto a clean towel, trim any excess dough from around the form and save to reroll. Arrange them in a single layer. Continue with the remaining dough and filling.

To make the ravioli by hand, roll each piece out on a lightly floured surface into a large rectangle about ⅛ inch thick. Space ½ teaspoon of the filling about 1½ inch apart on one sheet of dough. Cover with another sheet of dough, press down around the mounds of filling with your fingers to seal, and cut into ravioli with a ravioli wheel.

5. In a medium saucepan, melt the butter over medium heat. Add the garlic and cook, pressing on the cloves with a wooden spoon, until the garlic just begins to brown. Add the Fontina, peppercorns, and cream, cook, stirring constantly, until the cheese has melted and the sauce has thickened. Season the sauce with salt, cover and set aside.

6. Bring 8 quarts of salted water to a boil in a large pot. Add half the ravioli at a time and cook until al dente, 2 to 3 minutes. Drain well, and put them on a warm serving platter.

7. Meanwhile, reheat the sauce, stirring until smooth.

8. Pour the sauce over the ravioli and gently toss to coat them evenly. Serve immediately.

Note: The filling and sauce can be made 2 days ahead and refrigerated. The uncooked ravioli can be frozen: place on cookie sheets in a single layer and freeze until hard. Transfer to plastic bags and freeze. Cook the ravioli unthawed.

Ravioli con Peperoni Rossi e Ricotta

Ravioli Stuffed with Red Peppers and Ricotta

❧

Ask and you shall receive. I heeded that advice in Parma when I flagged a passerby and said, "Conosce un posto dove si mangia bene ma si paga poco (do you know a place where I can eat well and cheaply)?" "Ma certo" came the reply… and a personal escort to Trattoria Corrieri, where I succumbed to a wonderful dish of delicate ravioli with a roasted pepper and cheese filling. Here is my version of these delicate little pillows, which I serve as a first course on Christmas Day.

❧

Makes about 8 dozen ravioli (serves 10 to 12); makes about ⅔ cup sauce, enough to dress 4 dozen ravioli

FILLING

2 medium red bell peppers
2 ⅔ cups ricotta cheese, well drained
¼ cup freshly grated Parmigiano-Reggiano cheese
1 extra-large egg
3 tablespoons minced flat-leaf parsley
½ teaspoon fine sea salt

DOUGH

3 cups unbleached all-purpose flour
⅛ teaspoon fine sea salt
4 extra-large eggs

SAUCE

14 tablespoons (1 ¾ sticks) unsalted butter, melted and kept warm
Freshly grated Parmigiano-Reggiano cheese for sprinkling

1. Preheat the broiler. Place the peppers on a broiler pan and broil, turning, until blackened on all sides. Let cool. Peel, core, and seed the peppers and dice them. Place in a bowl, add the ricotta cheese, Parmigiano cheese, egg, parsley, and salt, and mix well. Refrigerate until ready to use.

2. Mound the flour on a work surface and sprinkle on the salt. Make a well in the center of the flour and add the eggs. With a fork, gently beat the eggs, then gradually incorporate the flour from the inside of the well. When the dough becomes too firm to mix with the fork, use your hands to knead it into a ball of dough that is soft but no longer sticky, adding more flour as necessary.

3. Push the excess flour aside and knead the dough for about 5 minutes. Cover the dough with a bowl and let rest for 10 minutes.

4. Divide the dough into 4 pieces. To make the ravioli using a ravioli form, flatten each piece of dough slightly with a rolling pin and run it through the rollers of a pasta machine on the thinnest setting. Cut the dough into 13-inch lengths. Place one sheet of dough over the bottom part of a ravioli form, making sure that the sheet overhangs the sides slightly. Use the top part of the form to make slight impressions in the dough. Place about 1 teaspoon of the filling in each impression. Cover with a second sheet of dough and carefully roll over the form with a rolling pin to create the ravioli. Gently push the ravioli out onto a clean towel and arrange in a single layer. Continue with the remaining dough and filling.

To make the ravioli by hand, roll out each piece into a 16 by 14-inch rectangle. Space teaspoons of the filling about $1\frac{1}{2}$ inches apart on one sheet. Cover with another sheet of dough. Press down around the mounds of filling with your fingers to seal, and cut into ravioli with a ravioli wheel.

5. Bring 8 quarts of water to a boil in a large pot. Add half the ravioli and cook just until they float to the top, about 1 minute. Scoop the ravioli out of the water with a strainer and place on a platter and drizzle with a little of the melted butter. Toss gently. Top with the remaining butter and a sprinkling of cheese. Serve immediately.

Note: To freeze the uncooked ravioli, place them in single layers on floured cookie sheets. Cover with aluminum foil and freeze until firm, about 1 hour. Transfer to plastic bags and freeze. Do not defrost before cooking.

Conchiglioni Ripieni al Forno

Large Stuffed Shells

The original recipe for these large stuffed pasta shells (conchiglioni) comes from the kitchen of Signora Alba d'Aurora in Rome. I was a little skeptical scanning the ingredients—so much heavy cream and butter.

I used low-fat milk for the besciamella (white sauce) and less cream. One or two of these rich ragu-stuffed shells are very filling, and I recommend serving them as part of a buffet. The shells are not cooked first but they are filled dry and then baked. The entire dish can be assembled a day ahead and refrigerated, leaving just the final steps of adding cream and milk before baking.

Makes 36 to 40 shells; serves 20 as part of a buffet, 8 to 10 as a pasta course

RAGU

1 tablespoon olive oil

³/₄ pound lean ground beef

¹/₂ cup dry red wine

1 cup Tomato-Basil Sauce (page 32)

WHITE SAUCE

4¹/₂ cups low-fat milk

8 tablespoons (1 stick) butter

¹/₂ cup unbleached all-purpose flour

¹/₂ teaspoon fine sea salt

One 12-ounce box large (2-inch) pasta shells

¹/₄ cup milk

1¹/₂ cups heavy cream

¹/₄ cup freshly grated Parmigiano-Reggiano cheese

1. In a large skillet, heat the olive oil over medium heat. Add the meat and cook, stirring, until browned. Raise the heat to high, stir in the wine, and let most of it evaporate. Lower the heat to medium, add the tomato sauce, and cook, uncovered, for 15 minutes, or until thickened. Set aside.

2. In a large saucepan scald the milk (bring to just under a boil). Set aside.

3. In another large saucepan, melt the butter. Whisk in the flour to make a smooth paste, and cook, stirring, for about 1 minute. Slowly whisk in the hot milk, and cook, whisking, until the sauce thickens enough to coat the back of a spoon. Stir in the salt. Remove from the heat, and stir in the ragu until well blended. Set aside.

4. Preheat the oven to 375°F. Lightly butter a 14 by 8-inch baking dish. Using a spoon, fill the shells with the ragu mixture and place them close together in the baking dish.

5. In a bowl, combine the milk and heavy cream. Slowly pour evenly over the shells. Sprinkle the cheese over the top. Cover with aluminum foil and bake for 40 minutes. Serve immediately.

3 tablespoons olive oil

1 large white onion, diced

2 cloves garlic, minced

1 green bell pepper, cored, seeded, and diced

2 medium zucchini, diced

1 medium eggplant, peeled and diced

1/4 cup minced fresh basil

1/4 cup minced flat-leaf parsley

2 medium potatoes, cooked, peeled, and diced

1 pound ripe tomatoes, diced

Fine sea salt to taste

Eight 7 by 6 1/2-inch no-boil lasagne noodles (see headnote)

1 cup diced Italian Fontina cheese

1 cup diced provolone cheese

1 cup diced mozzarella cheese

2 cups Tomato-Basil Sauce (page 32) or prepared sauce

1. In a large sauté pan, heat the oil over medium heat. Add the onion and garlic and cook until the onion begins to soften. Add the pepper, zucchini, and eggplant and cook until the vegetables soften. Stir in the basil and parsley. Add the potatoes and tomatoes, stir well, and season with salt. Cover the pan and let simmer until very soft, about 20 minutes. Remove from the heat.

2. Preheat the oven to 350°F. Lightly grease a 14 by 8 1/2 by 2-inch baking pan with olive oil.

3. Place 2 lasagne sheets in the pan, slightly overlapping them. Spoon about 2 cups of the vegetable mixture over the noodles. Scatter the Fontina cheese over the vegetables. Cover the cheese with 2 more lasagne noodles. Spread another 2 cups of the vegetable mixture on top. Scatter the provolone cheese over, cover with 2 more lasagne sheets, and top with the remaining vegetable mixture. Scatter the mozzarella cheese over the vegetables and top with the remaining 2 lasagne sheets.

continued

Lasagne di Verdure Fresche

Fresh Vegetable Lasagne

❦

A medley of just-picked summer vegetables layered between thin sheets of lasagne noodles gives this dish its garden-fresh taste. I like to use Del Verde brand no-boil lasagne sheets. For this recipe, you will need eight of the 7 by 6 1/2-inch sheets. If using another brand, adjust the number of lasagne sheets as necessary to make four layers in the pan.

❦

Serves 8 to 10

4. Press down on the top sheets with your hands to compact the layers. Spread the tomato sauce over the top. Cover the dish with aluminum foil and bake for 45 minutes.

5. Let the lasagne cool for about 5 minutes before cutting into squares. Serve immediately.

Note: Cooked lasagne can be frozen for as long as 3 months. Defrost in the refrigerator and reheat in a moderate oven for 20 to 30 minutes.

3 tablespoons extra-virgin olive oil

1³/₄ cups diced leeks

¹/₄ pound pancetta or bacon, diced

¹/₃ cup minced flat-leaf parsley

One 10-ounce package frozen petite peas, thawed

3 cups Tomato-Basil Sauce (page 32) or prepared tomato sauce

Fine sea salt and coarsely ground black pepper to taste

1 pound capellini or angel hair pasta, broken into thirds

2 cups freshly grated Asiago or Parmigiano-Reggiano cheese
    (5 ounces)

20 aluminum foil cupcake cups, 3 inches wide and 1¹/₂ inches deep

1. In a large skillet, heat the olive oil. Add the leeks and pancetta or bacon and cook over medium heat until the leeks begin to wilt and the panetta starts to brown. Add the parsley and cook for 1 minute. Add the peas and cook for 1 minute. Add 2 cups of the tomato sauce and stir well. Add the salt and pepper, cover the pan and set aside.

2. Preheat the oven to 350°F. Lightly oil the aluminum foil cups. Bring 6 quarts of salted water to a boil in a large pot. Add the pasta and cook just until al dente. Drain the pasta well and place it in a bowl. Add the leek mixture and cheese and mix well with a wooden spoon. Add the remaining 1 cup of tomato sauce and mix again.

3. Divide the mixture among the foil cups, making sure to distribute it evenly. Press down the pasta lightly with the back of a spoon to compact the ingredients. Place the cups on cookie sheets. Cover loosely with foil and bake for 15 to 20 minutes, or until the timballini are heated through.

4. To unmold, using a potholder or oven mitt, carefully invert the molds onto a large platter or onto individual dishes.

Variation: Instead of making timballini, use the leek mixture to sauce 1 pound of farfalle bow ties or other pasta for a simple supper for four.

Timballini di Pasta

Small Pasta Molds

Timballini are small neat molds made with meats, vegetables, or, as in this case, with pasta. These are flecked with bright green peas, pancetta, and parsley and bound together with fresh tomato sauce. They make a bright and unusual addition to a Christmas buffet. You can make the sauce several days in advance and assemble the timballini one day ahead, then bake just before serving.

Makes 20

Pasta Buffet for a Crowd

Riso e Melanzane alla Palermitana

Rice and Eggplant Palermo Style

֍

In this old Palermo recipe, rice is first browned in a skillet, before simmering, similar to the first steps in making a northern Italian risotto. Pecorino cheese and plum tomatoes, two other basic Italian ingredients, keep this dish firmly rooted in traditional Sicilian cuisine. The recipe makes enough to feed a crowd and is a good choice for a buffet menu.

֍

Serves 10 to 12 as part of a buffet; 8 as a pasta course

---

4 eggplants (about 2 pounds), sliced lengthwise into $1/2$-inch-thick slices

Coarse salt

4 tablespoons olive oil

2 medium onions, diced

$1 3/4$ cups long-grain rice

$2 1/2$ cups hot Homemade Beef Broth (page 16)

1 cup freshly grated Pecorino Romano cheese

1 tablespoon butter

$1/3$ cup chopped fresh basil

$1/3$ cup chopped flat-leaf parsley

3 pounds plum tomatoes (about 12), peeled, cored, and diced

Fine sea salt and freshly ground black pepper to taste

About 1 cup peanut oil

1. Layer the eggplant slices in a large colander, salting each layer. Set the colander on a plate and let the eggplant sweat for 1 hour.

2. In a large skillet, heat 2 tablespoons of the olive oil. Add half the onions and sauté for 2 minutes. Add the rice and stir to coat. Cook, stirring often, until the rice is "toasted," or browned, about 5 to 6 minutes. Add the beef broth, lower the heat, and simmer, covered, until all of the liquid is absorbed. Stir in $1/2$ cup of the grated cheese and set aside.

3. In a large saucepan, heat the remaining 2 tablespoons olive oil and the butter. Add the remaining onions, the basil, and parsley, and sauté until the onions are soft. Add the tomatoes, and salt and pepper and simmer, covered, for 25 minutes. Set the sauce aside.

4. Rinse the eggplant slices and dry well.

5. In a large skillet, heat $1/2$ cup peanut oil over medium-high heat. Add the eggplant slices, a few at a time, and fry until slightly browned on both sides. Remove the eggplant to brown paper to drain. Fry the remaining eggplant slices, adding additional peanut oil as needed.

6. Preheat the oven to 375°F. Generously grease a 13 $\frac{1}{2}$ by 8-inch casserole. Arrange one quarter of the eggplant over the bottom of the casserole, overlapping the slices. Cover with one third of the rice and one quarter of the tomato sauce. Continue layering the eggplant, rice, and sauce, ending with a layer of eggplant covered with sauce. Sprinkle on the remaining $\frac{1}{2}$ cup grated cheese.

7. Cover the casserole with aluminum foil and bake for 25 to 30 minutes until heated through. Serve immediately.

Note: To make ahead, bake the casserole, let cool completely, then wrap tightly and freeze for up to a month. To serve, defrost the casserole in the refrigerator, then reheat in the oven.

Sformato di Riso con Spinaci

Rice and Spinach Mold

❧

The gentle cooking of this spinach, rice, and dried tomato mold in a bagnomaría (water bath) guarantees that it will be moist and hold its shape. Besides making a nice presentation with its flecks of green, white, and red, this dish can accompany just about any type of main course.

Assemble it early in the day, refrigerate, and bake it just before serving (if refrigerated, bake for about ten minutes longer than the recipe specifies).

❧

Serves 8 to 10

4 tablespoons butter

1 medium white onion, diced

1 3/4 cups long-grain white rice

Two 10-ounce packages frozen chopped spinach, thawed and squeezed dry

5 cups hot Homemade Chicken Broth (page 14)

1/2 cup diced Dried Tomatoes (page 310)

1/2 cup freshly grated Asiago cheese

Fine sea salt to taste

1. Preheat the oven to 350°F. Butter a 7 1/2 by 3-inch round baking mold or a 1 1/2-quart soufflé dish.

2. In a large saucepan, melt the butter. Add the onions and cook until they begin to turn golden brown. Remove the onions to a plate. Add the rice to the saucepan and cook, stirring to coat it with the butter. Cook, stirring, until the rice begins to brown lightly, then add the spinach and stir well. Slowly stir in the broth, lower the heat, and simmer for 20 minutes, covered, or until all the liquid has been absorbed. Remove from the heat and add the onions, along with the dried tomatoes and cheese. Stir well and add the salt.

3. Pack the mixture into the mold, and smooth the top. Place a piece of foil over the top of the mold. Place the mold in a larger baking pan and add boiling water to come halfway up the sides of the mold. Bake for 30 minutes.

4. Remove the mold from the water, and discard the foil. Invert a serving dish over the top of the mold. Carefully turn the mold upside down, tap the bottom of the mold, and unmold the sformato. Serve at once.

1 ounce dried porcini mushrooms

1 cup hot water

6 tablespoons butter

½ cup diced white onion

2 cups Arborio rice

2 to 2 ½ cups hot Homemade Chicken Broth (page 14)

1 ½ cups dry white wine

½ cup mascarpone cheese

1 teaspoon fine sea salt, or more to taste

1. Place the porcini in a small bowl, pour the hot water over them, and let soak until soft, about 30 minutes. Drain the porcini, reserving the liquid, dice them, and set aside. Strain the liquid and add enough water to equal 1 cup. Set aside.

2. In a deep heavy earthenware pot or large heavy saucepan, melt the butter. Add the onions and cook over low heat until they are very soft. Add the rice and stir with a wooden spoon to coat with butter. Cook, stirring, for about 5 minutes. Slowly add a ¼ cup chicken broth and stir until all the liquid is absorbed by the rice. Add a little of the wine and continue stirring until it is absorbed, then add a little of the reserved porcini liquid. Continue adding broth, wine, and porcini liquid alternately, making sure that the rice absorbs each addition of liquid before adding another. When the rice is done, it should be firm but not hard to the bite, with a creamy consistency.

3. Add the cheese and stir until it is melted. Stir in the mushrooms and salt. Serve at once.

Risotto con Mascarpone

Risotto with Mascarpone

A risotto must be cooked properly, with constant stirring and a slow addition of the liquid, until the rice is "not thirsty anymore." This version uses creamy mascarpone cheese, which produces a velvety finish, and makes an elegant first course for a holiday dinner.

Serves 4 to 6

Northern Italian Dinner

....

Risotto with Mascarpone

Veal Scallops with Prosciutto and Fontina (page 155)

Green Bean and Fennel Salad (page 200)

Befana Cake (page 280)

Dried Fig, Pear, and Pine Nut Pie (page 258)

....

Risotto ai Funghi

Mushroom Risotto

❦

Wild funghi (mushrooms) are unearthed from wooded areas all over Italy. They come in various shapes, sizes, and textures, but their whereabouts are usually a well-kept secret. Porcini (literally "little pigs") are probably the most well known of the hundreds of species of Italian mushrooms.

But the deep brown, smooth-textured portobello mushroom, which is neither Italian nor wild, is a work of art and is wonderful grilled and sprinkled with just a whiff of balsamic vinegar. I use portobellos as a ravioli filling, to make mushroom pasta, and in this wonderful risotto. To clean mushrooms, use a mushroom brush or a damp clean sponge to wipe them off. Do not rinse them under running water.

❦

Serves 6 to 8

---

3 tablespoons olive oil

1 large portobello mushroom (about 6 ounces), stemmed, cleaned, and diced

Fine sea salt to taste

4 tablespoons butter

3 medium shallots, diced

2 cups Arborio rice

4 cups hot Homemade Chicken Broth (page 14)

1/2 cup dry white wine

1/4 cup mascarpone cheese

1/2 cup freshly grated Parmigiano-Reggiano cheese

1. In a medium skillet, heat the olive oil. Add the mushrooms and cook them over low heat until they are lightly browned, about 4 minutes. Season with salt and set aside.

2. In a large heavy saucepan or a Dutch oven, melt the butter. Add the shallots and cook over low heat until soft. Add the rice and stir to coat with the butter. Cook, stirring, for about 5 minutes. Add about 1/4 cup of the chicken broth and stir until the liquid is absorbed by the rice. Add a little of the wine and stir constantly until it is absorbed. Continue adding the broth and wine alternately and stirring until the rice is al dente, with a creamy consistency.

3. Add the mushrooms, mascarpone cheese, and Parmigiano cheese and stir to combine. Season with salt and serve immediately.

1 small pie pumpkin (about ¹/₂ pound)

6 tablespoons butter

1 large leek, white part only, halved lengthwise, well rinsed, and diced

1 cup Arborio rice

3¹/₂ cups hot Homemade Chicken Broth (page 14)

1 cup dry white wine

¹/₄ cup mascarpone cheese

¹/₃ cup freshly grated Parmigiano-Reggiano cheese

1. Cut off the pumpkin stem. With a vegetable peeler, remove the skin. Cut the pumpkin in half, and remove and discard the seeds and stringy flesh. Dice enough of the pumpkin to make 1 cup. (Save any remaining pumpkin for another use.)

2. In a large heavy saucepan, melt the butter. Add the pumpkin and leek and cook over medium heat, stirring often, until softened. Add the rice and stir to coat with the butter. Cook, stirring, until the rice begins to crackle, about 5 minutes; do not let brown. Slowly add ¹/₂ cup of the chicken broth and stir constantly until the rice absorbs all the liquid. Add a little of the wine and continue stirring until it is absorbed. Continue adding broth and wine alternately, stirring all the while, until the rice is al dente, with a creamy consistency.

3. Stir in the cheeses, blending well and stirring until the mascarpone melts. Serve immediately.

Risotto di Zucca

Pumpkin Risotto

Classic risotto usually gets its deep golden hue from saffron, but in this version from Terry Rozzi, whose home is Cremona, in northern Italy, diced pumpkin provides not only a delicate color but also a slightly sweet taste. Part of the process can be started in advance, by cooking the leeks, pumpkin, and rice in the butter; set aside at room temperature, or refrigerate if more than a few hours before serving time.

Serves 8

Italian-Style Thanksgiving

Pumpkin Risotto

Rolled Stuffed Turkey Breast
(page 166)

Rosemary-Cranberry Sauce
(page 188)

Green Beans and Fontina
(page174)

Mixed Stewed Vegetables
(page 177)

Roasted Chestnuts
(page 189)

Zuppa Inglese (page 296)

Polenta

☙

Polenta is enjoying great popularity in this country as a gourmet food, somewhat ironic for a staple long associated with Italian peasant cooking. Coarsely ground cornmeal is best in this basic recipe. Once polenta is cooked, it lends itself to many possibilities: It becomes the plate on which to serve stewed or grilled meats and vegetables. It can be cut into slices, fried in olive oil or butter, and topped with cheese or eaten plain. It is the perfect accompaniment to Spicy Chicken (page 163).

☙

Serves 8

4 ¹/₂ cups water

1 ¹/₂ teaspoons fine sea salt

1 ¹/₂ cups coarsely ground cornmeal

1. Lightly oil a wooden board or a platter.

2. In a large heavy pot, combine the water, salt, and cornmeal. Set over medium heat and cook, stirring vigorously all the while, until the polenta thickens and begins to leave the sides of the pan, about 15 to 25 minutes (depending on the cornmeal used).

3. Immediately pour the polenta onto the oiled board or platter. It can be served hot, or it can be refrigerated until chilled, then cut into slices and fried.

Pani Diversi

Pizzas, Tarts, and Filled Breads

Pizza di Verdure

Vegetable Pizza

❧

Top a basil-and-sesame-seed yeast dough canvas with fresh, seasonal vegetables to create this vibrantly colored pizza. The recipe makes two pizze, enough to serve twenty as an antipasto if cut into small squares.

❧

Makes 2 large pizze; serves 12

DOUGH

$1/4$ cup sesame seeds

1 tablespoon active dry yeast

1 teaspoon malt extract or sugar

2 cups warm (110° to 115°F) water

$5^1/2$ to $5^3/4$ cups unbleached all-purpose flour

$1/2$ teaspoon fine sea salt

$1/4$ cup finely minced fresh basil

TOPPING

$1/4$ cup olive oil

1 pound small zucchini, thinly sliced

2 pounds tomatoes, thinly sliced

Fine sea salt and freshly ground black pepper to taste

Dried oregano, optional

1. Preheat the oven to 400°F. Spread the sesame seeds on a cookie sheet and toast for about 5 minutes, until golden. Watch them carefully to prevent burning. Remove the seeds to a small dish and set aside.

2. In a large bowl, dissolve the yeast and malt extract or sugar in the warm water and let proof until foamy, about 10 minutes.

3. In another bowl, mix 5 cups of the flour and the salt. Add to the yeast mixture along with the basil. Using your hands, form a ball of dough that is smooth and no longer sticky, adding flour as needed. Knead the dough on a floured surface for about 5 minutes.

4. Lightly grease a large bowl with olive oil, add the dough, turning it to coat, and cover tightly with plastic wrap. Let the dough rise in a warm place until doubled, about $1^1/2$ hours.

5. Preheat the oven to 425°F. Lightly oil two $15^1/2$ by 14-inch baking pans or 15 by 11-inch cookie sheets. Spread the sesame seeds over the work surface. Punch the dough down and turn it out on top of the sesame seeds. Knead the seeds into the dough, adding a little flour to the work surface if necessary to prevent the dough from sticking.

6. Divide the dough in half. On a lightly floured surface, roll out each piece of dough to a rectangle the size of the prepared pans, and fit the pizzas into the pans.

7. Brush 1 tablespoon of the olive oil over the top of each pizza. Arrange alternating rows of the zucchini and tomatoes on each pizza, overlapping them slightly. Brush the vegetables with the remaining 2 tablespoons olive oil. Sprinkle the tops with salt and pepper, and with oregano if desired.

8. Bake for 45 minutes. Cool slightly. Cut the pizze into squares and serve warm.

Libretti di Olive

Little Olive Pizzas

☙

Libretti are small pizzas folded in half, like a book, and then eaten out of hand. The inspiration for this recipe comes from the many versions of libretti I've sampled all over Italy. Mine are made with a yeast dough that is first brushed with hot red and green peppers that have been cooked in olive oil, and then embedded with oil-cured black and brine-cured green olives. The recipe makes sixteen libretti; they never last long, but you can freeze any leftovers. You can also divide the dough in half rather than into smaller pieces and make two sixteen-inch pizze from this recipe.

☙

Makes 16

DOUGH

$2^{1}/_{4}$ *cups warm (110 to 115°F) water*

1 teaspoon active dry yeast

6 to $6^{1}/_{2}$ cups unbleached all-purpose flour

TOPPING

$^{1}/_{4}$ *olive oil*

1 small hot red pepper, diced

1 small hot green pepper, diced

$^{1}/_{2}$ *cup oil-cured black olives, pitted and chopped*

$^{1}/_{2}$ *cup Sicilian green olives in brine, drained, pitted, and chopped*

1. Pour $^{1}/_{4}$ cup of the warm water into a large bowl and stir in the yeast. Let the yeast proof for about 10 minutes, until foamy.

2. Add the remaining 2 cups warm water and 5 cups of the flour to the yeast mixture. Mix with your hands, add the additional flour as needed until a smooth ball of dough is formed. Turn the dough out onto a floured surface and knead for about 5 minutes.

3. Lightly grease a large bowl with olive oil, add the dough, and turn to coat with the oil. Cover the bowl tightly with plastic wrap and let rise in a warm place until doubled in size, about 2 hours.

4. In a small skillet, heat 3 tablespoons of the olive oil. Add the red and green peppers and cook for about 2 minutes, pressing on them with the back of a wooden spoon to release their flavor. Set aside.

5. Mix the black and green olives together in a small bowl.

6. Preheat the oven to 425°F. Lightly grease two cookie sheets. Punch the dough down and knead it on a floured surface for 4 to 5 minutes. Divide the dough in half and roll each piece into a 12-inch circle. Pour half the oil and pepper mixture over each piece and use a pastry brush to brush the mixture evenly over the dough. Roll each piece up like a jelly roll and then into a ball, and knead again until the peppers are well distributed.

7. Divide each piece of dough into 8 pieces. Roll each piece into a 5-inch circle. Sprinkle the olive mixture evenly over the pizze, pressing the olives into the dough with your fingers.

8. Brush the tops with the remaining 1 tablespoon olive oil. Place the pizze on lightly greased cookie sheets and bake for 20 to 25 minutes, or until the crust is nicely browned. Serve warm, and fold in half to eat.

Pizza Chena

Pizza chena (its name is a
Neapolitan dialect term meaning
"full pie") was always a part of
our Easter table when I was a
child. This enormous two-crusted
pie was stuffed with salami,
prosciutto, cheeses of all sorts,
bacon, and a dozen eggs! I have
reduced the number of eggs, but
this still remains a substantial
and memorable dish.

Serves 10 to 12

DOUGH

1 tablespoon active dry yeast

2 1/2 cups warm (110° to 115°F) water

5 1/2 to 6 cups unbleached all-purpose flour

1 teaspoon fine sea salt

2 1/2 teaspoons olive oil

FILLING

3/4 pound fresh mozzarella cheese (fior di latte), thinly sliced

1/2 pound ham, thinly sliced

1/2 pound provolone cheese, thinly sliced

1/2 pound Genoa salami, thinly sliced

1/2 pound Swiss cheese, thinly sliced

1/2 pound capocollo, thinly sliced

6 large eggs

1/2 cup freshly grated Parmigiano-Reggiano cheese

1/3 cup minced flat-leaf parsley

Fine sea salt and freshly ground black pepper to taste

1 egg beaten with 1 teaspoon water, for egg wash

1. In a large bowl, sprinkle the yeast over 1 cup of the warm water, stir well, and let proof for 5 to 10 minutes, or until foamy. Add the remaining 1 1/2 cups water and stir well.

2. In another bowl, mix 5 cups of the flour with the salt. Add to the yeast mixture along with 1 teaspoon of the olive oil. Mix with your hands, adding additional flour if necessary, until a soft and no longer sticky dough is formed.

3. Turn the dough out onto a floured surface and knead it until smooth and elastic. Lightly grease a large bowl with olive oil, add the dough, and turn to coat. Cover tightly with plastic wrap and let rise in a warm place until doubled in bulk.

4. Preheat the oven to 375°F. Brush the bottom and sides of a 15 by 13-inch baking dish or a 10 by 3-inch springform pan with the remaining 1 1/2 teaspoons olive oil. Punch down the dough and knead it on a floured surface for 3 or 4 minutes. Divide the dough in half. On a floured surface, roll one piece of the dough to a rectangle or round at least 2 inches larger than the pan. Fit the dough in the pan, stretching it up the sides so that it overhangs the rim.

5. Fill the pan with alternating layers of the sliced cheeses and meats (you should have at least 10 layers).

6. In a bowl, whisk together the eggs, and Parmigiano-Reggiano cheese, parsley, and salt and pepper. Pour the mixture evenly over the cheese and meat.

7. Break a lemon-size piece of dough off the remaining piece of dough and set aside. On a floured surface, roll the second piece of dough out to a rectangle or round at least 1 inch larger than the pan. Place the dough over the filling and seal the edges by pinching them closed and rolling the seam underneath itself. Divide the reserved piece of dough in half and roll each piece into a rope. Lay one piece across the center of the pie, and lay the second piece across it to form a cross.

8. Brush the top of the pie evenly with the egg wash. Bake for 35 to 40 minutes or until the crust is nicely browned. Remove from the oven and let cool completely.

9. If using a springform pan, release the spring, transfer the pie to a serving plate, and cut into wedges. If using a rectangular pan, cut the pie into pieces in the pan, then transfer them to a serving dish.

Note: This pie will keep for up to 1 week in the refrigerator. It is best served at room temperature or just slightly warm.

Pizza di Patate

Potato Pizza

❧

My son's favorite food is pizza, and for Chris's last birthday, I made his Great-grandmother Galasso's potato pizza, which looks like a pizza, but mashed potatoes are used as a crust. Fresh mozzarella cheese, meaty plum tomatoes, and dried oregano are the traditional toppings. This can also be served as a side dish.

❧

Serves 8

Christopher's Birthday Dinner

....

Pan-Cooked Chicken Breasts
(page 161)

Potato Pizza

Asparagus and Red Pepper
Salad (page 5)

Chocolate Pudding (page 212)

Chocolate Wafer Cookies
(page 233)

....

2 pounds white or all-purpose potatoes, unpeeled
4 tablespoons butter, softened
$\frac{1}{3}$ cup freshly grated Parmigiano-Reggiano cheese
Fine sea salt to taste
5 ounces fresh mozzarella (fior di latte) (1 large ball), diced
2 plum tomatoes, thinly sliced
1 teaspoon dried oregano
1 tablespoon olive oil

1. Place the potatoes in a pot, cover with water, and cook until tender, about 15 minutes. Drain. When cool enough to handle, peel and place in a bowl. Add the butter and mash the potatoes. Stir in the Parmigiano-Reggiano cheese, and salt. Set aside.

2. Preheat the oven to 350°F. Generously butter a 9½ by 2-inch round baking dish. Spread the potato mixture evenly in the dish. Arrange the top with the mozzarella cheese, then the tomato slices. Sprinkle the oregano over the top and drizzle with the olive oil. Bake until the cheese is melted and the tomatoes have softened, about 35 minutes.

3. Preheat the broiler. Place the pizza under the broiler for about 7 minutes, or until the top is nicely browned. Let stand for 5 minutes, then serve directly from the dish.

2 tablespoons extra-virgin olive oil

1 cup thinly sliced leeks, white part only (about 2 medium leeks)

¼ pound prosciutto, diced

Two 10-ounce packages frozen spinach, thawed and squeezed dry

1½ cups grated ricotta salata or Pecorino Romano cheese

2 sheets frozen puff pastry, thawed

1 egg beaten with 1 teaspoon water, for egg wash

1 tablespoon sesame seeds

Coarse sea salt to taste

1. In a skillet, heat 1 tablespoon of the olive oil. Add the leeks and prosciutto and cook over medium heat until the leeks are soft and the prosciutto begins to crisp. Remove to a bowl.

2. In the same pan, heat the remaining 1 tablespoon olive oil. Add the spinach and cook for about 5 minutes, stirring often. Add to the leek mixture. Stir in the cheese, and set aside.

3. Preheat the oven to 425°F. On a floured surface, roll one sheet of the dough out into a 16 by 12-inch rectangle. Lift the pastry up and place it on a 15 by 11-inch baking sheet, letting the edges hang over the sides. Spread the leek mixture evenly over the dough.

4. Roll the remaining sheet of dough out into a 16 by 12-inch rectangle and place it over the filling. Cut off the excess dough, leaving a 1-inch overhang. Pinch the edges of the dough together on all sides, then press the edges with a fork to seal. Reroll the scraps and cut out shapes to make a decorative design on the top of the tart if you wish.

5. Brush the egg wash evenly over the dough. Sprinkle the sesame seeds and salt over the top. Bake for 20 to 25 minutes, or until the pastry is golden brown.

6. Let cool slightly, then cut into pieces and serve.

Torta di Porri e Spinaci

Leek and Spinach Tart

No one will ever guess that it did not take you all day to make this spinach, leek, and prosciutto tart. It is perfect as a luncheon dish, can be cut into small squares for an antipasto, and is a nice addition to a buffet supper. Made with prepared puff pastry, the tart can be assembled hours ahead and takes less than a half hour to bake.

Serves 8

Holiday Buffet

Melon and Prosciutto
(page 12)

Leek and Spinach Tart

Fresh Sausage (page 151)

Escarole Salad (page 195)

Ricotta-Filled Pastry Cones
(page 276)

Torta di Spinaci

Spinach Tart

❧

Spinach is one of the first leafy vegetables to appear in my Italian garden. It is such a versatile vegetable I have many uses for it, including this tart, with a dense spinach and creamy cheese sauce filling.

❧

Serves 8

DOUGH

1 3/4 cups unbleached all-purpose flour

1/4 teaspoon fine sea salt

6 tablespoons cold butter, cut into pieces

2 to 2 1/2 tablespoons ice water

FILLING

1 pound spinach, stemmed, washed, and drained

1 cup milk

1 tablespoon butter

1 tablespoon unbleached all-purpose flour

1 teaspoon grated nutmeg

1 cup diced Swiss cheese (4 ounces)

1 large egg, slightly beaten

2 tablespoons freshly grated Parmigiano-Reggiano cheese

2 medium tomatoes, sliced 1/4 inch thick

1/2 cup pine nuts

1. In a large bowl or in a food processor, mix the flour and salt together. Cut in the butter until the mixture resembles coarse crumbs, or pulse to form a coarse mixture. Slowly add the water and mix or process just until a ball of dough begins to form. Do not overmix. Wrap the dough in plastic wrap and refrigerate for 15 minutes.

2. Preheat the oven to 425°F. Place the spinach in a saucepan without any additional water, cover, and cook over medium heat until wilted, about 5 minutes. Drain well and squeeze out as much water as possible. Coarsely chop the spinach and set aside.

3. In a small saucepan, heat the milk until hot. Set aside.

4. In a medium saucepan, melt the butter. Add flour and whisk to form a paste. Slowly whisk in the milk and cook, whisking continually, until the mixture starts to thicken and coats the back of a spoon, about 5 minutes. Using a wooden spoon, stir in the nutmeg and half the Swiss cheese, and stir until the cheese has melted and the sauce is smooth. Transfer the sauce to a medium bowl and cool for 5 minutes. Stir in the egg and blend well. Set the sauce aside.

5. Roll the chilled dough between two sheets of waxed paper to a 10½-inch round. Fit it into a 10-inch tart pan with a removable bottom. Trim the edges. Place a sheet of aluminum foil over the dough and fill it with uncooked beans, rice, or pastry weights to prevent puffing while baking. Bake the tart shell for 20 minutes, then remove the foil and weights and let cool for 10 minutes. (Leave the oven on.)

6. Add the spinach to the cream sauce and mix well. Stir in the Parmigiano-Reggiano cheese. Spread the spinach mixture evenly in the tart shell. Arrange the tomato slices in a circle on top of the filling, and sprinkle on the remaining Swiss cheese and the pine nuts.

7. Bake the tart for 20 to 25 minutes, or until the cheese has melted and the top is lightly browned. Cool the tart for 5 minutes, then cut into wedges and serve.

Spring Luncheon

....

Spinach Tart

Carrot Salad
(page 201)

White-and-Black Biscotti
(page 230)

Fresh Fruit

....

Pasticcio di Maccheroni

Macaroni and Chicken in a Pastry Crust

❧

Whenever I make pasticcio di maccheroni, an Italian version of chicken pot pie, I think of Giuseppe Lampedusa's novel The Leopard, *about the decline of the aristocracy in nineteenth-century Sicily. In his elegantly written book, Lampedusa describes lavish multicourse dinners at which "three lackeys in green, gold, and powder entered, each holding a great silver dish containing a towering macaroni pie." Pasticcio di maccheroni is easy to assemble if you make the slightly sweet dough a day ahead and have some cooked or leftover chicken on hand. Or the entire pie can be assembled in one day, covered with a sheet of buttered parchment paper, and baked the next day. Either way, this savory, deep-dish pie will be the centerpiece of your buffet table.*

❧

Serves 8 to 10

DOUGH

2 ³/₄ *cups unbleached all-purpose flour*

¹/₄ *cup sugar*

¹/₂ *teaspoon fine sea salt*

1 tablespoon grated lemon zest

8 tablespoons (1 stick) butter, cut into pieces and softened

3 large egg yolks

¹/₂ *cup water*

FILLING

1 pound penne rigate

One 10-ounce package frozen peas, thawed

2 cups freshly grated Asiago cheese

5 tablespoons butter, softened

1¹/₄ pounds cooked chicken, cut into bite-size pieces (about 2¹/₂ cups)

1 cup Homemade Chicken Broth (page 14)

Fine sea salt to taste

1 egg, slightly beaten

1. In a bowl mix together the flour, sugar, salt, and zest. Using a fork or pastry blender, work in the butter until the mixture resembles coarse crumbs.

2. In a small bowl, whisk together the egg yolks and water. Add the yolks to the flour mixture and mix with your hands until a soft dough is formed. If the dough seems dry, add a little water. Gather the dough into a ball. Divide it in half and wrap each piece in plastic wrap. Refrigerate overnight.

3. Bring 6 quarts of salted water to a boil in a large pot. Add the penne and cook until just al dente; the pasta should remain slightly undercooked. Add the peas to the boiling water during the last 3 minutes of cooking. Drain well and place in a large bowl. Add the cheese and butter and toss well. Set aside.

4. In another bowl, combine the chicken and chicken broth. Set aside.

5. Preheat the oven to 375°F. Butter a 10 by 3-inch springform pan. On a lightly floured surface, roll one piece of dough into a 16-inch round. Fit the dough into the pan, letting the excess hang over the sides.

6. Place one third of the pasta mixture in the pastry shell and sprinkle with salt. Spread half of the chicken and broth mixture over the pasta. Repeat with another layer of pasta and another layer of chicken. Spread the remaining pasta over the chicken and sprinkle with salt.

7. On a floured surface, roll out the remaining dough to a 12-inch round. Place the dough over the filling. Trim off the excess dough, leaving a 1-inch overhang and pinch the edges together to seal. If you wish, reroll the scraps and cut out shapes to make a decorative design on top of the pie. Brush the top of the pie with the beaten egg.

8. Bake for 45 minutes, or until the crust is nicely browned. Transfer the pan to a rack and let cool for 10 minutes for easier cutting. Release the spring on the side of the pan and transfer the pasticcio to a serving plate. With a sharp knife, cut into wedges and serve.

La Festa di Pasqua

Easter

❦

In Italy, the week before Easter is the most solemn and grandest of them all. During that week, known as *Settimana Santa* (Holy Week), religious drama and symbolism are centered around Christ's last days on earth. It is a time of reflection and special church services, beginning with the observance of the Last Supper on Holy Thursday and Good Friday services and culminating in the glorious celebration of Easter itself. The earth is crisp and fresh after a long, dark winter, and in the renewal of nature we find our own spiritual renewal.

In addition to the many religious observances at Eastertime, there is the celebratory Easter feast, and here, too, symbolism can be found in the foods prepared. No Easter table in Italy would be complete without eggs, lamb, and bread.

Eggs, symbolic of hope, fertility, and new beginnings, are abundantly present in the Easter breads and in the ever-present *Torta Pasqualina* (page 88), a dense Easter pie made with thirty-three layers of dough to signify the years of Christ's life, and twelve eggs, representing the apostles.

The lamb, representing innocence and the sacrificed Christ, is often referred to as the Pascal lamb. It is the meat of choice on an Italian table at Eastertime. Lamb no more than a few months old, and milk-fed, is the best. The Roman technique of roasting lamb with fresh rosemary, lemon, and a splash of wine is one of my favorites. Accompany the lamb with a sampler of spring vegetables such as tender baby artichokes, new potatoes, asparagus, tiny green beans, and *misticanza*, a mixture of greens including chicory, radicchio, and watercress.

Lamb keeps its place of honor on the Easter table even with dessert. The often-elaborate lamb-shaped Easter cake is traditionally sculpted from *pasta reale*, marzipan (see page 327). To make a lamb cake without almond paste, try the cake on page 270.

Bread is the most basic food, and its importance cannot be overstated. In its religious connotation, it is Christ who is "the bread of life," meaning everlasting life. Easter breads are sacred and are taken to local churches to be blessed for the Easter feast.

Easter Monday is a holiday in Italy known as "Little Easter," or *Pasquetta*. It is a time for Italians to transport their Easter foods (perhaps *Pizza Chena*, page 78) to the countryside to enjoy a quiet respite with family and friends.

Torta Pasqualina

Easter Pie

❦

Torta Pasqualina is a double-crust pie with a dense filling of spinach, eggs, and ricotta cheese. Assemble the pie a day ahead, then bake and let cool before serving.

❦

Serves 10

Easter Buffet

....

Easter Pie

Pizza Chena (page 78)

Grilled Skewered Pork Loin
(page 149)

Carrot Salad (page 201)

Oranges and Bananas in
Amaretto (page 205)

Chatters (page 247)

....

DOUGH

6 cups unbleached all-purpose flour

1 teaspoon fine sea salt

1½ to 2 cups ice water

2 tablespoons olive oil

FILLING

Four 10-ounce packages frozen spinach, thawed and squeezed dry

½ cup freshly grated Parmigiano-Reggiano cheese

3 cups skim-milk ricotta cheese, well drained

¾ cup half-and-half

2 tablespoons chopped fresh marjoram

⅛ teaspoon fine sea salt

Olive oil for brushing

8 large eggs

Fine sea salt and freshly ground black pepper to taste

5 tablespoons butter

2 tablespoons freshly grated Pecorino Romano or Parmigiano-Reggiano cheese

1 egg yolk beaten with 1 teaspoon water, for egg wash

1. In a large bowl, mix the flour and salt together. Add 1½ cups ice water, a little at a time, and mix with your hands to form a rough ball of dough. Add the olive oil and mix well. Add just enough additional ice water to form a smooth ball; the dough should not be sticky.

2. Transfer the dough to a floured surface and knead until very smooth and elastic, about 5 minutes. Divide the dough into 10 equal pieces. Set aside, covered, on a floured surface.

3. In a bowl, mix the spinach with the Parmigiano-Reggiano. Set aside. In another bowl, mix the ricotta cheese with the half-and-half, marjoram, and salt. Set aside.

4. Preheat the oven to 375°F. Butter a 10 by 3-inch springform pan. On a floured surface, roll one piece of the dough into a 12-inch circle. Brush with a little olive oil, and place in the bottom of the springform pan. Repeat with 4 more pieces of dough, brushing each one with a little olive oil.

5. Spread the spinach mixture evenly over the dough. Spread the ricotta cheese mixture evenly over the spinach. Use a whole egg to make 8 shallow impressions in the ricotta, then carefully crack 1 egg into each impression. Sprinkle the eggs with salt and pepper and put ½ tablespoon of the butter on each one. Sprinkle the Pecorino or Parmigiano cheese over the eggs.

6. One at a time, roll out the remaining 5 pieces of dough into 12-inch circles. Carefully lay the circles over the eggs, letting the edges hang over the pan, and brush each one with olive oil. Trim off the excess dough, leaving a 1-inch overhang. Tuck the top layers of dough in around the edges of the pan and pinch to seal. (At this point the pie can be covered with plastic wrap and refrigerated until ready to bake, or overnight.)

7. Two hours before serving time, brush the top of the torta with the egg wash. Bake the pie for 1 hour or until the top is nicely browned. Let cool to room temperature.

8. Release the sides of the springform pan and cut the torta into wedges.

Rotolo di Verdure

Country Vegetable Roll

❦

This whole wheat dough is filled with a collage of vegetables and cheese, rolled up like a jelly roll, and then baked and sliced. As part of a vegetarian summer buffet, serve slightly warm or at room temperature. Tote it to a picnic as well.

❦

Serves 8 to 10

Vegetarian Picnic

Country Vegetable Roll

Cauliflower Frittata (page 179)

Maria's Musakà (page 186)

Asparagus and Red Pepper Salad (page 5)

Small Carrot Cakes (page 285)

Whole Wheat Bread dough (page 95), prepared through step 5

1 large white onion, thinly sliced

$1/4$ cup plus 1 tablespoon olive oil

One 10-ounce package frozen spinach, cooked, drained, and squeezed dry

$1/2$ pound broccoli, cooked, well drained, and chopped (1 cup)

1 cup diced carrots, blanched in boiling water until tender

$1/2$ pound Asiago or Swiss cheese, diced

$1/3$ cup diced pitted oil-cured black olives

Fine sea salt and coarsely ground black pepper to taste

$1/4$ cup toasted sesame seeds

1. On a floured surface, roll out the dough to a rectangle about 26 by 14 inches and fit it into a 17 by 11-inch jelly-roll pan, letting the edges of the dough overhang the pan. Set aside.

2. In a large skillet, heat $1/4$ cup of olive oil. Add the onion and cook until it begins to soften. Add the spinach, broccoli, and carrots and cook for 2 minutes to blend the flavors. Transfer to a bowl and let cool.

3. Spread the cooled vegetables over the dough, and sprinkle the cheese on top. Scatter the olives over the cheese and sprinkle with salt and pepper.

4. Roll the dough up like a jelly roll, starting at a long side and tucking the ends in as you roll. Pinch the seam closed and turn the roll seam side down on the pan. Brush the top of the dough with the remaining 1 tablespoon olive oil and sprinkle the sesame seeds over the top. Cover the loaf with a clean towel and let rise in a warm place until almost doubled in size, about 25 minutes.

5. Preheat the oven to 375°F. Bake the loaf for 35 to 40 minutes or until golden brown. Let cool on the baking sheet for 10 minutes, then remove to a cooling rack. Serve warm or at room temperature, cut into slices.

FILLING

$^1/_3$ cup olive oil

1 large white onion, thinly sliced

Two 10-ounce packages frozen spinach, cooked, drained, and
squeezed dry

$^1/_2$ cup toasted pine nuts

1 cup grated provolone cheese (4 ounces)

$^1/_2$ cup raisins

DOUGH

$^1/_4$ recipe Carmelo's Sicilian Bread dough (page 99), prepared
through step 4 (let rise on a cookie sheet)

1 egg, beaten

Sesame seeds for sprinkling

Coarse sea salt for sprinkling

1. In a skillet, heat the olive oil over low heat. Add the onions
and cook until they are deep brown and lightly caramelized. Add
the spinach and pine nuts, and cook for 2 minutes. Transfer to a
bowl, and let cool, then add the cheese and raisins. Mix well and set
aside.

2. Preheat the oven to 375°F. Divide the dough in half. On a
floured surface, roll one piece into a 12-inch circle. Fit it into a 9-
inch pie pan. Spoon the filling into the pan.

3. Roll out the remaining dough to a 14-inch circle, and cover
the filling with the dough. Trim the excess dough and pinch the
edges to seal. Make a decorative border with your fingers. Brush
the top of the pie with the beaten egg, and sprinkle on the sesame
seeds and coarse salt.

4. Bake the pie for 25 to 30 minutes, or until the top is nicely
browned. Let cool slightly before cutting into wedges. Serve warm
or at room temperature.

Impanata

Rustic Sicilian Pie

*Impanata is a rustic Sicilian pie,
filled with spinach, cheese, pine
nuts, and raisins. You will need
only one quarter of the basic
dough for Carmelo's Sicilian
Bread for this two-crust pie; use
the remaining dough to make a
slightly smaller loaf of bread.
Since it can be made ahead and
transported with ease, impanata
is perfect picnic fare.*

Serves 6

Pane

Bread

Cresciuta

❧

This is my favorite recipe for a natural starter. It produces a loaf of bread with a crunchy crust, a chewy interior, and just the right amount of tang. Starters using natural yeast can be made in your kitchen from nothing more than flour, water, and something for the sugars in the flour to feed on. This could be a bunch of grapes, a bit of overrripe mashed banana, or naturally fermenting cider. Once you make the starter, keep it active by feeding it additional flour and water.

❧

Makes about 2 ½ cups

2 cups unbleached all-purpose flour

1½ cups water, at room temperature

2 tablespoons natural apple cider

1 generous cup seedless grapes, washed and dried

1. In a bowl or tall glass jar, stir together the flour, water, and cider until smooth.

2. Wrap the grapes in a piece of cheesecloth and tie the cloth into a knot. Press on the cheesecloth with your hand to slightly crush the grapes. Submerge the grapes in the flour mixture and cover the bowl or jar with a piece of damp cheesecloth.

3. Let this mixture sit in a warm place, preferably in a place where you make bread—this is where the air in your kitchen is filled with wild yeast spores, and keeping the starter there increases the likelihood that wild yeast spores will be "captured" by the starter.

Keep the cheesecloth covering the starter damp; after a day, remove the cheesecloth and cover the bowl or jar loosely with plastic wrap.

4. The starter is ready to use when you see many bubbles on the surface and it begins to smell very sour. It will take about 2 days to develop. Discard the grapes in cheesecloth, pour the starter into a glass jar with a lid, and refrigerate it.

5. To make Pane Rustico (page 96) with the starter, you will need 1 cup of starter. Put it in a bowl and let it come to room temperature. Stir ¾ cup flour and ¾ cup room-temperature water into the starter remaining in the jar. Cover the jar and refrigerate. Replenishing the starter will keep it active and strong; each time the starter is used, be sure to add equal amounts of flour and water to it.

1 package active dry yeast

1 ¾ cups warm (110° to 115°F) water

2 teaspoons malt extract or sugar

3 to 3 ¼ cups unbleached all-purpose flour

1 cup whole wheat flour

½ teaspoon fine sea salt

1 egg, lightly beaten

1 tablespoon wheat bran

1. In a large bowl, dissolve the yeast in ¼ cup of the warm water. Allow the yeast to proof until it is foamy, about 10 minutes.

2. Add the remaining 1½ cups water and the malt extract or sugar to the yeast and mix well. Set the bowl aside.

3. In a medium bowl, mix 2 cups of the all-purpose flour, the whole wheat flour, and salt together. Add to the yeast mixture and mix with a wooden spoon. The dough will be very soft. Add another cup of all-purpose flour and mix with your hands until a ball of dough is formed, adding additional flour as needed to make a soft dough.

4. Place the dough on a floured work surface and knead it for 5 to 10 minutes, until it is shiny and elastic. Cover the dough with a bowl and let rest for 5 minutes.

5. Grease a bowl with olive oil. Add the dough and turn to coat with the oil. Cover the bowl tightly with plastic wrap and then a towel, and let rise in a warm place until doubled in size, about 1 hour.

6. Preheat the oven to 375°F. Punch down the dough. On a floured surface, knead the dough a few times. Shape the dough into a round or oval and place it on a greased baking sheet. (Or divide the dough into 3 pieces, roll each piece into a rope, and create a braid according to the directions on page 120.) Cover the bread and let rise for about 20 minutes.

7. Just before baking, brush the top of the dough with the beaten egg and sprinkle on the wheat bran. Bake for 30 to 35 minutes or until the crust is nicely browned and the bottom sounds hollow when tapped. Remove the bread to a rack to cool completely.

❧

Many Italian bakers use malt extract, or barley malt syrup, to give color and a wonderful rise to bread. It is used in this dough for whole wheat bread and produces a regal-looking loaf. I use this dough for the Country Vegetable Roll on page 90.

❧

Makes 1 loaf

Pane Rustico

Rustic Bread

❧

*This dense country loaf, made
with a natural starter and malt
extract, available in health food
stores or through mail-order
sources (see page 331), gives a
boost to the rising dough. I bake
the bread directly on a hot baking
stone to ensure an evenly browned
loaf, and I achieve a crackling
crust by spraying water into the
oven while the bread is baking.*

❧

Makes 1 loaf

¹/₄ teaspoon active dry yeast

1 cup warm (110° to 115°) water

1 teaspoon malt extract

1 cup Starter (page 94), at room temperature

3 to 3¹/₂ cups unbleached all-purpose flour

1 teaspoon fine sea salt

Cornmeal for sprinkling (if using a baking stone)

1. In a large bowl, dissolve the yeast in ¹/₄ cup of the warm water. Let the yeast proof for about 10 minutes, or until foamy.

2. Add the remaining ³/₄ cup water to the yeast along with the malt extract and stir well. Stir in the starter. Mix 3 cups flour with the salt, and gradually add to the yeast mixture, mixing with your hands until a ball of dough is formed. Add additional flour only if necessary—this is a loose dough; it should remain slightly wet and sticky. Resist the temptation to add too much flour.

3. On a floured surface, knead the dough: Pick the dough up with one hand, using a pastry scraper to scrape it all up, and slam it back down on the work surface. Do this six or seven times, or until the dough is smooth and slightly less sticky.

4. Lightly grease a large bowl with olive oil and add the dough, turning it to coat. Cover the bowl tightly with plastic wrap and let rise in a warm place for at least 4 to 6 hours, or even overnight, to allow the bread to develop its sour tang.

5. Punch down the dough, and turn it out onto a floured surface. Knead the dough with floured hands until it is smooth and just barely sticky. Form the dough into a round or oblong. If using a baking stone, place the bread on a wooden peel heavily dusted with cornmeal or lined with parchment paper. Or place it on a baking sheet. Cover the dough with a clean cloth and let rise for about 40 minutes.

6. If using a baking stone, set the stone on the lowest oven rack and preheat the oven to 500°F at least 20 minutes before baking the bread. If baking the bread on a baking sheet, preheat the oven to 425°F.

7. Slash the top of the loaf in several places with a sharp knife, razor blade, or scissors. If baking the bread on a stone, sprinkle the stone with cornmeal. Slide the bread from the peel onto the stone, starting at the back of the oven and working forward; if the bread is on parchment, slide it on the paper onto the baking stone. Or place the baking sheet in the lower third of the oven.

8. Using a plant mister spray the oven several times with water, and close the oven door. Spray two or three more times during the first 10 minutes of baking. If using a stone, bake for 35 to 40 minutes, or until the bread is dark brown in color and sounds hollow when tapped with your hand. If using a baking sheet, bake for 40 to 50 minutes, or until the bread is nicely browned and sounds hollow. Remove the bread to a wire rack to cool.

Pane di San Francesco

Raisin Semolina Bread

❦

I first sampled this bread in Sicily at Eastertime in Santa Caterina Villarmosa, the birthplace of my Grandfather Saporito. Grano duro, a hard-wheat semolina flour, gives this bread its deep, shiny brown crust and golden interior. You can substitute unbleached all-purpose flour for the semolina, but the interior will be lighter.

❦

Makes 1 large loaf

1 tablespoon active dry yeast

1³/₄ cups warm (110° to 115°F) water

¹/₂ cup honey

1 tablespoon olive oil

4 to 4¹/₂ cups fine durum semolina flour

¹/₈ teaspoon fine sea salt

1 cup raisins

¹/₂ cup candied lemon peel, diced

Cornmeal for sprinkling (if using a baking stone)

1 egg yolk, lightly beaten

1. In a large bowl, dissolve the yeast in 1 cup of the warm water. Add the honey and let the yeast proof for 5 minutes or until foamy.

2. Stir in the remaining ³/₄ cup water and the olive oil. Add 3¹/₂ cups of the flour along with the salt and mix with your hands into a rough ball. Add the raisins and lemon peel and continue to work the dough, adding additional flour as necessary, until the dough is no longer sticky. Turn the dough out onto a floured surface and knead it until soft and very smooth, about 5 minutes.

3. Generously grease a large bowl with olive oil and add the dough, turning to coat. Cover the bowl tightly with plastic wrap and let rise in a warm place for about 2 hours until doubled in size.

4. Preheat the oven to 400°F. Set a baking stone on the lowest rack to preheat for at least 20 minutes, or butter a cookie sheet. Punch the dough down and turn it out onto a lightly floured surface. Knead the dough for about 5 minutes. Then roll it under your palms into a 26-inch-long log. Turn the dough in on itself from each end until the two ends meet in the middle, like a pretzel.

5. If using a baking stone, place the loaf on a peel dusted with cornmeal or place on a cookie sheet. Cover and let rise for 20 minutes.

6. Brush the top of the loaf with the beaten egg yolk. If using a baking stone, dust with cornmeal, and slide the loaf from the peel onto the stone. Bake for 35 to 40 minutes, or until the crust is golden brown and a cake tester inserted in the center comes out clean. If using a cookie sheet, bake for 35 to 45 minutes, until the crust is a shiny brown. Remove the bread to a wire rack to cool.

CRESCIUTA

¹/₂ cup warm (110° to 115°F) water
¹/₄ teaspoon active dry yeast
¹/₂ cup unbleached all-purpose flour

DOUGH

1 large cake fresh yeast (1 ounce) or 4 packages active dry yeast
3 cups warm (110° to 115°F) water
Prepared Cresciuta (above)
1 teaspoon fine sea salt
6¹/₂ to 6³/₄ cups fine durum semolina flour
Cornmeal for sprinkling
Olive oil for brushing
¹/₃ cup sesame seeds

1. To make the cresciuta, in a small bowl, dissolve the yeast in the water. Let it proof for 10 minutes, or until foamy. Stir in the flour, cover the bowl, and let the mixture sit in a warm place for at least 4 hours, or overnight.

2. In a large bowl, dissolve the yeast in 2 cups of the warm water. Let stand, covered, for 5 minutes, or until foamy.

3. Stir the remaining 1 cup water and the cresciuta into the yeast, blending well. Add 5 cups of the semolina flour and the salt to the yeast and mix with your hands until a ball of dough is formed, adding additional flour as needed until the dough is no longer too sticky.

4. Turn the dough out onto a floured surface and knead it with closed fists for about 20 minutes.

5. Form the dough into a round and place it on a peel sprinkled with cornmeal. Cover and let rise in a warm place for about 2 hours until doubled in size. Or place the dough in a 10 by 4-inch floured banneton (bread basket), cover, and let rise.

6. Preheat the oven to 425°F, and place a baking stone on the bottom rack to preheat for at least 30 minutes.

continued

Pane Siciliano di Carmelo

Carmelo's Sicilian Bread

🐟

I owe my love of this bread to Sicilian bread maker Carmelo Di Martino, who makes it weekly in his old wooden madia. *Carmelo mixes a starter dough, the cresciuta, with semolina flour and water, then kneads the dough with his fists for close to thirty minutes to achieve an elegant smoothness. Then he free-forms it into round loaves to rise. A banneton (reed basket) can also be used to shape the dough before turning it out onto a hot baking stone or a cookie sheet for baking. This bread freezes very well. Start the cresciuta early on the day you plan to bake the bread, or make it the day before.*

🐟

Makes 1 large loaf

7. Brush the top of the loaf with olive oil and sprinkle on the sesame seeds. Sprinkle the baking stone with cornmeal and slide the loaf from the peel onto the baking stone. Or, if using a basket, carefully turn the bread out onto the peel. Brush the top with olive oil, sprinkle on the sesame seeds, and slide the bread onto the baking stone. Bake the bread for about 35 minutes, or until nicely browned and hollow sounding when tapped on the bottom. Let the bread cool on a rack before slicing.

Note: To bake the bread using a cookie sheet, follow the instructions through step 3, then shape the dough into a round or oval loaf and place on a lightly greased cookie sheet to rise. Place the oven rack in the bottom third of the oven and preheat to 425°F. Bake for 40 to 45 minutes, or until the bread is golden brown and sounds hollow when tapped on the bottom. Cool the bread on a wire rack before slicing.

Pane Panierino

Bread in a Basket

❧

Pane Panierino, *bread in a basket, is so called because the dough is left to rise in a basket called a banneton. Before baking, the risen dough is turned out of the banneton onto a baking sheet or a baking stone. The ridges of the basket leave a decorative impression on the bread and also give the loaf its round country look.*

❧

Makes 1 round loaf

1 teaspoon active dry yeast
1½ cups warm (110° to 115°F) water
⅓ cup Cresciuta (page 94, or see step 5)
2 cups fine durum semolina flour
1 to 1¼ cups unbleached all-purpose flour
⅛ teaspoon fine sea salt

1. In a large bowl, sprinkle the yeast over ½ cup of the warm water and stir to dissolve. Let proof for 10 minutes, or until foamy.

2. Stir the cresciuta, the remaining 1 cup water, and the olive oil into the yeast mixture. Mix the semolina flour with 1 cup all-purpose flour and add it to the yeast. Mix with your hands until a ball of dough is formed, adding additional all-purpose flour if the dough seems sticky.

3. Turn the dough out onto a floured surface and knead with your hands for 5 minutes, or until soft and elastic.

4. Lightly grease a large bowl with olive oil. Place the bread in the bowl and turn to coat. Cover tightly with plastic wrap and let rise in a warm place for about 2 hours, until doubled in size.

5. Punch down the dough. Turn out onto a floured surface and knead for about 5 minutes. Pinch off a piece of dough the size of a small orange, put it in a jar, cover, and refrigerate; this is your cresciuta for the next time you make this bread.

6. Heavily flour a 10 by 4-inch banneton (bread basket), and spread a layer of cornmeal over the bottom. Form the dough into a round loaf and place it in the basket. Let rise for about 25 minutes.

7. Preheat the oven to 425°F, and place a baking stone on the bottom rack to preheat for at least 20 minutes.

8. Sprinkle the baking stone with cornmeal. Carefully turn the dough out of the basket onto the stone. Bake for 35 to 40 minutes, or until the bread is golden brown and sounds hollow when tapped on the bottom. Cool the bread on a wire rack before slicing.

Note: To bake the bread using a cookie sheet, follow the instructions through step 5, then shape the dough into a round or oval loaf and place on a lightly greased cookie sheet to rise. Place an oven rack in the bottom third of the oven and preheat to 425°F. Bake for 40 to 45 minutes, until the bread is golden brown and sounds hollow when tapped on the bottom. Cool the bread on a wire rack before slicing.

Viva San Giuseppe

Long Live Saint Joseph

❦

Certain saints have very special places in Italian and Italian-American families. Some people choose particular saints because fervent prayers have been answered; others revere saints whose names they bear; and still others favor saints whose job it is to perform miracles in an hour of need.

Saints' feast days can take on particularly special significance. Some, like Saint Joseph, the father of the Holy Family, are so important that the veneration of him, displayed on his feast day, March 19, reaches dramatic cult proportions.

This is especially true in Sicily, where Saint Joseph is the island's revered patron saint. Saint Joseph's tables, resembling stepped altars, are decorated with oranges, lemons, and foliage, along with foods representing the bounty of the land. These tables are offered by individuals, families, even entire communities in gratitude to the saint for, among other things, good fortune, deliverance from disaster, restored health, or a special favor.

Fervor for the Feast of Saint Joseph reaches a peak in the town of Salemi, in Sicily, which is known for its altars. For weeks before the feast day, the women of Salemi prepare a wide variety of foods for friends and strangers alike. Bread is the most important food because it is the most basic. One specialty is sourdough that is left to rise for seven hours before being shaped and intricately sculpted, using ordinary implements such as pastry wheels and hair combs, into hundreds of objects, including Saint Joseph's staff and beard, as well as the tools of his trade, carpentry. Letters of the alphabet, peas in the pod, crosses, baskets of flowers, and animals are some of the other bread ornaments made to cover the altars.

On the feast day, private homes displaying these tables are open for anyone to sample the array of food. A painting or statue of Saint Joseph has the place of honor at the head of each altar, with candles and flowers flanking the saint on either side. Beneath him stretches a tapestry of foods ranging from pasta with bread crumbs, sugar, parsley, and olive oil to fried cardoons to fava beans to the Saint Joseph's Day pastries called sfince. Before any eating can commence by the public, the local priest blesses the food. Then the Holy Family, Jesus, Mary, and Joseph, usually portrayed by children (called *virgineddi*), taste all the dishes first.

Some local schools also host the tables, to which parents and students are invited. One I visited had prepared more than one hundred dishes, representing a true composite of all the seasonal offerings (except meat, of course, since the feast day occurs during Lent). As each offering is tasted by the virgineddi, a drumbeat is sounded, and a loud *"Viva San Giuseppe"* is chanted to drive away all evil spirits.

When the banquet ends, the virgineddi cut a large consecrated loaf of bread into large pieces and give pieces to all those present. According to local tradition, eating the pieces of bread will ensure good fortune for the earth.

In Fairport, New York, far from her native Caltinasetta in Sicily, my Grandmother Maria Assunta Saporito kept the ritual for the Feast of Saint Joseph alive because of an answer to her prayers. Praying in church one day for my Grandfather Rosario to be cured of tuberculosis, she promised to make the table in exchange for the saint's intercession. To seal the pact, she knelt down at the back of the church and rolled her tongue on the floor all the way down the center aisle to the altar. The protector of the Holy Family did not fail her, and my grandfather was cured.

Frisedde

Pugliese Hard Biscuits

❧

Frisedda, a hard, dry biscuit from Puglia, was originally eaten by shepherds while tending their flocks. It provided a welcome snack that kept well for a long time. There are many ways to use it; my favorite is as the base of a fresh tomato salad (see page 199). Traditionally, frisedde are boiled first, then baked, split in half, and baked again until dry and hard; in this modern version, the boiling step is eliminated. The frisedde are topped with anything from diced plum tomatoes and herbs to marinated vegetables to a seafood salad of squid, shrimp, and clams.

❧

Makes 12

DOUGH

1 teaspoon active dry yeast

1 cup warm (110° to 115°F) water

About 3 cups unbleached all-purpose flour

⅛ teaspoon fine sea salt

1. In a large size bowl, sprinkle the yeast over the water and stir to dissolve. Let the yeast proof for about 5 minutes, until it swells and becomes bubbly.

2. Gradually add 2¾ cups flour and the salt to the yeast mixture and mix with your hands until a ball of dough is formed, adding additional flour as needed until the dough is no longer sticky. Turn the dough out onto a lightly floured surface and knead it for about 5 minutes, or until smooth.

3. Lightly oil a large bowl with olive oil. Place the dough in it, and turn to coat. Cover with a towel and let rest for about 20 minutes.

4. Preheat the oven to 400°F. Lightly grease two baking sheets.

5. On a floured surface, knead the dough for a few minutes. Roll it into a 24-inch rope and cut the rope into six pieces. Roll each piece into a 13-inch rope and bring the ends together to form a ring. Pinch the ends to seal. Place 3 rings on each baking sheet, spacing them well apart. Cover and let rise for 15 minutes.

6. Bake the rings for 10 minutes. Remove the baking sheets from the oven and let the rings cool slightly. (Leave the oven on.) With a sharp knife, cut the rings horizontally in half, and place on the baking sheets, cut sides up. Bake for 10 minutes. Remove the rings to a rack to cool completely.

7. To serve, dip each ring quickly in water and place on individual serving dishes. Fill the centers with your choice of ingredients.

Note: Any leftover rings can be frozen, well wrapped, for future use.

3 cups warm (110° to 115°F) water

*1 small cake fresh yeast (0.6 ounce) or 2 tablespoons active
dry yeast*

1/4 cup sugar

4 tablespoons butter, melted

2 large eggs, lightly beaten

8 1/2 to 9 cups unbleached all-purpose flour

1 teaspoon fine sea salt

3 cups Almond Paste (page 327)

GLAZE

1 1/2 cups confectioners' sugar

1 teaspoon vanilla

4 to 5 tablespoons light cream or milk

1. In a large bowl, dissolve the yeast in 2 cups warm water. Stir in the sugar, and proof yeast for about 10 minutes, until foamy.

2. Add the remaining 1 cup water, the butter, and eggs, and mix with a wooden spoon. Stir in 4 1/2 cups flour and the salt. Mix with a spoon. Gradually add 4 more cups of flour and mix with your hands to form a smooth ball, adding flour if necessary.

3. Turn the dough out onto a floured board and knead until shiny and smooth. Butter a large bowl, place the dough in the bowl, and turn to coat. Cover and let rise in a warm place until doubled.

4. Preheat the oven to 375°F. Lightly grease two cookie sheets. Punch down the dough and divide it in half. Working with one piece at a time, on a floured surface, roll the dough into an 18 by 15-inch rectangle. Spread 1 1/2 cups of the almond paste over the dough, leaving a 1/2-inch border. Starting at a long side, roll up the dough like a jelly roll. Cut the roll into 15 pieces and space the rolls about 1 inch apart on the cookie sheets.

5. Bake the rolls for 20 to 25 minutes, or until delicately browned on top. Let cool on wire racks for 10 minutes.

6. In a medium bowl, combine the confectioners' sugar, vanilla, and 1/4 cup cream or milk and stir until smooth. Add more if necessary. Use a spoon to drizzle the glaze over the rolls.

Panini Ripieni con Pasta Reale

**ALMOND PASTE
YEAST ROLLS**

❧

*These sweet yeast rolls are filled
with homemade almond paste.
Almond paste that has been
refrigerated should be allowed to
come to room temperature. To
make the job of spreading the
paste over the dough easier, soften
it in the microwave for about forty
seconds, or place it in a small
bowl and set it in a larger bowl
of hot water until soft.*

❧

Makes 30

Taralli Pugliesi

Biscuits with Pepper

❦

Pepper taralli from Puglia are great as a snack with cheese for an antipasto or as part of an Italian picnic. Unlike other types of taralli, these are not boiled before they are baked. They can be frozen for up to two months.

❦

Makes about 1 dozen

1 package active dry yeast

1 cup warm (110° to 115°F) water

¼ cup olive oil

3½ to 4 cups unbleached all-purpose flour

1 teaspoon fine sea salt

1½ teaspoons coarsely ground black pepper

1 egg beaten with 1 tablespoon water, for egg wash

1. In a large bowl, dissolve the yeast in ¼ cup of the warm water. Cover the bowl and let the yeast proof for about 10 minutes, until foamy.

2. Stir in the remaining ¾ cup water and the olive oil. Mix 3½ cups flour with the salt and pepper. Gradually add to the yeast mixture, mixing with your hands to form a ball of dough, and adding additional flour only if the dough is very sticky.

3. On a floured surface, knead the dough until it is smooth. Lightly grease a large bowl with olive oil, add the dough and turn to coat. Cover the bowl tightly with plastic wrap and let the dough rise for about 1½ hours, until doubled in size.

4. Lightly grease two cookie sheets. Punch down the dough and knead it for a few minutes. Divide the dough into 24 balls. On a floured surface, roll each ball under the palms of your hands into a rope 6 to 7 inches long. For each tarallo, braid 2 ropes together, and bring the ends together to form a ring. Pinch the ends to seal. Place the braids on the cookie sheets, spacing them about 1 inch apart. Cover and let rise for about 25 minutes.

5. Preheat the oven to 350°F. Brush the top of each tarallo with the egg wash. Bake for 22 to 25 minutes, or until golden brown.

6. Remove the taralli to wire racks to cool slightly. Serve warm or at room temperature.

4 to 4¹/₂ cups unbleached all-purpose flour

1 tablespoon active dry yeast

¹/₄ cup sugar

1 cup warm (110° to 115°F) milk

¹/₈ teaspoon fine sea salt

1 large egg, lightly beaten

5 tablespoons butter, softened

¹/₄ cup water

1. Mound 4 cups flour on a work surface and make a well in the center. Place the yeast and 1 tablespoon of the sugar in the well and mix together. Add ¹/₄ cup of the warm milk and, with your hands, begin incorporating the flour from the inside walls of the well into the yeast mixture. Use just enough of the flour to make a ball of dough about the size of an orange: This is the *panetto*. Leave the panetto in the well, cover with a clean cloth, and let rest for 15 minutes.

2. Add 2 tablespoons of the sugar, the salt, egg, the remaining ³/₄ cup milk, and the butter to the well. With your fingers, carefully break up the panetto into the other ingredients. Then incorporate the remaining flour from the sides of the well, working the mixture with your hands until a ball of dough is formed, adding additional flour if necessary. Knead the dough until smooth and elastic.

3. Cover the dough with a bowl and let rise until doubled in size, about 45 minutes.

4. Generously butter two cookie sheets. Punch down the dough and divide it into 12 equal pieces. On a floured surface, shape each piece into a 4-inch oval, and place the rolls 1 inch apart on the cookie sheets. Cover the rolls with clean cloths and let rise for 30 minutes.

5. Preheat the oven to 375°F. In a small bowl dissolve the remaining 1 tablespoon sugar in the water.

6. Brush the rolls with the sugar glaze. Bake for about 20 minutes, or until the rolls are nicely browned on top. Remove to racks to cool.

Panini

Little Rolls

These versatile oval-shaped rolls make wonderful dinner rolls. Or fill for sandwiches, serve with soup, or toast and eat for breakfast. The dough is strengthened by a panetto, a small bit of dough, and set in a well in the middle of the flour and left to rise for 15 minutes.

Makes 1 dozen

Pani Tradizionali di Natale

Traditional Christmas Breads

❧

As the Christmas season approaches, my senses stir with memories of the rich variety of celebration breads that were always made at home. Long before Christmas, New Year's Day, or the Feast of the Epiphany arrived, I had lost count of the number of panettoni, pandori, torte di Befana, and torte di frutte secche stored in the freezer.

Making these breads in advance and freezing them was the only way to have a spectacular display and variety. I still employ that method today, and I can assure you that flavor is not sacrificed by freezing if the breads are carefully wrapped.

I start baking my holiday breads two months before I will need them, for my own use and for gifts. Some of the breads in this chapter begin with a starter, or *madre* (mother), and it is best to begin the process early in the day, since many of them require several risings.

Some of these breads, like the pandoro, are baked in star-shaped molds, and panettone is traditionally baked in a high-sided mold. If these are not available, you can use two-pound coffee cans, clean clay flowerpots, a crockpot insert, or other deep baking pans. You can also use aluminum foil cupcake tins, or small cans, to make miniature versions of the breads.

To ensure that the breads will unmold without coming apart, butter and flour each mold very well. For star-shaped or other molds with hard-to-reach crevices, use nonstick vegetable spray, and then flour the mold.

Be sure that all ingredients are at the proper temperature before you begin. Butter and eggs should be at room temperature; should the recipe call for separated eggs, do this step upon taking the eggs from the refrigerator, since they are easier to separate when cold.

As with any baking, the quality of the ingredients will determine the outcome. Do not make substitutions. For breads calling for yeast, make sure it is fresh: Look on the package for the expiration date. If possible, use filtered or bottled water for these recipes. Chemically treated water can give an unwanted taste to your bread.

Measure the flour accurately. To do this, lightly spoon the flour from the bag or canister into your measuring cup and level it off at the top. Dipping a measuring cup into the flour container will compact the flour too much and give you more than you need. Better still, invest in a good kitchen scale and weigh the flour, as the Italians do. Weight of different flours can vary, but a general rule to follow is that four ounces of flour equals one cup.

To freeze, make sure the breads have cooled completely. Use heavy-duty foil and wrap each loaf tightly. Label the outside with the name of the bread and the date. Then place the foil-wrapped bread in plastic bags, seal, and freeze for up to two months. Do not freeze bread directly in plastic bags, and do not store bread used on a daily basis in plastic bags: Bread needs to breathe, and if stored in plastic bags for too long, it tends to stale and even mold. It is better to keep bread for immediate consumption in paper bags.

To give as gifts, let freshly baked breads cool, then use clear or colored cellophane to wrap each loaf. Tie with a colorful bow and include the recipe and a note on the tradition surrounding the bread. (You can find cellophane in florist shops, where it is usually sold by the sheet. Or see Mail-Order Sources, page 331.)

In Italy, no Christmas or other celebration would be complete without the appropriate bread, and over the years, folktales have been handed down about the origins of some of them, such as panettone and torta di Befana. You will find my story about Befana on page 282, and one story about the origins of Colomba, an Easter bread, on page 124. If you have children, read the stories with them, then make some of the breads in this chapter together. In that way, you can start your own holiday tradition to be passed on.

Panettone

❧

Whether you call it a big bread or Tony's bread, panettone is a sweet fruit bread from Milan. Today panettone is found all over Italy, but the Motta shop in Milan is the most famous for its panettone.

❧

**Makes 1 large bread
or 2 smaller ones**

SPONGE

1 package active dry yeast

¹/₄ cup warm (110° to 115°F) water

¹/₂ cup unbleached all-purpose flour

²/₃ cup golden raisins

¹/₄ cup grappa or brandy

5 tablespoons butter, softened

2 large eggs

4 large egg yolks

³/₄ cup sugar

¹/₄ cup warm (110° to 115°F) water

1 tablespoon vanilla

4¹/₂ to 5 cups plus 1 tablespoon unbleached all-purpose flour

Grated zest of 1 medium orange

Grated zest of 1 medium lemon

¹/₂ cup chopped candied citron

1. To make the sponge, in a medium bowl, dissolve the yeast in the warm water. Add the flour and stir with a spoon or your fingers to make a loose, almost liquid, dough. Cover the bowl with plastic wrap and let rise in a warm place for at least 6 hours, or overnight.

2. In a small bowl, combine the raisins and grappa or brandy, and let marinate for at least 4 hours, or overnight.

3. In a large bowl, stir the butter, eggs, yolks, sugar, warm water and vanilla together. Drain the marinated raisins in a small strainer set over a bowl and press on the raisins with a spoon to extract as much liquid as possible. Set the raisins aside and add the liquid to the egg mixture. Add the sponge and mix well with your hands. Add the flour about 2 cups at a time, mixing with your hands until a ball of dough forms.

4. Turn the dough out onto a floured work surface and knead for 5 to 10 minutes, or until smooth and elastic, adding additional flour as needed.

5. Butter a large bowl, place the dough in the bowl, and turn to coat. Cover with a clean cloth and let rise for 6 hours in a warm place.

6. Butter and flour a panettone or other deep mold at least 6½ inches tall and 7 to 8 inches wide (The ceramic insert to a crockpot is ideal. Or you can use two 2-pound coffee cans and make 2 smaller loaves. Panettone can also be baked in two greased and floured 6 by 6-inch clay flowerpots.)

7. Punch down the dough and turn it out onto a floured surface. Flatten the dough out with your hands and sprinkle on the lemon and orange zest. In a small bowl, mix the raisins and citron with the 1 tablespoon flour, and sprinkle the mixture over the dough. Fold the dough in half, press the edges together, and knead to distribute the fruits. Continue to knead for 5 to 10 minutes or until the dough is smooth, adding additional flour if necessary. Place the dough in the mold, cover with a clean cloth, and let rise for 35 minutes in a warm place.

8. Preheat the oven to 400°F. Cut an X in the top of the bread. Bake for 5 minutes, reduce the heat to 375°F, and bake for 10 minutes. Reduce the heat to 350°F, and bake for 30 to 35 minutes longer, or until a skewer inserted in the center of the bread comes out clean. If the top begins to brown too much, cover the bread loosely with a piece of foil.

9. Cool the bread on a rack for about 30 minutes before removing it from the mold.

Note: There are many versions of panettone. Some use Vin Santo, a sweet dessert wine, instead of grappa. Some are made with olive oil instead of butter, and some include pine nuts and anise seed instead of raisins and citron. Try it using these variations.

Gubana

Holiday Fruit Bread

❦

This impressive spiral-shaped bread is my version of an old Italian standby, the classic sweet nut-and-fruit-filled bread of Friuli called gubana. *I've added malt extract to fortify the proofing yeast and mascarpone cheese to create a delicate texture. If you can't find these ingredients, you can use sugar in place of the malt extract and cream cheese instead of mascarpone (see page 331 for Mail-Order Sources).*

❦

Makes 2 spiral-shaped breads

DOUGH

1³⁄₄ cups warm (110° to 115°F) water

1 tablespoon active dry yeast

2 tablespoons malt extract or sugar

4 tablespoons butter, softened

¹⁄₄ cup sugar

2 large eggs

¹⁄₂ cup mascarpone cheese

6 to 7 cups unbleached all-purpose flour

¹⁄₄ teaspoon fine sea salt

FILLING

2¹⁄₂ cups dried mixed fruits (such as apricots, pears, prunes, and/or apples), diced

¹⁄₃ cup coarsely chopped hazelnuts

¹⁄₄ cup raisins

2 tablespoons sugar

1 teaspoon ground cinnamon

¹⁄₄ cup sweet marsala wine

1 cup apricot or orange marmalade

1 egg, lightly beaten

¹⁄₄ cup turbinado (coarse brown) sugar

1. In a large bowl dissolve the yeast in ³⁄₄ cup of the warm water, stir in the malt extract, and let proof for about 10 minutes, until foamy.

2. In a medium bowl, whisk together the butter, sugar, eggs, and mascarpone cheese until smooth. Stir the remaining 1 cup water into the yeast mixture, then stir in the mascarpone mixture. Slowly add 5 cups of the flour and the salt, and mix with your hands to form a ball of dough, adding additional flour if necessary, until the dough is smooth and no longer sticky.

3. Turn the dough out onto a floured surface and knead for about 5 minutes. Place the dough in a lightly oiled bowl and turn to coat. Cover tightly with plastic wrap and let rise in a warm place for about 2 hours.

4. Generously grease two 2-quart soufflé dishes or round baking dishes (you could also use 10-inch springform pans; I use oven-safe pottery bowls). In a bowl, combine all the filling ingredients except the marmalade and mix well.

5. Punch down the dough and divide it in half. On a well-floured surface, roll each piece into a 16-inch circle. Spread ½ cup of the marmalade over each circle, leaving a ½ inch, then sprinkle on half of the fruit mixture. Roll up each piece like a jelly roll, tucking the edges in as you roll. Pinch the seam tightly closed. Turn each bread seam side down, and shape into a spiral. Place the breads in the soufflé or baking dishes, cover, and let them rise for 30 minutes in a warm place.

6. Preheat the oven to 375°F. Brush the tops of the spirals with the beaten egg, and sprinkle 2 tablespoons of the turbinado sugar over each one. Bake for 35 to 40 minutes, or until the tops are nicely browned and a cake tester inserted in the middle comes out clean. Let cool for 30 minutes.

7. Run a knife around the edges of each dish and carefully turn the breads out. This bread is best eaten warm; the breads can be reheated in a warm oven.

Note: The breads can be frozen. Let cool completely, then wrap tightly in foil and freeze for up to 3 months. To serve, unwrap and let thaw, then reheat in a warm oven.

Orsi Piccoli

Little Bears

❧

These bear-shaped breads are a favorite at holiday time, and they make unique favors for a children's party. Dress them up with brightly colored bows around their necks.

❧

Makes 6

1⅓ cups milk

1 tablespoon active dry yeast

⅔ cup sugar

5 to 5¼ cups unbleached all-purpose flour

1 teaspoon fine sea salt

8 tablespoons (1 stick) butter, cut into pieces

1 egg beaten with 1 tablespoon milk, for egg wash

Turbinado (coarse brown) sugar for sprinkling

Raisins or currants

1. In a saucepan, scald the milk (bring almost to a boil). Let cool until warm (110° to 115°F). Pour the milk into a large bowl, add the yeast and 1 teaspoon of the sugar and stir to blend. Cover and let proof for about 10 minutes, until the yeast is foamy.

2. In another bowl, mix 5 cups flour, the salt, and the remaining sugar together. Add the butter and work it into the flour mixture until it resembles coarse meal. Slowly add the yeast mixture, and mix with your hands until a ball of dough is formed, adding additional flour only if the dough is very sticky. Turn the dough out onto a floured surface and knead until smooth, about 10 minutes.

3. Lightly butter a bowl, place the dough in the bowl and turn to coat. Cover tightly with plastic wrap and let rise in a warm place until doubled in size, about 1 hour.

4. Grease two cookie sheets. Punch down the dough and divide it into 24 equal pieces. Use 4 pieces for each bear: Roll 3 pieces of dough into balls about 2 inches in diameter. Place the balls of dough together in a line on one of the cookie sheets, as if making a snowman: one for the head, one for the upper body, and one for the lower body. Divide the fourth piece of dough into 7 pieces for the ears, nose, feet, and hands, and attach to the bear. Repeat with the remaining dough, placing the bears 3 inches apart on the sheets. Cover with a towel and let rise for 20 minutes.

5. Preheat the oven to 350°F. Insert raisins or currants into the heads for the bears' eyes. Brush the bears with the egg wash and sprinkle the bodies with the coarse sugar. Bake for 20 to 25 minutes, or until golden brown.

6. Cool on wire racks, then tie ribbons around the necks.

Note: You can make more bears by using smaller pieces of dough. These freeze beautifully and can be made 2 to 3 weeks ahead. Wrap them individually in foil and place in freezer bags (add the ribbons after thawing). Or use the bears as placecards at children's birthday parties: Print each child's name on a paper flag made from a toothpick and a small piece of paper, and insert into the bears' paws.

Pani di Pasqua

Easter Breads

❧

"Easter, Easter, come soon. Children are imploring and imploring with all their hearts for *scaredda* (bread) with an egg, *scaredda* with an egg." This old Pugliese saying is a reminder of the importance that bread plays in the celebration of Easter, not only in Puglia but throughout Italy, where Easter bread making is an ancient tradition and taken very seriously.

Hand-fashioned egg-decorated breads vary from region to region and go by many different dialect names; some of the more familiar ones are corrucolo, ciambella, and pupazze. But the commonality of baking whole eggs twisted or braided into bread dough is part of the theme of Easter, eggs being the symbol of fertility and new beginnings.

There are also Easter breads that do not include these baked whole eggs in the dough. Some of my favorites are Gubana (page 112), a swirled nut-filled bread; Treccia (page 120), a braided bread topped with poppy seeds or coarse sugar; and the classic Colomba, Easter dove bread, studded with whole almonds, although here I have included a non–yeast dough version of colomba with whole eggs nestled on top (page 121).

Throughout the year, I collect a variety of baskets in different shapes to give as part of my Easter gifts, and then when my Easter baking begins, I make and freeze an assortment of these breads for each basket.

Besides breads, Crostoli (page 249), fried dough puffs, which are a Lenten Carnevale treat, are also popular at Easter. To make the puffs ahead, cool them completely after baking, then freeze unsugared in an airtight container. Sugar them after they are completely defrosted, wrap them in pairs in clear cellophane, and tie with colorful ribbon.

Another good choice for a gift basket is Panini Ripieni con Pasta Reale (page 105), almond paste yeast rolls, made with homemade almond paste. To make ahead, after baking and cooling, wrap the unglazed rolls well in aluminum foil. Glaze them when completely thawed, and let the glaze dry completely before wrapping.

To create an Italian Easter bread basket, make one or more of the suggested Easter breads, wrap in cellophane, and combine in an attractive basket with half a dozen almond paste rolls and half a dozen fried puffs. Add copies of the recipes to the basket as well, along with a jar of homemade Almond Paste (page 327) for a unique gift.

Pane di Giovedi Santo

Good Friday Bread

❧

These small loaves, also called pagnottelle, are traditionally made in observance of Good Friday. Their slightly sweet taste is enhanced by a thin veil of anise seeds sprinkled over the top. The top of each loaf is marked with a small cross to signify the solemnity of the day. There is only one rising for this bread, which results in a somewhat dense loaf. You can shape the dough into one large loaf if you prefer; bake it for forty to forty-five minutes.

❧

Makes 4 small round loaves

2 cups warm (110° to 115°F) water

1 small cake fresh yeast (0.6 ounce) or 1 tablespoon active dry yeast

1 cup plus ¼ teaspoon sugar

About 6 cups unbleached all-purpose flour

⅛ teaspoon fine sea salt

1 teaspoon olive oil

1 egg white beaten with 1 tablespoon water, for egg wash

2 teaspoons anise seed

1. In a large bowl, combine 1 cup of the warm water, the yeast, and ¼ teaspoon of the sugar. Stir well, cover the bowl, and let the yeast proof for about 10 minutes, or until foamy.

2. Stir in the remaining water and sugar and mix well. Add 5 cups of the flour with the salt and mix with your hands to make a soft ball of dough, adding additional flour as needed.

3. Turn the dough out onto a floured surface and knead until smooth, about 10 minutes. Let the dough rest, covered with a bowl, for about 10 minutes.

4. Lightly grease two cookie sheets. Divide the dough into 4 pieces on a floured surface, roll each piece into a 5-inch round, and place 4 inches apart on cookie sheets. Cover the rounds and let rise in a warm place for 1½ hours, or until doubled in size.

5. Preheat the oven to 400°F. With a sharp knife, make a cross about 3 inches long in the center of each round. Brush the egg wash over the top and sides of each round. Sprinkle the anise seeds over the rounds.

6. Bake for 25 to 30 minutes, or until the rounds are nicely browned on top. Remove to a cooling rack.

Note: The breads may be frozen for 2 to 3 months. Let cool completely and wrap in aluminum foil.

1 tablespoon active dry yeast

¼ cup warm (110° to 115°F) water

¼ cup warm (110° to 115°F) milk

8 tablespoons (1 stick) butter or margarine, softened

7 large eggs, at room temperature, well beaten

1 cup freshly grated Pecorino Romano cheese (5 ounces)

1 teaspoon freshly ground black pepper

6½ to 7 cups unbleached all-purpose flour

1. In a large bowl, sprinkle the yeast over the warm water, and stir to dissolve. Cover and let the yeast proof for about 10 minutes, or until foamy.

2. Add the milk to the yeast mixture, and whisk in the butter. Whisk in the eggs, then add the cheese and pepper. Add 6½ cups flour, about a cup at a time, and mix with your hands until a soft ball of dough is formed, adding additional flour if necessary until the dough is no longer sticky.

3. Turn the dough out onto a floured surface and knead until smooth, about 5 minutes.

4. Generously grease a large bowl with olive oil, place the dough in the bowl, and turn to coat. Cover the bowl with a towel and let the dough rise in a warm place until doubled in size, about 1½ hours.

5. Punch down the dough and place it on a lightly floured work surface. Knead it into a smooth ball. Place the bread on a greased cookie sheet or in a greased tube pan and let rise for about 30 minutes.

6. Preheat the oven to 375°F. Bake the crescia for 30 to 35 minutes, or until it is nicely browned. If using a tube pan, let the crescia cool slightly, then carefully remove it to a cooling rack. Serve the crescia warm, cut into slices.

Crescia

❦

This recipe is from an old friend of my mother, Rena Petregani, who came from the village of Famo in the region of the Marches. She prepared all the food for my mother's wedding over fifty years ago. Crescia—its name comes from the word for "to grow"—is traditionally made for the Easter holiday and eaten with sausage. This makes a beautiful ten-inch round bread.

❦

Makes 1 large round bread

Treccia

Braided Bread

❦

Whether dressed with whole eggs baked into the dough for Easter, studded with citron or candied orange peel and nuts for Christmas, filled with juicy raisins for a special breakfast bread, or served plain, braided breads are always festive.

❦

Makes 1 loaf

¹/₄ cup warm (110° to 115°F) water

3 tablespoons warm (110° to 115°F) milk

1 teaspoon active dry yeast

2 tablespoons sugar

2 large egg yolks, lightly beaten

2 tablespoons extra-virgin olive oil

2 to 2¹/₄ cups unbleached all-purpose flour

¹/₈ teaspoon fine sea salt

1 egg, lightly beaten

1 tablespoon poppy seeds

1. In a medium bowl, combine the warm water and milk. Add the yeast and sugar and stir to dissolve. Cover the bowl with a towel and let the yeast proof for about 5 minutes, until foamy.

2. Add the egg yolks, olive oil, 2 cups flour, and the salt to the yeast mixture and mix with your hands until a ball of dough is formed, adding more flour if the dough is very soft. Turn the dough out onto a floured surface and knead until smooth.

3. Lightly grease a large bowl with olive oil. Add the dough, turn to coat, and cover tightly with plastic wrap and then a towel. Let rise in a warm place for about 1 hour, or until doubled in size.

4. Punch down the dough, turn it out onto a floured surface, and knead it for a few minutes. Divide the dough into 3 equal pieces. Roll each piece into a 16-inch-long rope. Pinch the ropes together at one end. Lay the rope on the left over the one in the middle, then lay the rope on the right over the middle, and so on to the ends of the ropes, creating a braid. Pinch the ends together. Grease a cookie sheet, and place the braid on the sheet.

5. Gently brush the entire surface of the braid with the beaten egg and sprinkle on the poppy seeds. Let the braid rise in a warm place for about 1 hour, until doubled in size.

6. Preheat the oven to 375°F. Bake the braid for about 25 minutes, or until the crust is golden brown. Remove to a rack to cool.

Note: Once the bread has cooled completely, it can be wrapped tightly in foil and frozen for up to 3 months.

6¹/₂ to 7 cups unbleached all-purpose flour

1¹/₄ cups sugar

1 tablespoon baking powder

1 teaspoon fine sea salt

5 large eggs plus 4 hard-boiled large eggs

8 tablespoons (1 stick) butter, melted

1¹/₄ cups milk, or more as necessary

1 tablespoon vanilla

2 whole cloves

Colored sprinkles

1. Preheat the oven to 350°F. Lightly grease two cookie sheets. On a piece of cardboard, make a template: Draw a dove that is 12 inches long from tail to beak and 7 inches across at its widest point. Cut out the form with scissors.

2. Sift together 6½ cups flour, the sugar, baking powder, and salt into a large bowl. In another bowl, whisk together 4 of the eggs, the butter, milk, and vanilla until well combined. Add to the flour mixture and mix with your hands to form a ball of dough that is smooth and no longer sticky, adding more flour if necessary.

3. Turn the dough out onto a floured surface and knead until it is smooth. Divide the dough into 2 pieces.

4. Roll each piece of dough out into a 13 by 11-inch rectangle and transfer to the cookie sheets. Place the template on each piece of dough and cut around it with a pastry wheel or small sharp knife. Remove the scraps of dough. With scissors, cut small V's in the tails to resemble feathers. Stick 1 clove in each head for the eyes. Place 2 of the hard-boiled eggs side by side in the middle of each dove's body. Cut 4 narrow 6-inch-long strips of dough from the dough scraps and cross 2 of them over each egg.

5. In a small bowl, lightly beat the remaining egg. Brush the doves with the beaten egg and sprinkle with the colored sprinkles.

6. Bake the doves for 20 to 25 minutes, or until they are lightly browned and firm to the touch. Let them cool slightly on the cookie sheets before removing them to cooling racks.

Colomba

EASTER DOVE BREAD

Colomba is an Easter bread, shaped like a dove. Regional versions are found all over Italy. They may be "free-formed" by hand or baked in special dove-shaped molds. Some have a cake-like texture, while those made with yeast have the consistency and texture of bread dough. In this version, hard-boiled eggs are nestled in the dough before baking. Place the doves in a colorful basket and use as a centerpiece on your Easter table.

They also make a nice Easter gift.

These can be frozen once completely cool, but the eggs will not be edible.

Makes 2 breads

Le Pupazze di Nonna Fall-River

Nana Fall-River's Easter "Dolls"

❧

Easter bread in Calabria is shaped like dolls or babies called pupazze. *My good friend Tomie dePaola, the noted children's author and illustrator, who often sets his stories in Italy, gave me his grandmother's recipe in which the dough is braided and an egg is nestled in the top of the braid, like a small baby wrapped in a blanket. When Tomie makes these, he freezes them to give away to dear friends.*

❧

Makes 10

3 packages active dry yeast

½ cup warm (110° to 115°F) water

3 cups plus ½ teaspoon sugar

2 cups milk

31 eggs

1 pound solid vegetable shortening, melted and cooled to lukewarm

5 pounds unbleached all-purpose flour, sifted

1 tablespoon ground cinnamon

1 tablespoon fine sea salt

2 egg yolks beaten with 2 tablespoons water, for egg wash

1. In a large bowl, dissolve the yeast in the water. Sprinkle on ½ teaspoon of the sugar and stir to dissolve. Let the yeast proof, covered, for 10 minutes, or until foamy.

2. In a medium saucepan, scald the milk (bring to just under a boil).

3. In a heavy-duty electric mixer, beat 21 of the eggs until frothy. Add the milk and the remaining 3 cups sugar and blend well. Add the yeast mixture and stir to blend.

4. Sift the flour, cinnamon, and salt together. Using a dough hook, gradually add the flour mixture to the egg mixture, mixing until a ball of dough forms. Turn the dough out onto a floured surface and knead until smooth and elastic.

5. Place the dough in a large oiled bowl. Brush the top of the dough with oil and cover the dough with plastic wrap and then a towel. Let the dough rise in a warm place until it is doubled in size, about 1½ hours.

6. Lightly butter two cookie sheets. Punch down the dough. Turn the dough out onto a lightly floured surface and knead for 2 to 3 minutes. Divide into 30 equal balls. Roll each ball into a rope about 12 inches long.

7. For each bread, braid 3 ropes together (see page 120), then nestle an egg in the top of the braid. Place the braids on the cookie sheets and brush with the egg wash. Cover the braids with a towel and let rise in a warm place for about 20 minutes.

8. Preheat the oven to 350°F. Bake the braids for 40 to 45 minutes, or until golden brown. Transfer to wire racks to cool.

Note: When completely cool, these may be frozen, well-wrapped in aluminum foil.

Variation: Make braided wreaths instead of pupazze.

La Colomba di Pasqua

The Easter Dove

Marco walked carefully along the stone path, his sandals making a flapping sound as he hurried along. He carried a basket of bread dough, made just a few hours earlier by his mother, Costanza. After it had risen, she had asked him to take it to the *panificio* (bakery) in the center of town to be baked. It was to be the Easter bread for their table.

Gaetano, the roly-poly bread baker, welcomed Marco with a loud *buon giorno*, and Marco returned the greeting.

"Well, my lad," said Gaetano, brushing the flour from his hands, "I see that your mamma has been up early getting the dough made."

"*Sì, signore*," laughed Marco, "*mia mamma è sempre in gamba* (my mother is always on the ball)."

Gaetano took the basket from Marco and with a small knife carved the letter C for Costanza on the top of the dough to make sure that Marco got the right loaf when it came from the oven. Many people in the village brought their dough to Gaetano for communal baking since fuel was so expensive they could not afford their own. Gaetano put the dough onto a long wooden shovel, then pushed it off the shovel into the hot oven.

"How long will it take to bake, *signore*?" asked Marco.

"Come back before *mezzogiorno*, and it will be ready," Gaetano assured him.

Marco decided to get a lemonade at one of the shops and amuse himself while he waited. The whole town looked very festive, because it was just a few days before the celebration of Easter. Beautiful lilies in pots lined the doorways of the houses and the smell of Easter pies made with ricotta cheese wafted through the streets. Marco stopped by a shop displaying birdcages with canaries, pigeons, and doves. One bird in particular, a snowy white dove, caught his attention. Marco put his fingers near the cage to pet it.

"You interested in that bird, little boy?" inquired the shopkeeper. "It's only a few lire and would make a nice pet."

Marco had no money, but he knew that he wanted that dove. "No, *signore*, I don't have enough money," he answered with sadness in his voice, and walked out the door. The church bells were chiming and Marco realized that it was noontime; the bread would be ready. As he entered the panificio, Gaetano was taking hot loaves from the oven.

"Tell your mamma this is her most beautiful loaf, such a high loaf, and look at the golden crust. It is a loaf more precious than gold," he said, with excitement in his voice. Marco paid him for baking the bread, put it, wrapped in brown paper, in his basket, and said good-bye. The smell of the bread comforted him, and as he made his way home, an idea occurred to him. He turned around and headed for the bird shop.

"*Signore*," he said, "will you take this loaf of bread in exchange for this dove?" The shopkeeper looked stunned.

"A loaf of bread for a bird?"

"Oh, yes, *signore*, it is a loaf more precious than gold. Look at how high the loaf is, the color of its crust; it is worthy to be eaten at only the finest of feasts."

The shopkeeper wrinkled his brow and put his hand to his chin. Hmmm, he thought. The boy is right. I do need something special for my Easter table and it *is* the most beautiful loaf that I have ever seen. "Done," he said, "the bird for the bread."

Marco was thrilled. He handed the loaf to the shopkeeper, who handed him the dove. Marco cradled the dove in his arms and started home. So happy was he that he almost did not realize what he had just done. How will I explain this empty basket to mamma? he thought. She will have to make more dough. She will be angry. I'll say that robbers stole the bread, or that Gaetano burned it in the oven, or... as ideas raced into his head, he heard a small voice say, "You will tell her the truth." It was the dove, talking to him. Marco could not believe his ears.

"You," he exclaimed, "you can talk?"

"Only when I know that someone is not at peace," said the dove in a soothing voice, and then it was silent.

Marco knew the dove was right. He held the bird even closer to him, and when he reached home, he found his mother sitting at the table, busily cleaning dandelion greens. She did not look up from her basket as she asked to see the bread. Marco, his

Pane 🐑 *Bread*

hands trembling, placed the dove on the table.

"What is this?" came her startled question. "Where is my bread for the Easter table?"

"Mamma," he cried, "I gave your bread away because I wanted this beautiful dove. I know that I deserve to be punished."

His mother reached out her arms and pulled Marco toward her. With her apron, she wiped the tears streaming down his face, and in a soft voice said, "You were wrong not to ask me first about the bird, but you told me the truth, and that is what matters. Come, Marco, we will make more dough." Together they mixed the water, yeast, and flour until they had a mound of soft dough. Marco's mother cut the dough in half and gave him a piece to form into his own loaf. Marco looked over at the dove, cooing softly nearby, and instead of making a loaf, he shaped his dough into a dove; his mother smiled and made hers the same.

Once more, Marco took the breads to the bakery. This time Gaetano did not need to put a C or M on the breads because they were the only ones shaped like doves. All the townspeople who had come to the panificio to pick up their loaves were curious about Marco's bread, and so they waited until the golden-brown doves came out of the oven.

"How beautiful!" everyone shouted, clapping their hands, and how clever. "We want to make a colomba too," they all said. Marco was so happy that people liked his bread. He told them how to shape the dough and they hurried off to create their own.

That Easter was the best one Marco ever had. The table was full of good things to eat, roast lamb and potatoes, tender artichokes, Easter pie, and Marco's bread. His mother said that it was the most beautiful bread she had ever seen, and every Easter from that time on, Marco, his mother, and all the townspeople always made their bread in the shape of a dove.

Pesce

Fish

Salmone con le Erbe

Poached Salmon with Herbs

❦

Aromatic fennel leaves infuse salmon with their delicate flavor in this simple dish. It's easiest to cook the salmon in a fish poacher, but a large deep frying pan will also work. I like to serve boiled artichokes and Potato Croquettes (page 182) with the salmon.

❦

Serves 4

Bridal Luncheon

....

Pasta "Caramels" (page 42)

Poached Salmon with Herbs

Fried Asparagus (page 6)

Zuppa Inglese (page 296)

....

Leafy tops and stalks of 2 large bulbs fennel

2 pounds salmon fillet, in one piece

2 bay leaves

5 tablespoons butter

6 large fresh basil leaves

Fine sea salt and freshly ground black pepper to taste

1. Fill a fish poacher with 1½ inches of water. Place half the fennel leaves and stalks on the poaching rack and lay the salmon skin side down on the leaves. Place the bay leaves on the salmon, and cover with the remaining fennel leaves and stalks. Cover the poacher, bring the water just barely to a simmer, and cook the fish for 8 to 10 minutes, or until it is light pink in color and opaque throughout.

Alternatively, use a steamer basket set in a large frying pan to cook the salmon.

2. Meanwhile, melt the butter in a small saucepan. Snip the basil leaves with scissors, add to the pan, and swirl the leaves in the butter for a few minutes with a wooden spoon to release their flavor. Season with salt and pepper.

3. Carefully lift the poaching rack or steamer out of the poacher or frying pan. Discard the fennel and bay leaves and transfer the salmon to a warm platter. Pour the sauce over the salmon, and serve immediately.

¼ cup plus 1½ tablespoons Thyme-Peppercorn Oil (page 308)

2 pounds swordfish, cut into 4 pieces and patted dry

4 medium red onions, thinly sliced

2 tablespoons red wine vinegar

1. Early in the day, marinate the fish: Pour 2½ tablespoons of the oil into a glass dish large enough to hold the fish in one layer. Add the fish, turning to coat. Cover and refrigerate until ready to grill.

2. Preheat a charcoal or gas grill. In a skillet, heat the remaining 3 tablespoons oil. Add the onions and cook over low heat, stirring occasionally, until they have darkened and are caramelized, about 20 minutes. Raise the heat to high, stir in the vinegar, and let the vinegar evaporate. Reduce the heat to low and keep warm.

3. Grill the fish for about 4 minutes on each side, basting with the marinade, just until a knife is easily inserted. Remove the fish to a serving dish. Place the onions on top and serve immediately.

Pesce Spada alla Griglia con Cipolle Rosse

Grilled Swordfish with Red Onions

❧

Thyme-peppercorn oil and slow-cooked red onions give this dish exquisite flavor. To make a quick version of the oil, smash a few peppercorns with a heavy skillet, chop a handful of thyme, and combine with olive oil. A dash of red wine vinegar provides just the right agrodolce *—sweet-and-sour—balance of flavors.*

❧

Serves 4

Summer Dinner

Zucchini Mint Soup
(page 20)

Grilled Swordfish with Red
Onions

Green Bean, Chickpea, and
Tomato Salad (page 202)

Strawberry Tart (page 262)

La Serata gli Animali Hanno Parlato

The Night the Animals Talked

Near the town of Bethlehem lived a farmer named Guido and his wife, Giulia, who could not speak. Their few possessions consisted of an ox, a donkey, and two sheep. Their small house was made from mud and straw and they slept on a dirt floor. To keep warm at night, Guido would make a small fire from bits of twisted olive tree branches, then heat stones near the fire, which radiated warmth while he and Giulia slept. During the day, Guido took care of feeding the animals, while Giulia spun the wool from the sheep and then wove it into cloaks and blankets to be sold in the town.

One day as they were making their way to town, Guido and Giulia saw a man leading a donkey on which a young woman rode. As they approached the man, Guido said good morning and Giulia nodded.

"Kind sir," said the man, "do you have any water with you? My wife is very thirsty." Guido reached over to the side of his own donkey for a leather pouch full of water and handed it to the man.

The man took the water and gave it to his wife to drink. Afterward he took a drink himself and handed what was left to Guido. Then he asked, "How far is it to Bethlehem?"

Guido told him it was a half a day's journey ahead. "Come, follow me," offered Guido. "We are on our way there now to sell our blankets and cloaks."

"Thank you," said the man, "my wife and I are looking for a place to stay for the night in Bethlehem." So together they continued their journey to town.

Finally, as the sky was darkening, they reached Bethlehem and they parted company. Guido and Giulia went to their usual spot in the town, outside a traveler's inn, and set out their blankets and cloaks on the ground for people to see. Each time someone made a purchase, Giulia clapped her hands. It was getting late now, and Guido and Giulia packed up their things to make the journey home. The money they had made was needed to buy food and seeds.

As they were leaving, Guido saw the man he had guided into town earlier. Approaching him again, he said, "Did you find what you came here for?"

The man looked at him, shaking his head, and said, "Kind sir, I needed a room in the inn, but they are all taken, and my wife, Mary, is with child."

Guido could see that the man was very worried. "Wait here," he said, "I will be right back," and he quickly turned toward the inn. Meanwhile, Giulia, who had overheard this, felt sorry for the young woman. Unable to speak, she walked over and handed her a blanket to keep warm. The woman smiled and took the blanket, and Giulia thought that she was the most beautiful woman she had ever seen.

Guido returned and said, "The innkeeper is a friend of mine, he will let you stay in the stable behind the inn for the night."

The man took Guido's hand and said, "How can I ever thank you?"

"There is no need," replied Guido, and he motioned them toward the stable.

The stable was as cold as a tomb. The man helped Mary off the donkey and, with Giulia's blanket over her shoulders, guided her into the stable. Guido rushed about trying to find a few twigs and stones to make a fire. Giulia took the two donkeys into the stable, then she went back outside to help Guido. They were so busy gathering twigs and stones that they did not realize how much time had passed. As they made their way back to the stable, they noticed a bright star overhead, casting a warm glow below. It seemed to light up the stable. When they reached the stable door, their bundles fell from their arms as they stood in amazement. Before them knelt the beautiful woman, her face ringed with light. The man stood beside her. He too was bathed in soft light, and at his feet lay a magnificent child wrapped in Giulia's blanket. Even the donkeys seemed to glow in light, and their warm breath kept the stable warm.

Guido and Giulia slowly came closer. The Child seemed to smile at them, reaching out to touch them with His tiny hand. Then a strange thing happened. The donkeys raised their heads and spoke: "This is Jesus, the son of God. Do not fear, for He has come to do great things for all mankind."

Peace 🐟 *Fish*

Guido was so taken aback by the animals talking that he was, for the moment, speechless, but then Giulia began to speak, saying, "Welcome, blessed Child." When Guido heard his wife speak for the first time, he was overcome with joy, and both he and Giulia fell to their knees in prayer.

Then the donkeys spoke again: "Because of your kindness to Mary and Joseph, the Lord blesses you."

Then Giulia and Guido understood why Giulia could now speak. "Go out and tell your neighbors that the Lord has come."

Guido and Giulia did as the donkeys said, praising the Lord to everyone they met. In fact, for the rest of their lives, Guido and Giulia never stopped talking about the Christ Child.

La Vigilia di Natale

Christmas Eve

~

Weeks of preparation set the stage not only for the celebration of Christmas but also for *la vigilia*, Christmas Eve. Many special foods, pasta, breads, and cookies are made in anticipation of the holidays, and the day before Christmas Eve is reserved for the purchase of the other food for the Christmas Eve meal.

Topping the list is fish. Traditionally the meal is meatless, and the number of fish courses may run anywhere from seven to nine. The number seven represents the seven sacraments, and nine is a multiple of the Holy Trinity. Other traditions hold that seven courses represent the week before Christmas, the last week of Advent. Over the years the number of courses served by most families has decreased as generations shy away from the traditions, but fish remains the central feature of the meal.

In Italy, eel is regarded as a delicacy and a must for *la vigilia*, but it is really the cook's choice as to what will be prepared. Serving seven fish courses requires organization, but it can be a family activity in which everyone helps. Some dishes can be prepared a day ahead, such as Marinated Seafood Salad (page 138) or Sole in Lemon and Oil (page 134). Some prep work for the other fish dishes can be done ahead as well. For example, the vegetables and sauce for Stewed Cod (page 135) can be made ahead since the fish is the last thing to go into the dish and cooks in just a few minutes. Likewise, the sauce for Pasta with Sardines (page 137) can be cooked ahead and refrigerated, then reheated while the pasta is cooking.

For a simpler meal, Beans, Mussels, and Pasta Soup (page 24) is perfect with crusty bread. Any or all of these dishes can be accompanied by a Mixed Green Salad (page 192), a Green Salad (page 193), or an Arugula and Radicchio Salad (page 197).

Customs vary in Italy, but traditionally, assorted fresh fruits, pomegranates, dried figs, dates, nuts, and torrone end the meal.

Sogliola al Limone ed Olio

Sole in Lemon and Oil

❧

The ancient Romans gave the name solea *to sole because this flatfish reminded them of the sole of a sandal. A carryover of the ancient Roman practice of preserving fish is sole marinated in lemon juice and olive oil, prepared for* la vigilia. *Dover or gray sole, both mild in flavor and delicate in texture, are good for this dish, but the firmer petrale sole, which is really flounder, is a good substitute.*

❧

Serves 8

1/4 cup plus 3 tablespoons extra-virgin olive oil

Juice of 2 large lemons

2 teaspoons minced garlic

1/3 cup finely minced flat-leaf parsley, plus sprigs for garnish

Fine sea salt and freshly ground black pepper to taste

2 pounds sole or flounder fillets

Lemon wedges

1. In a glass dish large enough to hold the fish in one layer, mix together 1/4 cup of the olive oil, the lemon juice, garlic, parsley, and salt and pepper. Set aside.

2. In a skillet, heat the remaining 3 tablespoons olive oil until smoking hot. Add the fish, a few pieces at a time, and fry until golden brown, turning once or twice. Remove the fish to a cutting board and let cool. Set the pan aside.

3. Cut the fish into small squares and place them in the marinade. Strain any oil remaining in the frying pan and pour it over the fish. Cover the dish tightly with plastic wrap and refrigerate overnight, occasionally spooning the marinade over the fish.

4. Bring the fish to room temperature before serving. Arrange the fish on a platter and garnish with lemon wedges and sprigs of parsley.

2 tablespoons olive oil

1 onion, diced

2 ribs celery, diced

2 cups coarsely chopped plum tomatoes

1 tablespoon capers in brine, drained and minced

1 bay leaf

2 tablespoons chopped flat-leaf parsley

2 pounds fresh cod, cut into chunks

Fine sea salt to taste

In a large skillet, heat the olive oil over medium heat. Add the onion and celery and cook until soft. Stir in the tomatoes, capers, bay leaf, and parsley and simmer, covered, for 3 to 4 minutes. Add the cod, cover, and cook over low heat for about 8 minutes, or until the fish flakes easily with a fork. Add salt to taste and serve.

Variation: The fish can also be served as a sauce over spaghetti.

Merluzzo Stufato

Stewed Cod

❧

It required patience to prepare dried salt cod (baccalà), stiff as a board, for la vigilia. A few days before Christmas Eve, we would place it in the sink and turn the faucet on to a lazy drip to allow the fish to rehydrate slowly before stewing it. Now I save time by using fresh cod instead of dried.

❧

Serves 4

Traditional Christmas Eve Seafood Dinner

Anguille Fritte

Fried Eel

❧

The best anguille (eels) in Italy come from the Po River area. With their white meat and delicate flavor, they are a treat reserved for la vigilia. In Rome, December 24 is not only Christmas Eve but also a holiday known as the Cottio, the day the eel markets open. If you are lucky enough to be able to purchase eel, you are in for a unique treat, whether you roast, smoke, stew, or deep-fry them.

❧

Serves 4

Vegetable oil for deep-frying

1 cup unbleached all-purpose flour

Fine sea salt to taste

2 pounds eels, skinned, cleaned, cut into 2-inch pieces, and patted dry

Lemon wedges

1. In a deep fryer or a large heavy pot, heat the vegetable oil to 375°F.

2. Mix the flour and salt together on a plate. Dredge the eel pieces in the flour, turning to coat them well, and shake off the excess. Fry the eels in batches until golden brown. Remove the eel to brown paper to drain. Serve immediately, with lemon wedges.

¹/₃ cup olive oil

²/₃ cup dried bread crumbs

2 medium onions, finely minced

*Three 4-ounce cans sardines in olive oil, drained and coarsely
chopped, oil reserved*

¹/₄ cup pine nuts

¹/₄ cup currants

1 pound bucatini or spaghetti

Leafy tops of 1 bulb fennel, tied together with kitchen string

¹/₂ teaspoon powdered saffron

Fine sea salt to taste

1. In a large skillet, heat 2 tablespoons of the olive oil. Add the
bread crumbs and cook, stirring, until golden brown. Drain on
paper towels.

2. Add the remaining olive oil to the pan, then add the onions
and cook until the onions are soft. Add the sardines with their oil
and cook gently for about 3 minutes. Stir in the pine nuts and currants. Remove from the heat.

3. Bring 6 quarts of salted water to a boil in a large pot. Add
the fennel tops and bucatini or spaghetti, and cook until the pasta
is al dente. Just before the pasta is cooked, remove ¹/₂ cup of the
cooking water and dissolve the saffron in it; set aside. Scoop out the
fennel, untie it, and chop the leaves fine. Set aside.

4. Drain the pasta and add it to the sardine mixture. Heat the
pasta and sardines over medium-low heat, stirring constantly. Stir
in the saffron water and fennel leaves and add the salt.

5. Place the pasta and sardine mixture on a large serving platter. Sprinkle with the bread crumbs and serve immediately.

Note: It is not customary to serve grated cheese on fish pastas.

Pasta con le Sarde

Pasta with Sardines

❧

*Sardines with pasta called
bucatini, a thick hollow
spaghetti, was always part of the
seven-course fish dinner Nonna
Saporito served on Christmas
Eve. In this version of her recipe,
I've substituted Florence fennel
for her beloved wild fennel, and
canned sardines for fresh, both
of which are difficult, if not
impossible, to find here.*

❧

Serves 6

Frutta di Mare

Marinated Seafood Salad

❧

Several preparations of squid were served on Christmas Eve at home. My favorite has always been frutta di mare, a marinated medley of squid, shrimp, and octopus. I use scallops in this recipe in place of octopus. This should be made a day before it is served to allow the marinade to fully flavor the fish.

❧

Serves 8

MARINADE

Juice of 2 to 3 lemons (to taste)
¹/₂ cup extra-virgin olive oil
4 cloves garlic, crushed
¹/₄ cup chopped flat-leaf parsley
¹/₃ cup chopped fennel leaves
1 cup diced red bell peppers
2 tablespoons red wine vinegar
Fine sea salt and coarsely ground black pepper to taste

2 pounds small squid (4 to 6 inches long)
1 teaspoon coarse sea salt
¹/₂ pound medium shrimp, peeled
1 pound bay scallops

1. In a shallow nonmetal dish, combine all the marinade ingredients. Mix well and set aside.

2. Remove the head of each squid by pulling it away from the body. Cut off the tentacles below the eyes and discard the heads. Pull out the interior membranes from each squid body and remove the plastic-like spine bone from the inside. Pull off the outer skin. Wash the squid bodies and tentacles thoroughly in cold water. Cut the bodies into ¹/₄-inch rings and dice the tentacles. Set aside.

3. Bring 4 cups of water to a boil in a large saucepan and add the salt. Add the shrimp and boil until they turn pink, about 3 minutes. With a slotted spoon, remove the shrimp and let cool.

4. Add the scallops to the boiling water and boil for 3 minutes. Remove the scallops with a slotted spoon and let cool. Add the squid rings to the water and boil until tender, 12 to 15 minutes. About 5 minutes before the rings are cooked, add the diced tentacles. The squid should be tender, not chewy. Drain well.

5. Toss the squid, shrimp, and scallops in the marinade. Add salt if necessary. Cover and let marinate overnight in the refrigerator, turning the mixture occasionally.

6. To serve, transfer the salad to a decorative platter, cover, and let come to room temperature before serving.

Vegetable oil for deep-frying

About 1 cup unbleached all-purpose flour

Fine sea salt to taste

*3 pounds assorted firm fish fillets and shellfish, fish cut into
uniform pieces*

Lemon wedges

1. In a deep-fryer or large heavy pot, heat the oil to 375°F.

2. Mix the flour and salt on a plate. Dredge the fish and shell-fish in the flour, shaking off the excess. Fry in batches until golden brown, and remove to brown paper to drain.

3. Place the fish and shellfish on a platter, sprinkle with salt, and squeeze the lemon wedges over. Serve immediately.

Fritto Misto di Pesce

Mixed Fish Fry

Fritto misto di pesce, a dish composed of several types of fish, clams, shrimp, squid, and smelts, was always the last dish to be served on Christmas Eve. Any firm fish, however, is well suited to this cooking method. To make a successful fritto misto remember the cardinal rules: Maintain the cooking oil at a constant temperature to ensure even browning, and fry pieces of fish or shellfish of the same size together to ensure even cooking.

Serves 6 to 8

Carne e Pollame

Meat and Poultry

Brasato all' Aceto di Vino

Braised Beef Roast in Wine Vinegar

❧

I make this braised roast using an old homemade red wine vinegar, but any good-quality commercial brand will lend the right zing to the sauce.

❧

Serves 4

One 2-pound top round roast

2 cloves garlic, slivered

Fine sea salt and coarsely ground black pepper to taste

1 tablespoon olive oil

1 large onion, diced

¼ cup red wine vinegar

1 tablespoon minced flat-leaf parsley

3 tablespoons minced fresh basil

1 large carrot, peeled and shredded

1 tablespoon tomato paste

2 tablespoons dry red wine

1. Dry the roast well with paper towels. Make slits all over the roast and insert the garlic slivers. Rub the roast with salt and pepper.

2. In a Dutch oven, heat the olive oil over medium heat. Brown the roast slowly on all sides. Add the onions and cook for 5 minutes, or until they begin to wilt. Add the vinegar, parsley, basil, and carrot, and cook for 5 minutes.

3. Mix the tomato paste and wine together in a small bowl and add to the roast. Bring to a simmer, cover, and cook for about 1 hour and 45 minutes, or until a knife is easily inserted into the meat.

4. Remove the meat to a cutting board and let rest for 10 to 15 minutes. Strain the pan juices through a sieve set over a bowl, pressing on the solids with a wooden spoon to extract as much liquid as possible. Set the pot aside.

5. Cut the roast into ¼-inch slices. Return the meat to the pot, add the strained juices, and bring the juices to a simmer. Serve immediately, with some of the juices poured over the meat.

2 ¹/₂ tablespoons olive oil

1 teaspoon fine sea salt

1¹/₂ teaspoons coarsely ground black pepper

One 4-pound boneless rib roast, tied

2 shallots, finely diced

2 tablespoons Homemade Beef Broth (page 16) or canned beef bouillon

10 black peppercorns, smashed

¹/₂ cup dry red wine

¹/₄ cup heavy cream

1. In a small bowl, combine the olive oil, salt, and pepper. Dry the beef with paper towels and rub the pepper mixture all over the roast. Place the roast in a dish, cover with plastic wrap, and refrigerate for 2 to 3 days.

2. Preheat the oven to 350°F. Place the meat on a rack in a roasting pan and insert a meat thermometer into the center of the roast. Roast for about 1¹/₂ hours (20 to 25 minutes per pound), or until the thermometer registers 160°F, for a well-done roast; or cook it to your personal preference. Remove the meat to a cutting board and let rest for 10 to 15 minutes.

3. Meanwhile, spoon 3 tablespoons of the pan drippings into a medium skillet. Heat the drippings, add the shallots, and cook until they are soft. Add the beef broth, wine, and peppercorns. Bring to a boil, reduce the heat, and stir in the heavy cream. Let simmer for 3 to 4 minutes. Pour the sauce into a sauceboat and keep warm.

4. Slice the roast and pass the sauce on the side.

Costata al Forno con Pepe Nero

Rib Roast with Black Pepper

❧

This is a delicious contemporary dish that I enjoyed on a visit to northern Italy. The roast marinates for several days and is served with a simple sauce made from the pan drippings and black peppercorns.

❧

Serves 8

A Supper for Company

....

Rib Roast with Black Pepper

Potatoes with Dried Tomatoes and Thyme (page 184)

Fruit Salad with Greens (page 194)

Rafaella's Apple Cake (page 267)

....

Farsumagru

Stuffed Beef Rolls

❦

The word farsumagru *literally translated means "false lean," and in Sicily it is the name given to stuffed and rolled beef. In other regions of Italy, it is called* braciolone. *Farsumagru was the Italian's answer to lean but not so tender cuts of meat like round or flank steak. Stuffed with a filling* a piacere *(according to your liking) and simmered in a sauce for nearly two hours, the meat becomes very tender. To cut neat slices, allow the meat to stand for a few minutes.*

❦

Serves 6 to 8

1½ pounds top round or flank steak, cut ¼ inch thick

1 teaspoon fine sea salt, or more to taste

1 tablespoon coarsely ground black pepper

3 cloves garlic, cut into thin slivers

½ cup packed minced flat-leaf parsley

½ cup freshly grated Pecorino Romano cheese

1 red onion, thinly sliced

3 hard-boiled eggs, optional

½ cup chopped pitted Sicilian oil-cured black olives

SAUCE

2 tablespoons olive oil

1 tablespoon lard or olive oil

1 clove garlic, minced

4 cups fresh or canned crushed plum tomatoes

½ cup water

1 cup dry red wine

1 bay leaf

Fine sea salt and freshly ground black pepper to taste

1. Lay the meat on a cutting board and pound it with a meat mallet to flatten it to a uniform thickness. Be careful not to tear the meat. Pat the meat dry with paper towels, and rub it all over with the salt and pepper.

2. Lay the meat flat and sprinkle the garlic over it, then sprinkle on the parsley, cheese, and onion. Place the eggs in a row lengthwise down the center of the meat and sprinkle the olives over. Starting at a long end, roll up the meat like a jelly roll. Tie the roll with string every inch or so.

3. In a large deep saucepan, heat the olive oil and lard over medium-high heat. Add the garlic and cook until it is soft. Add the meat and brown it on all sides. Lower the heat, add all the remaining ingredients, and stir to blend. Bring to a simmer, cover, and cook for 1½ hours, or until the meat is tender. Remove the meat to a cutting board and let rest.

4. Cut the meat into ½-inch slices, place on a serving platter, and spoon the tomato sauce over the top. Serve immediately, or keep warm in a low oven on an ovenproof platter, covered with aluminum foil, until ready to serve.

Controfiletto Freddo e Picante

Spicy Cold Beef Rolls

❦

These neat rolled packages of roast beef are a good example of cucina rapida (effortless cooking). The flavor-packed, slightly spicy filling is the perfect foil for the meat. This is a great choice for a summer luncheon.

❦

Serves 8 as a lunch main course, 12 as an antipasto

Cold Lunch

Marinated Fish (page 11)

Spicy Cold Beef Rolls

Sorrel and Endive Salad (page 198)

Pane Rustico (page 96)

Biscuits with Pepper (page 106)

Cantaloupe and Bananas with Ricotta (page 206)

$1^1/_2$ cups minced celery

1 marinated red bell pepper, drained and diced

1 tablespoon capers in brine, drained and finely minced

2 marinated artichoke hearts, drained and diced

$^1/_2$ cup good-quality mayonnaise

1 teaspoon Worcestershire sauce

1 teaspoon Dijon mustard

24 thin slices cooked roast beef (about $2^1/_2$ pounds)

Extra-virgin olive oil for brushing

1. In a bowl, mix the celery, red pepper, capers, and artichokes together.

2. In a small bowl, whisk together the mayonnaise, Worcestershire sauce, and mustard. Pour the sauce over the vegetables and mix gently.

3. Spread about $1^1/_2$ tablespoons of the mixture evenly over each slice of roast beef and roll up like a jelly roll. Place the rolls seam side down on a decorative serving plate, brush the top of each one with a little oil, and serve.

1/4 pound pancetta, thinly sliced

1 large shallot, peeled

2 pork tenderloins (about 2 1/2 pounds)

Fine sea salt and coarsely ground black pepper to taste

1 medium onion, thinly sliced

2 bay leaves

1 teaspoon juniper berries, crushed

1/3 cup dry white wine

2 teaspoons olive oil

1. Place the pancetta and shallot in a food processor and pulse to a paste. Or mince together with a sharp knife until a fine paste is obtained. Season with salt and pepper.

2. Pat the meat dry with paper towels. With a sharp knife, make 1/2-inch-long and 1/2-inch-deep slits along the length of each tenderloin on both sides. Insert the pancetta mixture into the slits, packing it in well. Season the tenderloins with salt and coarse pepper. Set aside.

3. In a dish large enough to hold the tenderloins in one layer, mix together the onion, bay leaves, juniper berries, wine, and olive oil. Add the tenderloins and turn them once or twice in the mixture. Cover and refrigerate for at least 3 hours, or overnight, basting occasionally with the marinade.

4. Preheat the oven to 350°F. Drain the tenderloins, reserving the marinade. Place the tenderloins in a roasting pan and roast for 45 minutes to 1 hour, basting from time to time with the reserved marinade.

5. Remove the tenderloins to a cutting board, reserving the pan juices, and let rest for about 10 minutes. Then cut into thin slices, place on a platter, and pour the pan juices over the top.

Arrosto di Lonza di Maiale al Ginepro

Roast Pork Tenderloin with Juniper Berries

The faint scent of juniper berries and aromatic roasting pork tenderloin is a sign in my kitchen that fall cooking has begun. This dish tastes best if you can let the meat marinate overnight, but this is not essential. Pork tenderloins are usually sold two to a package and weigh about one and a quarter pounds each.

Serves 8

Lombata di Maiale con Rosmarino e Vino

Pork Loin with Rosemary and Wine

❧

Lombata di maiale (*pork loin*) is usually roasted in the oven with a few herbs and wine. In this version, I make a battuto, or fine mince, of fresh rosemary and garlic to cover the meat, then braise the meat in a Dutch oven so that it remains moist. Cooking it this way produces a very flavorful roast.

❧

Serves 4 to 6

Christmas Dinner

Ravioli Stuffed with Red Peppers and Ricotta (page 60)

Pork Loin with Rosemary and Wine

Potato Fritters (page 183)

Arugula and Radicchio Salad (page 197)

Ricotta Cheesecake with Pomegranate Sauce (page 278)

3 tablespoons fresh rosemary leaves

2 large cloves garlic, peeled

One 2 1/2-pound boneless pork loin roast, tied

Fine sea salt to taste

1 tablespoon olive oil

1 large onion, cut into wedges

1 large green bell pepper, cored, seeded, and cut into chunks

3/4 cup dry red wine

Juice of 1 lemon

1/3 cup diced Dried Tomatoes in Olive Oil (page 312)

1. On a cutting board, mince the rosemary and garlic together.

2. Pat the meat dry with paper towels and roll the meat in the rosemary and garlic mixture, coating it on all sides. Season with salt.

3. In a Dutch oven, heat the olive oil. Brown the roast on all sides over low heat. Add the onion and green pepper and cook until the onion is soft. Raise the heat to high, add 1/3 cup of the wine, and let most of it evaporate. Cover the pot, lower the heat to a simmer, and cook for 45 minutes.

4. Add the remaining wine and continue cooking, covered for 15 minutes. Add the lemon juice and tomatoes and cook, covered, for 30 minutes longer, or until the meat is fork-tender.

5. Remove the meat to a cutting board and let rest for 15 to 20 minutes. Set the pot aside. Cut the pork into 1/4-inch slices, return the meat to the pot, and reheat it with the juices over low heat. Transfer the meat with the juices to a serving platter and serve immediately.

Juice of 2 lemons

¹/₄ cup plus 2 tablespoons olive oil

1 tablespoon Worcestershire sauce

2 teaspoons Spicy Mustard (page 305)

Fine sea salt and freshly ground black pepper to taste

2¹/₂ pounds boneless pork loin, cut into 1-inch cubes

²/₃ pound pancetta, cut into 1-inch cubes

1 pound small button mushrooms, stemmed and cleaned

10 small fresh sage leaves

1. In a glass dish large enough to hold the pork in a single layer, mix the lemon juice, olive oil, Worcestershire sauce, mustard, and salt and pepper. Add the pork, turning to coat, cover, and refrigerate for at least 3 hours, or overnight.

2. Drain the meat, reserving the marinade. Thread the pieces onto 10 skewers, alternating the meat with the pancetta and mushrooms and adding 1 sage leaf to each skewer.

3. Prepare the grill. Grill the spiedini, turning and basting occasionally with the remaining marinade, for 5 to 8 minutes. Remove the skewers and serve immediately.

Spiedini di Lonza di Maiale

Grilled Skewered Pork Loin

❧

Spiedini, skewered grilled meats, are the perfect solution for the harried cook. I like to serve these marinated pork loin spiedini as an alternative to lamb on an Easter buffet, but they are also perfect for a summer barbecue. Let the meat marinate for at least three hours before grilling.

❧

Serves 6

Borsette di Maiale

Little Pork Purses

❧

Italian cooks are very fond of stuffing vegetables, meats, fish, and fowl. In this recipe for borsette, "little purses," of stuffed pork chops, the savory filling is made from Fontina cheese, prosciutto, leeks, and thyme. The dish can be assembled early in the day, covered, and refrigerated until ready to bake. Veal chops can be used in place of pork.

❧

Serves 6

Elegant Anniversary Dinner

....

Little Pork Purses

Mushrooms and Cream
(page 175)

Fried Asparagus (page 6)

Mixed Green Salad
(page 192)

Zuppa Inglese (page 296)

....

1½ tablespoons olive oil

1 cup thinly sliced leeks

¼ cup diced fennel

1 teaspoon fresh lemon juice

¼ pound Italian Fontina cheese, diced

¼ pound prosciutto, diced

1½ tablespoons finely minced fresh thyme

Fine sea salt and freshly ground black pepper to taste

Six ¾-inch-thick center-cut pork chops, with 2-inch-deep pockets (about 2½ pounds)

1. In a medium skillet, heat 1 tablespoon of the olive oil. Add the leeks and fennel and cook over low heat until they just begin to color. Raise the heat, add the lemon juice, and let it evaporate. Remove the mixture to a bowl to cool slightly.

2. Preheat the oven to 350°F. Brush a casserole dish large enough to hold the pork chops in a single layer with the remaining olive oil. Add the cheese, prosciutto, and thyme to the leek mixture and mix well. Season with salt and pepper.

3. Fill the pork pockets with the mixture, packing it in firmly. Close the openings with toothpicks or sew closed with cooking string. Lay the pork in the prepared dish, and season with salt and pepper.

4. Bake, uncovered, for 45 minutes, or until nicely browned. Serve immediately.

Natural hog casings (see Note)

5 pounds boneless pork butt, ground (see headnote)

2 tablespoons fine sea salt

2 tablespoons coarsely ground black pepper

3 tablespoons fennel seeds

1 to 2 tablespoons hot red pepper flakes

1. In a bowl, soak 3 or 4 casings in several changes of cold water for about 10 minutes to remove the salt. If the casings are very long, cut them into 24-inch segments.

2. In a large bowl, combine the pork with all the remaining ingredients and mix well. Test a small piece for seasoning by frying it in a hot skillet, and correct the seasoning if necessary.

3. Drain the casings. Slip one end of a casing over the narrow opening of a sausage funnel. Place the funnel under the faucet and run cold water through it. With your hands, slide the casing up onto the funnel, leaving about 2 inches free at the end. Remove the funnel from the faucet and tie a knot in the end.

4. Push the sausage mixture, a little at a time, through the funnel with your thumbs, and fill the casing, leaving about 2 inches free at the end. Tie a knot in the end and release any air bubbles in the casing by pricking it with a sterilized safety pin. Repeat with the remaining meat.

5. To bake the sausages, preheat the oven to 350°F. Place the sausages in a baking dish and add just enough water to cover the bottom of the pan. Bake, uncovered, for 35 to 40 minutes, or until nicely browned. As excess water and fat accumulate in the pan, drain it off; after about 20 minutes, the sausage will begin to brown in its own juices. Remove the sausage to paper towels to drain. Cut into pieces and serve.

To fry, place the sausages in a large skillet and add just enough water to cover the bottom of the pan. Cook over medium heat, turning occasionally, for about 20 minutes, or until browned. As excess water and fat accumulate in the pan, pour them off. Cut into pieces and serve.

Note: Natural hog casings are available in the meat section of some grocery stores and in butcher shops. Keep any unused casings, still packed in salt, in the refrigerator for future use.

Salsiccia Fresca

Fresh Sausage

On Christmas Eve, while we're attending Midnight Mass, my fennel seed–flavored pork sausage slowly cooks in the oven. Traditionally it is the first thing we eat on returning home, signaling the end of the meatless fast of la vigilia. For the most succulent sausage, buy pork butt that has about one third fat, or it will be too dry. Have the butcher grind it once coarse and once fine. You can make the sausage ahead and freeze it in airtight plastic bags. These are great cooked on an outdoor grill.

Makes 5 pounds

Salsiccia e Lenticchie

Sausage and Lentils

❧

For Capodanno (New Year's Day), it is traditional to eat lentils and zampone, pork sausage stuffed into the skin of a pig's foot. Here I use natural hog casings because they are more readily available. Because they resemble tiny coins, lentils are eaten as a symbol of good luck for the coming year.

❧

Serves 4 to 6

Traditional Dinner
....

Sausage and Lentils

Arugula and Radicchio Salad
(page 197)

Bread in a Basket (page 100)

Befana Cake (page 280)
....

1 1/2 cups lentils

1 tablespoon olive oil

1/4 pound pancetta, diced

1 large onion, diced

1 carrot, peeled and diced

1 rib celery, diced

1 pound Fresh Sausage (page 151)

1/2 cup Tomato-Basil Sauce (page 32)

1 bay leaf

Fine sea salt to taste

1. Put the lentils in a bowl, add water to cover, and let soak for several hours, or overnight. Drain.

2. Place the lentils in a soup pot, add 2 quarts of water, and bring to a boil. Lower the heat and simmer, covered, for about 35 minutes, or until tender. Drain and set aside.

3. In a skillet, heat the olive oil. Add the pancetta, onion, carrot, and celery, and cook until very soft, about 6 minutes. Remove to a dish.

4. In the same skillet, cook the sausage, turning frequently, until nicely browned. Remove the sausage to paper towels to drain, then place in another dish and cover to keep warm.

5. Discard the fat in skillet. Return the vegetables to the skillet, and add the tomato sauce, lentils, and bay leaf. Cook over low heat, covered, for 5 minutes. Season with salt, and remove from the heat.

6. Cut the sausage into pieces. Pour the lentil mixture into the center of a serving platter, arrange the sausages around it, and serve immediately.

Capodanno

New Year's Day

❧

Italians cling to their holiday rituals, reluctant to change them in any way. Tradition, pageantry, religion, and folklore, the threads that have made up the very fabric of the Italian character for centuries, are a way of life in Italy. In every season of the year, Italians express the richness of their traditions by celebrating life and nature and the spiritual connection in their lives.

The cyclical rhythms of these celebrations begin on New Year's Day, when families gather to celebrate endings and new beginnings. In some regions of Italy, lentils are eaten on the first day of the year to ensure good fortune for all the days to follow. Some households prepare a special bread, similar to panettone, which is cut into pieces by the head of the family and passed to each person, who eats it as a symbol of hope and prosperity for the coming year. In some towns *la vampa*, a bonfire, is set to symbolize the casting away of old cares and misfortunes of the past year. Italy's *piazze* are the settings for fairs, selling everything from local food specialties to the popular witch doll known as Befana.

The end of the Christmas holiday season is marked by the Feast of the Epiphany on January 6. On that day children wait in anticipation for a visit from Befana, the tired, toothless, and lovable old witch who lives in chimney tops and is more popular than Babbo Natale (Santa Claus). Her popularity stems from an old folktale, reinterpreted on page 282.

Vitello in Umido

Stewed Veal Shoulder Roast

❦

I am always experimenting with new ways to serve inexpensive cuts of veal, and this one is a favorite. The sauce gives this slowly simmered roast unique character. Rolling the roast in a battuto, *or fine mince, of parsley and garlic before browning adds flavor to a somewhat bland cut of meat. I like to use meaty portobello mushrooms. Button, cremini, or shiitake mushrooms may be substituted.*

❦

Serves 4

Country Dinner

....

Stewed Veal Shoulder Roast

Polenta (page 72)

Mixed Green Salad (page 192)

Orange Cream Bavarian
(page 211)

....

3 cloves garlic, peeled

8 large sprigs flat-leaf parsley, stems trimmed

One 2½-pound boneless veal shoulder roast, tied

Fine sea salt and coarsely ground black pepper to taste

¼ pound pancetta, diced

1 large red onion, diced

¼ teaspoon diced hot red pepper

4 tablespoons butter

½ cup dry red wine

¼ pound portobello mushrooms, trimmed, cleaned, and diced

1 tablespoon red wine vinegar

1. Finely mince the garlic and parsley together on a cutting board.

2. Wipe the veal dry with paper towels. Rub salt and pepper all over the meat and roll the roast in the garlic and parsley, making sure to coat on all sides. Set aside on a plate.

3. In a Dutch oven, cook the pancetta, without any additional fat, until it has browned and given off its fat. Add the onions and hot pepper and cook over low heat until the onions are browned. Remove the onion mixture to a plate.

4. Add 1 tablespoon of the butter to the pot and raise the heat. Add the veal roast and brown it on all sides. Add the wine and let most of it evaporate. Return the onion mixture to the pan, lower the heat to a simmer, cover, and cook for 1½ hours, or until the meat is fork-tender.

5. Meanwhile, in a skillet, melt the remaining 3 tablespoons butter. Add the mushrooms and cook until they are soft and begin to exude their juices. Add the wine vinegar and let it evaporate.

6. Add the mushrooms to the veal roast and simmer to blend the flavors. Remove the meat to a cutting board and let rest for 10 minutes. Keep the sauce warm over very low heat.

7. To serve, cut the roast into thin slices and spoon the mushrooms and sauce over the top.

1/3 cup unbleached all-purpose flour

Fine sea salt to taste

2 large eggs

1 teaspoon fresh lemon juice

1 cup dried bread crumbs

1 pound veal, cutlets (cut from the top round)

4 tablespoons butter

1/4 pound prosciutto

1/4 pound Italian Fontina cheese, thinly sliced

1 small head radicchio, separated into leaves

1. Mix the flour and salt together on a plate. In a shallow bowl, lightly beat the eggs and lemon juice together with a fork. Spread the bread crumbs on a plate.

2. Pound the veal slices with a meat pounder so that they are 1/4 inch thick. Be careful not to tear the meat. Dry the slices with paper towels.

3. Dredge the slices in the flour, shaking off the excess. Coat each slice in the egg mixture, then in the bread crumbs. Place the slices in a single layer on a cookie sheet. (The veal can be prepared to this point up to 2 hours ahead. Cover with a sheet of wax paper and refrigerate.)

4. Preheat the broiler. In a large skillet, melt the butter over medium-high heat. Brown the veal, in batches if necessary, on both sides and place on a lightly greased broiler pan.

5. Layer the prosciutto slices over the veal and top with the cheese. Broil the scallopine just until the cheese melts and begins to turn a light golden brown. Remove to a serving plate lined with the radicchio, and serve immediately.

Scaloppine Val d'Aostana

VEAL SCALLOPS WITH PROSCIUTTO AND FONTINA

❧

Gianni Tofolon is a master cheesemaker from Cremona, Italy, who now makes cheese in Denmark, Wisconsin. His wife, Cinzia, hosted an elegant dinner party one night and served scaloppine Val d'Aostana, a dish from Valle d'Aosta, one of the provinces of the Piedmont region. The success of this dish depends upon the cut of the veal. Ask your butcher for scallopine from young, milk-fed veal, cut against the grain.

❧

Serves 4

Quick Supper

....

Veal Scallops with Prosciutto and Fontina

Spinach with Cream (173)

Sorrel and Endive Salad (page 198)

Oranges and Bananas in Amaretto (page 205)

....

Rotolo di Vitello Ripieno

Rolled Stuffed Veal Breast

❧

One summer night, I made a pilgrimage to a small trattoria in Boston's Little Italy called Il Panino. Since I knew the owner, I left it up to the chef to prepare whatever he liked for me. To my delight, a succulent stuffed veal breast, fragrant with porcini mushrooms and wine, arrived on the table. I have created this version from my memory of that wonderful dish.

❧

Serves 8

$2/3$ cup (about 1 ounce) dried porcini mushrooms

$1\,2/3$ cups hot water

3 cloves garlic, peeled

2 teaspoons green peppercorns in brine, drained

1 small bunch flat-leaf parsley, stems removed (about $1/2$ cup)

$1/2$ cup olive oil

$1\,1/2$ cups thinly sliced cremini or button mushrooms (about 6 ounces)

One 4-pound boneless veal breast

Fine sea salt and freshly ground black pepper to taste

1 medium white onion, thinly sliced

1 red bell pepper, cored, seeded, and cut into thin strips

$1/2$ cup dry white wine

1. Place the porcini in a bowl, add the hot water, and let soak for about 30 minutes until soft. Drain, reserving the liquid, and dice the porcini. Strain the liquid through cheesecloth and set aside.

2. Finely chop the garlic, peppercorns, and parsley together. Place in a small bowl and set aside.

3. In a large Dutch oven, heat 3 tablespoons of the oil. Add the sliced mushrooms and cook until soft. Add the mushrooms to the garlic mixture. Set the pot aside.

4. Lay the veal breast open flat, and, if necessary, pound the meat so that it is an even thickness. Spread the garlic mixture over the meat. Sprinkle with salt and pepper. Roll the meat up tightly like a jelly roll and tie with kitchen string in several places. Season the outside of the meat. Set aside.

5. Heat 2 tablespoons of the oil in the Dutch oven. Add the onion and red pepper and cook until soft. Add the diced porcini and cook for about 2 minutes. Remove the vegetables to a dish.

6. Add the remaining 3 tablespoons olive oil to the pot and heat over medium-high heat. Add the veal roll and brown on all sides. Add the wine and bring to a simmer. Cover the pot, reduce the heat, and simmer for 1 hour.

7. Add the onion mixture and the reserved porcini liquid, cover, and continue cooking until the meat is tender, about 45 minutes. Remove the meat to a cutting board and let rest for about 10 minutes. Cover the vegetables and keep warm over low heat.

8. Slice the meat and place on a platter. Pour the vegetables and juice over the top. Serve immediately.

1/4 cup unbleached all-purpose flour

2 eggs

1 1/2 cups toasted bread crumbs

1/4 cup finely ground walnuts

2 tablespoons finely minced fresh sage

Fine sea salt to taste

6 veal loin chops, about 3/4 inch thick

6 tablespoons butter

Lemon wedges

1. Heat the oven to 350°F. Spread the flour on a plate. In a shallow bowl, lightly beat the eggs. On another plate, mix together the bread crumbs, walnuts, sage, and salt. Dry the meat with paper towels. Dredge the chops in the flour, shaking off the excess. Coat the chops in the beaten egg, then coat them with the bread crumb mixture, patting the mixture so it adheres. Set the chops aside on a plate.

2. In a large flameproof baking dish, melt the butter. Add the chops in a single layer. Bake, uncovered, for 30 to 35 minutes, or until the chops are nicely browned. Serve at once with lemon wedges.

Costolette al Forno

Oven-Fried Veal Chops

Traditional Milanese-style breaded veal cutlets are the inspiration behind the delicious crunchy coating on these oven-fried chops, a family favorite when dinner calls for something special.

Serves 6

Scaloppine con Gorgonzola

Veal Scallops with Gorgonzola

❧

Gorgonzola cheese paired with thin slices of veal cutlet is an elegant New Year's Eve main course. Gorgonzola, a cow's milk cheese, has been made for centuries in the provinces of Lombardy and Piedmont. Its distinctive taste is created not only by aging but also by the injection of penicillum yeast mold into the heated milk. It is wonderful eaten alone, or in a sauce for delicate veal.

❧

Serves 4 to 6

1½ pounds veal cutlets

Fine sea salt to taste

3 tablespoons butter

5 ounces Gorgonzola cheese, diced

1 cup fresh or frozen peas, blanched

1 teaspoon grated lemon zest

Radicchio leaves for garnish

1. Pound the veal slices until they are ¼ inch thick. Sprinkle each with a little salt. Set aside.

2. In a skillet large enough to hold all the veal pieces in a single layer, melt the butter over medium-high heat. Quickly brown the veal pieces on both sides. Remove the slices to a warm dish.

3. Reduce the heat to low, add the cheese to the skillet, and stir until melted. Add the peas and lemon zest and heat through.

4. Arrange the radicchio leaves around the outside edge of a serving platter. Place the veal slices in the center of the platter and pour over the sauce. Serve immediately.

STUFFING

¹/₂ pound ground veal

1 large egg

¹/₂ cup diced zucchini

¹/₂ cup diced leeks

¹/₂ cup diced carrots

2 tablespoons chopped fresh mint

1¹/₂ tablespoons chopped fresh rosemary

Fine sea salt and freshly ground black pepper to taste

One 4¹/₂ pound leg of lamb, boned, bone reserved

Fine sea salt and freshly ground black pepper to taste

¹/₄ cup plus 2 tablespoons olive oil

2 carrots, peeled

2 ribs celery

1 large onion, quartered

2 cloves garlic, halved

2 sprigs fresh rosemary

1 cup dry white wine

1. Preheat the oven to 350°F. In a bowl, combine the veal, egg, zucchini, leeks, carrots, mint, rosemary, and salt and pepper and mix well.

2. Lay the leg of lamb out flat on a work surface. Rub all over with salt and pepper. Pat the stuffing over the inside of the leg. Fold the long sides of the lamb over to enclose the filling and tie with kitchen string in several places. Reposition the bone at the end of the lamb and secure with string. (This will make a nice presentation when the lamb is served.)

3. Pour 3 tablespoons of the olive oil into a roasting pan. Add the carrots, celery, onion, garlic, and rosemary sprigs, and toss in the oil. Add the lamb and brush the top and sides with the remaining 3 tablespoons olive oil. Sprinkle with salt and pepper.

4. Roast for about 1¹/₂ hours (20 minutes per pound) for medium. Baste the roast with the wine every 15 minutes.

5. Remove the roast to a cutting board and let rest for 10 minutes. Cut into slices and serve.

Cosciotto d'Agnello Ripieno

Stuffed Leg of Lamb

❧

This boned leg of lamb stuffed with fresh mint and rosemary, and roasted with aromatic vegetables, is one that I like to prepare for Easter dinner. I team it with fresh asparagus and tiny potatoes oven roasted with garlic. Be sure to use young spring lamb for best results.

❧

Serves 6 to 8

Formal Easter Dinner

Bread Gnocchi (page 52)

Stuffed Leg of Lamb

Asparagus and Prosciutto (page 170)

Oven-Roasted Mixed Vegetables (page 176)

Endive, Radicchio, and Escarole Salad (page 196)

Bread in a Basket (page 100)

Ricotta Pie (page 266)

Pollo al Cartoccio

Chicken in Paper

❧

The Italians' fondness for hunting and cooking game birds is especially evident on the Capodanno (New Year's) table, when game birds such as guinea fowl are traditionally served. I use chicken in this recipe because it is readily available, but other types of game, such as pheasant and capon, produce delicious results too. Parchment paper helps to keep the meat from drying out, and "the package" makes a dramatic presentation when it is opened at the table.

❧

Serves 4

New Year's Dinner

Cheese Rind Soup (page 21)

Chicken in Paper

Oven-Roasted Mixed Vegetables (page 176)

Sicilian Salad (page 193)

Befana Cake (page 280)

One 3-pound roasting chicken

Fine sea salt and freshly ground black pepper to taste

1 large lemon

1/4 pound prosciutto, thinly sliced (about 8 slices)

1 tablespoon fresh thyme leaves

6 fresh sage leaves

1 1/2 tablespoons fresh rosemary leaves

1 tablespoon olive oil

Parchment paper

1. Preheat the oven to 350°F. Wash and dry the chicken. Sprinkle the cavity with salt and pepper. With a skewer, poke holes all over the lemon and place it inside the chicken cavity. Tie the legs together with string and set aside.

2. Place a sheet of aluminum foil large enough to enclose the chicken on a baking pan and lay a sheet of parchment paper on top of the foil. Cut the prosciutto slices in half crosswise and overlap the slices in the middle of the parchment paper. Cover the prosciutto with half the herbs. Place the chicken on top of the prosciutto and brush with the olive oil. Sprinkle the remaining herbs over the top. Fold the parchment paper up over the chicken and fold the edges over to seal, then fold over the foil, making a tight seal.

3. Bake the chicken for about 1 1/4 hours, or until an instant-read thermometer inserted in the thigh registers 165° to 170°F.

4. Place the wrapped bird on a serving platter. Cut through the foil and parchment paper at the table with scissors. Carve the chicken and serve with the cooking juices and the prosciutto.

¹/₃ cup unbleached all-purpose flour

1 teaspoon fine sea salt

¹/₂ teaspoon coarsely ground black pepper

2 pounds cutlets, cut into serving pieces

¹/₄ cup plus 1 tablespoon olive oil

¹/₂ pound pancetta, diced

²/₃ cup diced Dried Tomatoes in Olive Oil (page 312)

²/₃ cup dry white wine

2 tablespoons fresh lemon juice

1. On a plate, mix together the flour, salt, and pepper. Dry the chicken pieces with paper towels. Dredge each piece in the flour mixture shaking off the excess.

2. In a skillet large enough to hold the chicken in one layer, heat the olive oil over medium heat. Add the chicken and sauté for about 3 minutes, turning once or twice. Add the pancetta and cook until the chicken is nicely browned. Remove the chicken to a dish.

3. Add the dried tomatoes to the pan and cook for 2 minutes. Add the wine, raise the heat to medium-high, and stir until well blended. Return the chicken to the skillet along with the lemon juice and cook for 2 to 3 minutes, or just until the chicken is heated through.

4. Spoon the chicken and sauce onto a platter and serve immediately.

❧

Earthy and succulent, this chicken dish gets its inspiration from La Buca, an Italian restaurant in Seattle. Flamboyant chef/owner Luigi De Nunzio, a southern Italian, cooks and serves peasant food with a passion. Although Luigi will never divulge his recipe, this version is very close to the original. Use pancetta (Italian bacon) if at all possible; if it is unavailable, you can substitute unsmoked bacon.

❧

Serves 6

Pollo Compresso in Padella

Pressed Chicken

❧

From Tuscany comes this simple chicken dish, flavored with a few herbs and fennel. It's great fun to make because the technique — cooking the chicken under bricks — is so unusual. Be sure to cook the chicken over low heat.

❧

Serves 4

2 pounds chicken breasts, split

Fine sea salt and coarsely ground black pepper to taste

3 tablespoons olive oil

2 cloves garlic, peeled

1 sprig fresh rosemary

2 shallots, quartered

1 small bulb fennel, sliced crosswise into ¼-inch-wide strips

1. If you have them wrap three clean bricks in aluminum foil and set aside.

2. Wash the chicken and dry with paper towels. Sprinkle with salt and pepper.

3. In a skillet large enough to hold the chicken in a single layer, heat the olive oil over medium heat. Add the garlic and rosemary and, with a wooden spoon, swirl them in the oil, pressing on them to release their flavor. When the garlic is golden brown, discard the garlic and rosemary. Reduce the heat to low, add the chicken pieces, skin side down, and scatter the shallots and fennel around them. Place the bricks or a cast-iron skillet on top of the chicken and cook for about 20 minutes, until the chicken is browned on the underside.

4. Remove the bricks and turn the chicken pieces over. Replace the bricks and cook until the chicken is fork-tender, about 20 minutes longer.

5. Transfer the chicken to a platter, spoon the pan juices and fennel over, and serve immediately.

¼ cup olive oil

2 large onions, diced

1½ cups diced pumpkin or butternut squash

3 cloves garlic, minced

3 small hot red peppers, cut into strips

3 large sprigs fresh rosemary

5 pounds chicken breasts, split and skin removed

Fine sea salt and coarsely ground black pepper to taste

1 cup dry white wine

3 cups pureed fresh tomatoes (about 1½ pounds) or canned plum
   tomatoes

1. In a large skillet, heat the oil. Add the onions, pumpkin, garlic, hot peppers, and rosemary, and cook over low heat until the onions are soft and golden brown. Transfer to a dish and set aside.

2. Season the chicken pieces with salt and pepper. In batches, add the chicken to the hot skillet, skin side down, and brown well, turning once or twice. Return all the chicken to the pan, add the onion mixture and the wine, and raise the heat to high. Cook for 5 minutes. Add the tomatoes, reduce the heat, cover, and simmer for 40 minutes, or until the chicken is easily pierced with a knife. Uncover the pan, and cook for 10 minutes longer.

3. Transfer the chicken and sauce to a casserole dish, let cool, cover, and refrigerate overnight.

4. To serve, remove the bones from the chicken. Return the chicken and sauce to a skillet and heat over medium heat until hot.

Pollo Arrabbiato

Spicy Chicken

❧

This spicy stewed chicken is most flavorful made a day ahead, but can be served right away. Cooking the chicken with the bone in helps to give body to the sauce and adds flavor to the stew. Serve over soft Polenta (page 72) for a perfect fall dinner.

❧

Serves 8

Country Supper

Spicy Chicken

Polenta (page 72)

Fava Bean Puree with
Chicory (page 171)

Green Salad (page 193)

Pears with Mint (page 204)

Petti di Pollo con Spinaci

Spinach-Stuffed Chicken Breasts

Nutmeg, spinach, and Fontina cheese are favorite ingredients in northern Italian cooking. Chicken cutlets stuffed with a mixture of the three and served with a white wine sauce make a perfect company dish. Prepare a few hours in advance if you like and then reheat before serving.

Serves 4

8 chicken cutlets (about 2 pounds)

Two 10-ounce bags fresh spinach, stemmed, rinsed, and drained

4½ tablespoons olive oil

1 medium onion, diced

1 large clove garlic, diced

1 cup diced Italian Fontina cheese

¼ teaspoon grated nutmeg

¼ teaspoon fine sea salt

SAUCE

3 tablespoons butter

2 tablespoons unbleached all-purpose flour

⅔ cup Homemade Chicken Broth (page 14)

½ cup dry white wine

1 teaspoon fresh lemon juice

Fine sea salt to taste

1. With a meat pounder, flatten the cutlets to a ¼-inch thickness, being careful not to tear the meat. Set aside.

2. Place the spinach in a dry large skillet, cover, and cook over medium heat until wilted, about 5 minutes. Drain and squeeze dry. Coarsely chop and set aside.

3. In the same skillet, heat 2½ tablespoons of the olive oil. Add the onions and garlic and cook until the onions are lightly browned. Add the spinach and cook, stirring, for about 2 minutes. Transfer the mixture to a bowl and let cool slightly. Wipe out the skillet and set aside.

4. Stir the cheese, nutmeg, and salt into the the spinach. Spread the mixture evenly over the cutlets. Roll each one up like a jelly roll and tie with string or fasten with toothpicks.

5. Return the skillet to medium-high heat and heat the remaining 2 tablespoons olive oil. Add the chicken rolls and cook until nicely browned on all sides, about 5 minutes. Remove the rolls to a serving dish and cover to keep warm.

6. Reduce the heat to medium and melt the butter. Stir in the flour and cook, stirring, until the mixture forms a paste, about 1 minute. Slowly add the broth and wine, whisking until the sauce is smooth. Remove from the heat and stir in the lemon juice and salt. Pour the sauce over the chicken and serve immediately.

Note: The dish can be prepared a few hours in advance, covered with foil, and refrigerated. To serve, heat, covered, for about thirty minutes in a preheated 350°F oven.

3 1/2 pounds free-range chicken pieces

1 tablespoon fresh rosemary leaves

1 tablespoon fresh sage leaves

1 teaspoon fresh oregano leaves

1/2 cup olive oil

3 tablespoons fresh lemon juice

Fine sea salt to taste

1 teaspoon coarsely ground black pepper

1. Wash and dry the chicken.

2. Mince the rosemary, sage, and oregano together.

3. In a dish large enough to hold the chicken in a single layer, mix the olive oil and lemon juice. Add the herbs, salt, and pepper. Add the chicken pieces and turn to coat. Cover and let the chicken marinate in the refrigerator for at least 3 hours.

4. Prepare the grill. When it is hot, grill the chicken, basting 5 to 6 times with the marinade, until just cooked through.

Pollo Sulla Brace

Grilled Chicken

Grilled chicken sounds so ordinary, but the best chicken I have ever eaten was cooked simply on a wood-fired grill in Fiesole, Tuscany. Prepare this dish with free-range chickens — their taste and tenderness make all the difference. For best results, marinate the chicken for several hours before grilling.

Serves 4

Rollato di Tacchino

Rolled Stuffed Turkey Breast

❧

Thanksgiving is my favorite holiday. I am in the kitchen many days before making preparations so the holiday dinner runs as smoothly as possible. On our table, traditional turkey has given way to a stuffed turkey breast, prepared the way Italians like to have it in Perugia, the capital of Umbria. The beauty of this recipe is that it can be made two days ahead and reheated or served at room temperature.

❧

Serves 8

²/₃ pound whole chestnuts

¹/₂ cup olive oil

1¹/₂ cups fresh bread crumbs

¹/₄ pound prosciutto, diced

¹/₄ cup fresh rosemary leaves

3 tablespoons chopped flat-leaf parsley

2 large cloves garlic, minced

¹/₃ cup freshly grated Parmigiano-Reggiano cheese

One 4-pound turkey breast, butterflied

Fine sea salt and coarsely ground black pepper to taste

1¹/₂ cups dry white wine

1. Preheat the oven to 450°F. With a small knife, make an X in the top of each chestnut. Place on a rimmed baking sheet and roast for about 25 minutes, or until the skins split. Remove and let cool. Reduce the oven temperature to 400°F.

2. Crack the chestnuts open with a nutcracker and remove the nutmeats. Coarsely chop the nutmeats and put in a large bowl.

3. In a skillet, heat ¹/₄ cup of the olive oil. Add the bread crumbs and fry until lightly browned. Add to the chestnuts.

4. Add 1 more tablespoon of the oil to the skillet, and sauté the prosciutto until crispy. Add to the bread crumbs. Add the rosemary, parsley, garlic, cheese, and 1 tablespoon of the oil and mix well. (The stuffing can be covered and refrigerated for up to 2 days.)

5. Lay the turkey breast out flat on a cutting board. Place a large piece of wax paper over the turkey and pound it with a meat pounder to flatten it to an even thickness. Rub the inside of the turkey with salt and pepper. Spread the stuffing mixture evenly over the turkey breast to within 1 inch of the edges. Do not worry if all of the stuffing does not fit; save any excess for topping the breast after it is rolled.

6. Starting at a long side, roll the turkey up like a jelly roll and tie it with string in four or five places.

7. In a large skillet, heat the remaining 2 tablespoons olive oil over medium heat. Brown the turkey roll on all sides. Transfer the turkey roll to a rack in a roasting pan and add the pan juices from the skillet. Sprinkle with salt and pepper, and pat on any remaining stuffing over the top.

8. Add ½ cup of wine to the pan. Roast for 1 hour and 10 minutes, or until the internal temperature registers 175° to 180°F on an instant-read thermometer. Baste the meat occasionally with the pan juices, adding the remaining 1 cup wine to the pan halfway through the cooking time.

9. Let the meat rest for 15 minutes before slicing it. Then cut the roll into ½-inch slices, arrange them on a platter, and pour any pan juices over the meat. Serve hot, or let cool completely and serve at room temperature.

Verdure, Contorni, e Condimenti

Vegetables, Side Dishes, and Condiments

Asparagi e Prosciutto

Asparagus and Prosciutto

❦

Asparagus is the obvious choice
of vegetable for an Easter or
springtime buffet. Look for stalks
with tightly closed tips. In this
quickly made dish, asparagus
spears are combined with crisp
pieces of fried prosciutto
and sprinkled with grated
Parmesan cheese.

❦

Serves 8

2 pounds asparagus, stalks trimmed

1 teaspoon fine sea salt

2 tablespoons butter

1 tablespoon olive oil

¼ pound prosciutto, chopped

Freshly grated Parmigiano-Reggiano cheese for sprinkling

1. Make a slash in the bottom of each asparagus stalk.

2. Bring a large pot of water to a boil and add the salt. Add the asparagus and cook, uncovered, until a knife is easily inserted in the stalk. Carefully drain the asparagus.

3. In a large skillet, heat the butter and olive oil. Add the prosciutto and fry until it begins to crisp. Add the asparagus and heat through. Carefully transfer the asparagus and prosciutto to a serving platter. Sprinkle with the cheese and serve.

2 cups (8 ounces) dried split fava beans

2 medium all-purpose potatoes, peeled and quartered

1 teaspoon fine sea salt

¹/₂ cup extra-virgin olive oil

1 pound chicory, stemmed, washed, and drained

1. Put the beans and potatoes in a pot, add enough water to cover, and add the salt. Bring to a boil and boil uncovered for about 30 minutes, or until the beans are tender but not mushy. Drain, reserving ¹/₄ cup of the cooking water.

2. Transfer the beans and potatoes to a food processor. Add ¹/₄ cup plus 2 tablespoons of the oil and the reserved cooking water, and puree smooth. Remove the puree to a saucepan and keep warm over very low heat.

3. Bring a large pot of water to a boil. Add the chicory and cook until tender, about 20 minutes. Drain well, and spread the chicory on a serving platter.

4. Spoon the fava bean puree over the chicory. Drizzle the remaining 2 tablespoons olive oil over the top and serve immediately.

Variations: Serve the puree topped with strips of roasted red and yellow bell peppers.

Pack the fava puree into an oiled 4-cup mold, then unmold it onto the chicory for a party presentation. Or use individual molds and served on small portions of chicory.

Fave e Cicoria

Fava Bean Puree with Chicory

❦

I'm fond of this dried fava bean dish from Puglia, made with nothing more than cooked and pureed fava beans, flavored with the dense, fruity olive oil of the region and served with boiled chicory.

❦

Serves 8

Spinaci Fritti

Fried Spinach

At first this seems like a strange treatment for spinach, just fried in vegetable oil until crisp, and then topped with a sprinkling of grated Pecorino cheese, but it is truly delicious. Be sure to dry the spinach leaves very well before frying them. I serve this with a medley of other quickly fried vegetables, such as zucchini and yellow squash sticks, for a colorful buffet presentation.

Serves 6 to 8

Vegetable oil for deep-frying

Two 10-ounce bags fresh spinach, stemmed, washed, and thoroughly dried

$^1/_3$ to $^1/_2$ cup freshly grated Pecorino Romano cheese

1. In a deep-fryer or a deep heavy pot, heat the vegetable oil to 375°F. Carefully add the spinach a handful at a time, and fry until dark green and crisp. Drain on paper towels and keep warm in a low oven while you fry the remaining spinach.

2. Transfer the spinach to a serving dish and sprinkle with the cheese. Serve immediately.

Variation: Fry slices of tomatoes, zucchini, and squash, dredged in flour, in the oil after frying the spinach. Sprinkle with salt and serve immediately.

Two 10-ounce bags fresh spinach, stemmed, washed, and drained

2 tablespoons butter

$1/3$ heavy cream

$1/2$ teaspoon grated nutmeg

Fine sea salt to taste

$1/4$ cup freshly grated Parmigiano-Reggiano cheese

1. Put the spinach in a large pot with just the water clinging to its leaves, cover, and cook until wilted, 3 to 4 minutes. Drain well and squeeze dry.

2. In a skillet, melt the butter over medium heat. Add the spinach, cream, nutmeg, and salt and stir well. Sprinkle on the cheese. Turn off the heat, cover the pot, and let sit for a few minutes, until the cheese melts. Serve immediately.

Spinaci alla Panna

Spinach with Cream

❧

Fresh spinach in the northern Italian style — butter, a touch of cream, and a dash of nutmeg — becomes a sophisticated contorno *(vegetable side dish) when served with Chicken in Paper (page 160) or Grilled Chicken (page 165).*

❧

Serves 4

Fagiolini e Fontina

Green Beans and Fontina

❦

Whether this combination of Fontina cheese and green beans exists in Italy I do not know, but it is a favorite on our Thanksgiving table each year. This cheese works beautifully in so many cooked dishes because of its creamy texture, allowing it to melt easily. Be sure to buy Italian Fontina, which has a brown rind and a seal confirming that it was made in the Valle d'Aosta.

❦

Serves 8

2 pounds green beans, cleaned
1 tablespoon butter
½ pound Italian Fontina cheese, diced

1. Bring a large pot of salted water to a boil. Add the beans and boil, uncovered, until tender but still firm. Drain.

2. In a large skillet, melt the butter over medium-low heat. Add the beans and toss well. Add the cheese and stir to coat the beans with the cheese as it melts. Place the beans on a platter and serve.

*2 pounds small mushrooms, trimmed, cleaned, and
halved lengthwise*

¹/₂ cup dry white wine

¹/₂ cup water

Juice of ¹/₂ lemon

8 tablespoons (1 stick) butter

1 beef bouillon cube, crushed

Fine sea salt to taste

Freshly ground black pepper to taste

1 cup heavy cream

2 tablespoons unbleached all-purpose flour

1. In a skillet, combine the mushrooms, wine, water, and lemon juice, and bring to a boil. Cook for 5 minutes. Drain the mushrooms, reserving ¹/₄ cup of the liquid.

2. In the same pan, melt the butter. Add the mushrooms, bouillon cube, the reserved mushroom liquid, and a pinch of pepper and stir well. Cook over medium heat for 2 to 3 minutes.

3. In a small bowl, whisk the cream with the flour. Add to the mushrooms and cook, stirring, until the sauce is smooth. Add salt and pepper to taste and serve immediately.

Funghi e Crema

Mushrooms and Cream

Mushrooms in a smooth cream sauce make an elegant accompaniment to almost any poultry and meat dish. This delicate dish is best served at once.

Serves 6 to 8

Verdure Miste al Forno

Oven-Roasted Mixed Vegetables

❧

This colorful medley of oven-roasted vegetables requires little effort to put together. Serve it with Chicken in Paper (page 160). Put the vegetables in the oven fifteen minutes after the chicken.

❧

Serves 4

1 large white onion, thinly sliced

1 large bulb fennel, cut into 1/2-inch-thick pieces

1 medium zucchini, cut into 1/4-inch dice

3 large plum tomatoes, quartered

1 red bell pepper, cored, seeded, and cut into 1-inch-wide strips

1 yellow bell pepper, cored, seeded, and cut into 1-inch-wide strips

2 large cloves garlic, minced

1 tablespoon dried oregano

Fine sea salt and coarsely ground black pepper to taste

3 tablespoons olive oil

1. Preheat the oven to 375°F. Place all the vegetables and the garlic in a 2-quart baking dish. Season with the oregano and salt and pepper. Drizzle on the olive oil and toss with a wooden spoon.

2. Cover the dish with aluminum foil and bake for 45 minutes. Uncover the dish and bake for 15 minutes longer. Serve immediately.

Celebration Luncheon

Mushroom Ravioli
(page 58)

Chicken in Paper
(page 160)

Oven-Roasted Mixed
Vegetables

Mixed Green Salad
(page 192)

Three-Fruit Pudding
(page 210)

¹/₂ cup olive oil

1 large Spanish onion, diced

2 ribs celery, diced

¹/₂ cup packed fresh basil leaves, chopped

5 plum tomatoes, peeled, seeded, and pureed

1 ³/₄ pounds potatoes, peeled and diced

1 pound eggplant, peeled and diced

1 pound zucchini, diced

¹/₂ cup water

Fine sea salt and coarsely ground black pepper to taste

1 large yellow bell pepper, cored, seeded, and cut into thin strips

1. In a large deep skillet or a Dutch oven, heat the olive oil over medium heat. Add the onion and sauté until it is soft. Add the celery and basil and sauté until the celery is soft. Add the tomatoes, potatoes, eggplant, zucchini, water, and salt and pepper, and stir well. Cover and cook over low heat for 20 minutes.

2. Add the pepper strips and cook for about 10 minutes more, or until the vegetables are tender but not mushy. Serve immediately.

Ciambotta

MIXED STEWED VEGETABLES

Ciambotta, similar to French ratatouille, is a hearty vegetable stew of eggplant, zucchini, tomatoes, and, unlike ratatouille, potatoes. The slow cooking blends the flavors of the vegetables and prevents them from losing their shape.

Serves 12 to 16

Cavolfiore Fritto

Fried Cauliflower

❦

A Christmas Eve meal without cauliflower was unthinkable in my family. We had it marinated in salads, mixed with seafood and spaghetti, and batter-fried, which still gets my vote for the best way to eat it. Adding anisette to the batter gives it its unusual taste.

❦

Serves 8

$^1/_2$ cup unbleached all-purpose flour

$^1/_4$ teaspoon salt, plus more to taste

2 large eggs

3 tablespoons anisette liqueur

1 medium head cauliflower (about 2 pounds), rinsed and cut into 1-inch florets

Vegetable oil for deep-frying

1. In a bowl, whisk together the flour, salt, eggs, and liqueur. Cover and set the batter aside for 1 hour.

2. In a large pot of boiling salted water, cook the cauliflower for about 4 minutes, or until tender but still somewhat firm. Drain well and set aside to cool.

3. In a deep fryer or deep heavy pot, heat the oil to 375°F. In batches, dip the florets into the batter, and fry until golden brown. Drain on brown paper. Sprinkle with salt and serve immediately.

¹/₄ cup plus 2 tablespoons extra-virgin olive oil

1 large onion, thinly sliced

1 medium head cauliflower (about 2 pounds), washed and cut into small florets

4 large eggs

¹/₄ cup freshly grated Parmigiano-Reggiano cheese

¹/₄ cup diced Dried Tomatoes (page 310)

¹/₄ cup minced flat-leaf parsley

Fine sea salt and freshly ground black pepper to taste

1. In a large skillet, heat ¼ cup of the olive oil. Add the onions and cook until they begin to soften. Add the cauliflower and cook, stirring, for 2 to 3 minutes. Cover the pan, lower the heat to medium-low, and cook until tender, about 8 minutes. Remove the onions and cauliflower to a dish, and set the pan aside.

2. In a large bowl, beat the eggs, cheese, tomatoes, and parsley together. Season with salt and pepper. Add the cauliflower mixture and blend well.

3. Set the skillet over medium heat, and add 1 tablespoon of the oil. Add the frittata mixture, distributing the cauliflower evenly in the pan. Cook until the frittata holds together when the skillet is shaken.

4. Place a large dish or a pizza pan over the top of the skillet and invert the frittata onto the dish. Add the remaining 1 tablespoon olive oil to the skillet, slip the frittata back into the pan, and cook until lightly browned on the bottom. Turn the frittata out onto a serving plate, cut into wedges, and serve immediately.

Frittata di Cavolfiori

Cauliflower Frittata

❧

Cauliflower Frittata is one of my reserve recipes for busy holiday cooking days. The florets are cooked in olive oil, then combined with onions, eggs, and cheese. Bits of dried tomatoes and parsley give it a Christmas look. Add a salad and bread and dinner is ready.

❧

Serves 6 to 8

Porri al Forno con Senape

Leeks with Mustard Sauce

❦

Leeks grow beautiful and tall in my garden. One of my favorite ways to serve them is baked and then dressed in a citrus-mustard sauce.

❦

Serves 6 to 8

Spring Dinner

....

Oven-Fried Veal Chops
(page 157)

Leeks with Mustard Sauce

Fried Asparagus
(page 6)

Zuppa Inglese
(page 296)

....

SAUCE

1½ teaspoons Spicy Mustard (page 305)

1 teaspoon sugar

Fine sea salt to taste

⅓ cup fresh orange juice

¼ cup fresh lemon juice

¼ cup extra-virgin olive oil

2 teaspoons minced fresh marjoram

1¼ pounds leeks (about 4 medium), white parts only, halved lengthwise and then crosswise, well rinsed, and patted dry

Freshly ground black pepper to taste

½ cup water

⅓ cup dry white wine

1. In a medium bowl, mix together the mustard, sugar, and salt. Whisk in the orange and lemon juices. Whisk in the olive oil, drop by drop, until emulsified and smooth. Whisk in the marjoram. Cover the sauce and let sit for 1 hour to allow the flavors to mingle.

2. Preheat the oven to 350°F. Butter a baking dish. Place the leeks in a single layer in the baking dish. Season with salt and pepper. Mix the water and wine together and pour over the leeks.

3. Cover the dish with foil, and bake for 35 minutes, or until the leeks are tender.

4. Pour off any excess liquid from the baking dish. Stir the sauce and pour it over the leeks. Serve immediately.

2 medium bulbs fennel (about 2 pounds)

2 tablespoons butter

3 tablespoons unbleached all-purpose flour

1 3/4 cups milk

1/4 teaspoon grated nutmeg

Fine sea salt to taste

1/2 cup toasted bread crumbs

1/4 cup freshly grated Parmigiano-Reggiano cheese

1. Remove the feathery leaves and tough stalks from the fennel. Wash the bulbs and cut each into quarters.

2. Fill a large pot with water, add 1 tablespoon salt, and bring to a boil. Add the fennel, cover, and cook for about 20 minutes, or until a knife can easily be inserted into the fennel. Drain in a colander.

3. Preheat the oven to 350°F. In a medium saucepan, melt the butter over medium heat. Add the flour, whisking to a smooth paste, and cook for about 1 minute. Slowly whisk in the milk and cook, whisking until the sauce and comes to a simmer and thickens. Remove from the heat and stir in the nutmeg and salt.

4. Spread a thin layer of the sauce in a 12 by 8-inch casserole dish. Add the fennel, cut sides down, in a single layer. Pour the remaining sauce over the fennel. Sprinkle the bread crumbs and cheese evenly over the top. Bake, uncovered, for 25 to 30 minutes, or until the sauce and cheese are lightly browned. Serve immediately.

Finocchio al Forno

Baked Fennel

Fennel, the licorice-tasting celery-like vegetable, has an important place in Italian cooking. Long thought to have medicinal properties, it is still eaten raw as a digestivo *after meals, a practice my family continues today. In this recipe, it is blanketed in a simple cream sauce, topped with bread crumbs, and baked in the oven. Serve it as an accompaniment to Rolled Stuffed Veal Breast (page 156). You can assemble the dish ahead and bake it the next day.*

Serves 8

Croquette di Patate

Potato Croquettes

❧

These nutmeg-scented oven-baked potato croquettes can be prepared up to two hours ahead and refrigerated until ready to bake. Do not mash the potatoes in a food processor; they will turn to glue.

❧

Serves 6

2 pounds all-purpose potatoes, peeled and quartered

4 tablespoons butter, melted

3 large egg yolks

³/₄ teaspoon grated nutmeg

¹/₂ teaspoon fine sea salt

About ¹/₂ cup unbleached all-purpose flour

1 large egg, beaten

1. In a large pot of boiling salted water, cook the potatoes until tender. Drain well, return them to the pot, and let them dry in the heat of the pot, shaking occasionally.

2. Place the potatoes in a bowl and mash until smooth. Add 2 tablespoons of the butter, the egg yolks, nutmeg, and salt, and blend well.

3. Lightly butter a cookie sheet. Spread the potato mixture evenly on the sheet. Brush the top of the potatoes with the remaining butter, cover with wax paper, and refrigerate until cold, about 25 minutes.

4. Preheat the oven to 350°F. Butter a 12 by 9-inch baking dish. Sprinkle a work surface with ¼ cup flour. Dip your hands in the flour, then pull off a piece of the cold potatoes about the size of an egg, and form it into a cylinder. Roll the cylinder lightly in the flour, and place in the baking dish. Repeat with the remaining potato mixture, adding flour to the work surface as necessary.

5. Brush the tops of the croquettes with the beaten egg. Bake for 25 to 30 minutes, or until nicely browned. Serve immediately.

5 medium all-purpose potatoes (about 1 1/2 pounds)

2 large eggs

1/4 cup freshly grated Pecorino Romano cheese

2 tablespoons unbleached all-purpose flour

1 teaspoon fine sea salt

1/4 teaspoon freshly ground black pepper

Vegetable oil for deep-frying

1. Peel the potatoes and grate fine. (You should have 3 cups.) Place in a bowl, add the remaining ingredients (except the oil), and mix well.

2. In a deep-fryer or deep heavy pot, heat the oil to 375°F. Drop tablespoonfuls of the potato batter into the oil, and fry the fritters until nicely browned. Remove them with a slotted spoon and drain on brown paper. Serve hot.

Frittelle di Patate

Potato Fritters

✎

These golden-brown, crusty potato fritters have a wonderful Old World look about them, and making them always becomes a family affair. As soon I make them, they are gone! Finely grating the potatoes allows the fritters to cook evenly and quickly.

✎

Serves 8

Patate con Pomodori Secchi e Timo

Potatoes with Dried Tomatoes and Thyme

❧

These twice-cooked potatoes, flavored with dried tomatoes and thyme, are a good accompaniment to Roast Pork Tenderloin with Juniper Berries (page 147), and you can cook the potatoes along with the roast for a no-fuss company meal.

❧

Serves 6

6 medium all-purpose potatoes, peeled

2 tablespoons butter, softened, plus 4 tablespoons butter, melted

3 tablespoons fresh thyme leaves

Fine sea salt to taste

¹/₂ cup diced Dried Tomatoes in Olive Oil (page 312)

1. Put the potatoes in a large pot, cover with salted water, and bring to a boil. Cook until tender enough for a fork to pierce them easily. Drain and let cool.

2. Preheat the oven to 350°F. Brush a baking dish with the softened butter, and sprinkle the thyme over the butter.

3. Wrap the potatoes, one at a time, in a clean dish towel and, using a meat pounder, flatten into disks about ¹/₂ inch thick. Place them carefully in the baking dish, sprinkle with salt, and drizzle the melted butter over the top.

4. Bake the potatoes, uncovered, for about 35 minutes, or until nicely browned. Sprinkle the tomatoes over the potatoes and bake for 5 minutes longer. Serve immediately.

1½ pounds all-purpose potatoes, peeled and cut into 1-inch pieces

1½ pounds Swiss chard, tough stems removed

2 ounces prosciutto or ham, diced (¾ cup)

¾ cup freshly grated Pecorino Romano cheese

3 tablespoons olive oil

1 large egg white

2½ tablespoons minced flat-leaf parsley

⅓ cup toasted pine nuts

Fine sea salt to taste

1. Put the potatoes in a large pot, cover with cold salted water, and bring to a boil. Cook until tender. Drain well.

2. Meanwhile, bring a large pot of salted water to a boil. Wash the Swiss chard well, being careful not to tear the leaves. Add the chard to the boiling water, cover, and boil for about 10 minutes, or until tender. Carefully drain in a colander and let cool.

3. Place the potatoes in a bowl, add the prosciutto, cheese, olive oil, and egg white, and beat until smooth. Mix in the parsley, pine nuts, and salt.

4. Preheat the oven to 350°F. Lightly grease eight 4-ounce ramekins or 3 by 1½-inch aluminum foil baking cups with olive oil. Line each cup with Swiss chard, making sure that no gaps remain and that the chard overhangs the edges by about ½ inch. Divide the potato mixture evenly among the lined molds, and smooth the tops. Fold the overhanging edges of the Swiss chard over to enclose the filling.

5. Place the molds on a baking sheet and cover each one tightly with a piece of aluminum foil. Bake for about 15 minutes or until heated through. Carefully remove the aluminum foil and invert the molds onto a serving platter or individual dishes. Serve immediately.

Timballi di Patate e Coste

Potato and Swiss Chard Molds

❧

These charming little round molds of Swiss chard are filled with a potato, prosciutto, and pine nut filling. They can be assembled two hours before baking.

❧

Serves 8

Musakà di Maria

Maria's Musakà

❧

The recipe for this layered potato and eggplant dish with two sauces was sent to me by my Italian friend Maria. It goes together very quickly if the sauces are made a day before you assemble the musakà. Cut into small squares, it is a good choice for a buffet.

❧

Serves 6 to 8

WHITE SAUCE

5 tablespoons butter

¼ cup plus 2 tablespoons unbleached all-purpose flour

4 cups milk

1 teaspoon fine sea salt

1 pound russet or red-skinned potatoes (about 4 medium), unpeeled

1 eggplant (about 1¼ pounds), sliced into ¼-inch-thick rounds

Fine sea salt to taste

2 cups Tomato-Basil Sauce (page 32)

⅔ cup freshly grated Pecorino Romano cheese

1. In a large saucepan, melt the butter. Stir in the flour and cook over medium heat, stirring until well blended. Lower the heat and slowly whisk in the milk until smooth. Add the salt, raise the heat to medium-high, and cook, stirring, until the sauce has thickened. Cover and set aside. (The sauce can be made a day ahead, cooled, covered, and refrigerated. Thin it with a little milk if it has thickened too much, and reheat over low heat before assembling the musakà.)

2. Put the potatoes in a large pot, cover with cold salted water, and bring to a boil. Cook until tender. Drain and let cool, then peel and thinly slice. Set aside.

3. Layer the eggplant in a large pot, sprinkling each layer with salt. Cover and cook the eggplant over low heat for about 5 minutes, or just until it starts to get soft. Remove the lid and cook for another 10 minutes. Drain in a colander and set aside.

4. Preheat the oven to 350°F. Spread a thin layer of the white sauce in an 11 by 8-inch casserole dish or baking pan. Add a layer of eggplant and a thin layer of tomato sauce. Sprinkle on a little of the grated cheese and add a layer of potatoes. Cover with another layer of white sauce and continue layering, ending with a layer of potatoes covered with white sauce and sprinkled with cheese.

5. Bake for 20 to 30 minutes or until the sauce is bubbly and the top has browned. Let sit for 10 minutes before scooping out or cutting into squares.

1 firm eggplant (about 1¼ pounds), about 8 inches long

About 3 tablespoons extra-virgin olive oil

Fine sea salt to taste

¼ cup minced fresh mint or basil

⅔ cup chopped Dried Tomatoes in Olive Oil (page 312)

½ cup freshly grated Parmigiano-Reggiano cheese

Coarsely ground black pepper to taste

1. Preheat a charcoal or gas grill or the broiler. Trim off the ends of the eggplant, and stand the eggplant on end. With a sharp knife, cut lengthwise into ¼-inch-thick slices. You should have 10 to 12 slices.

2. Grill or broil the eggplant slices until golden brown on both sides, about 4 minutes on each side. Remove to a dish and let cool.

3. Preheat the oven to 350°F. Lightly grease a baking dish. Lay the eggplant slices on a work surface and brush each slice with ½ teaspoon olive oil. Sprinkle with a little sea salt. Sprinkle the mint or basil, tomatoes, and cheese evenly over the slices. Starting from a narrow end, roll each slice up like a jelly roll, and place the bundles seam side down in the baking dish. Drizzle a little olive oil over the top, and sprinkle with pepper.

4. Cover the dish with foil. Bake for about 20 minutes, or until the rolls are heated through. Serve immediately.

Involtini di Melanzane

Stuffed Eggplant Bundles

☙

Involtini *are neat bundles of stuffed meat, fish, or vegetables. The fillings can be as varied as the cook's imagination. Eggplant works especially well as involtini, and grilling the eggplant first imparts a wonderful roasted flavor. If dried tomatoes in olive oil are not at hand, substitute thinly sliced fresh tomatoes.*

☙

Serves 4 to 6

Rustic Dinner

Grilled Chicken
(page 165)

Bread in a Basket
(page 100)

Stuffed Eggplant Bundles

Peppina's Cake
(page 290)

Salsa di Mortella di Palude con Rosmarino

Rosemary-Cranberry Sauce

❧

Everyone loves this fresh cranberry sauce infused with the flavor of fresh rosemary. Serve it with the Rolled Stuffed Turkey Breast on page 166 as part of your Thanksgiving dinner. Do not attempt to make this with dried rosemary; it just will not work.

❧

Makes 5 cups

6 cups cranberries

$^1/_2$ cup sugar

$^1/_4$ cup water

$^1/_4$ teaspoon fine sea salt

2 large rosemary sprigs, plus additional sprigs for garnish

1. Combine all the ingredients in a large saucepan, and cook over medium heat until the cranberries burst and the mixture thickens, about 10 to 12 minutes. Let cool.

2. Remove the rosemary sprigs from the sauce and discard. Transfer to an attractive bowl and garnish with fresh rosemary sprigs.

3 to 4 pounds chestnuts

1. Preheat the oven to 450°F. With a small sharp knife, cut an X in the top of each chestnut to prevent it from exploding in the oven. (Once in a while, this fails to work.)

2. Spread the chestnuts on a baking sheet and roast for 15 to 20 minutes, or until the shells are puffed and split. Transfer to a bowl and let cool.

3. Crack the shells with your hands or use nutcrackers and picks to remove the nutmeats.

Castagne al Forno

Roasted Chestnuts

❦

Roasted chestnuts are a final statement to the Thanksgiving dinner. There are many theories as to the proper way to prepare chestnuts for roasting. Some insist on parboiling them first; others will only roast them in a wooden-handled chestnut roaster in the fireplace, but most take the less dramatic approach and roast them in the oven.

❦

Serves 8 to 12

Insalate

Salads

Insalata Mista

Mixed Green Salad

✦

Insalata mista, one of the basic salads eaten daily in Italy, often contains one or more varieties of bitter lettuce and vegetables like tomatoes and cucumbers. Simple as this sounds, there is an art to making this salad. The dressing must contain nothing but the best extra-virgin olive oil, a good, aged red wine vinegar, and fine sea salt. The leaves must be cleaned and dried thoroughly for the dressing to adhere.

✦

Serves 6

1 small head romaine lettuce, washed, dried, and torn into pieces

1 small head curly chicory, washed, dried, and torn into pieces

3 ripe plum tomatoes, quartered

1 cucumber, peeled and sliced

$1/4$ cup extra-virgin olive oil

$2 1/2$ tablespoons red wine vinegar

Fine sea salt to taste

Place the lettuce leaves, tomatoes, and cucumber in a salad bowl. Drizzle on the oil and toss gently. Add the vinegar and salt and toss again. Serve immediately.

2 cups packed torn romaine lettuce, washed and dried

1 cup torn arugula, washed and dried

1 cup packed torn escarole, washed and dried

1 small head radicchio, washed, dried, and torn into pieces

1/4 cup extra-virgin olive oil

2 tablespoons red wine vinegar

Fine sea salt to taste

Place all the lettuces in a salad bowl. In a small bowl, mix the oil and vinegar together with the salt and pour the dressing over the salad. Toss well and serve immediately.

1 head curly chicory or romaine lettuce, washed, dried, and torn into pieces

1 large orange, peeled, sectioned, and cut into small pieces

1 grapefruit, peeled, sectioned, and cut into small pieces

1 pomegranate, seeds only

1/4 cup extra-virgin olive oil

Juice of 1 medium orange

Fine sea salt to taste

1. Place the lettuce leaves in a bowl, and add the orange and grapefruit sections and pomegranate seeds.

2. In a small bowl, whisk together the olive oil and orange juice. Pour over the salad, sprinkle with salt, and toss gently. Serve immediately.

Insalata Verde

Green Salad

Fresh and crunchy bitter greens without the addition of raw vegetables characterize a classic insalata verde. Dress with the best extra-virgin olive oil and red wine vinegar you have.

Serves 6

Insalata Siciliana

Sicilian Salad

This eye- as well as palate-pleasing citrus and lettuce salad takes its inspiration from Sicily. Crisp lettuce leaves are combined with tart pomegranate seeds and orange and grapefruit sections, all tossed in a dressing of fruity extra-virgin olive oil and orange juice.

Serves 4 to 6

Insalata alla Frutta

Fruit Salad with Greens

❧

A fruit salad with greens is a welcome change of pace from a traditional greens-only salad. For this winter salad, pomegranate seeds, grapes, and blackberries, which are becoming more readily available year-round, are tossed with olive oil and homemade raspberry vinegar, and sprinkled with sunflower seeds.

❧

Serves 6

$1/4$ cup extra-virgin olive oil

Fine sea salt to taste

2 tablespoons Raspberry-Mint Vinegar (page 304)

1 teaspoon sugar

2 tablespoons finely chopped flat-leaf parsley

1 medium head romaine or red leaf lettuce, washed, dried, and torn into pieces

1 pomegranate, seeds only

1 cup seedless white grapes, cut in half

1 cup blackberries, optional

$1/4$ cup sunflower seeds

1. In a small bowl, whisk the olive oil and salt together. Gradually whisk in the vinegar and sugar. Stir in the parsley. Cover the bowl and let sit at room temperature for 1 hour.

2. Place the lettuce leaves in a salad bowl. Add the pomegranate seeds, grapes, and blackberries. Whisk the dressing and pour over the salad. Toss gently. Sprinkle the sunflower seeds over the top and serve immediately.

2 to 3 heads escarole, washed, dried, and torn into pieces

4 1/2 tablespoons extra-virgin olive oil

2 1/2 tablespoons balsamic vinegar

Fine sea salt to taste

1/3 cup thinly shaved Parmigiano-Reggiano cheese

Place the leaves in a salad bowl. Drizzle the olive oil over the leaves and toss gently. Sprinkle on the vinegar and salt and toss again. Scatter the cheese over the top, and toss again. Serve immediately.

Insalata di Scarola

Escarole Salad

Escarole, a slightly bitter-tasting chicory, is added to soups, stuffed and braised, or cooked and seasoned with olive oil. Its sturdy leaves do not wilt as quickly as other lettuces, making it a perfect salad green as well. In this salad, the escarole is complemented by the sweet-sour taste of balsamic vinegar and the not-too-piquant flavor of Parmigiano-Reggiano cheese.

Serves 10

Insalata d' Indivia, Radicchio, e Scarola con Pecorino

Endive, Radicchio, and Escarole Salad with Pecorino Cheese

❧

The flavor of this colorful salad, a combination of three kinds of chicory (cicoria), is enhanced by the addition of Pecorino (sheep's milk) cheese embedded with black peppercorns.

❧

Serves 6 to 8

2 heads Belgian endive, washed, dried, and cut into julienne strips

1 small head radicchio, washed, dried, and torn into pieces

¼ pound escarole, washed, dried, and torn into pieces

¼ cup extra-virgin olive oil

3 tablespoons white cider vinegar

2 ounces Pecorino cheese with black peppercorns, diced

Fine sea salt to taste

Place all the greens in a salad bowl. Add the olive oil and toss well. Add the vinegar and toss again. Sprinkle the cheese and salt over the top and toss again. Serve immediately.

1 clove garlic, mashed

4 anchovies in oil, drained and chopped

3 tablespoons red wine vinegar

1 tablespoon fresh lemon juice

Fine sea salt and freshly ground black pepper to taste

¹/₄ cup plus 2 tablespoons extra-virgin olive oil

1 pound arugula (about 1 bunch), stemmed, washed, and dried

2 small heads radicchio, washed, dried, and torn into pieces

1. In a bowl, mash the garlic and anchovies with a fork until a paste is formed. Whisk in the vinegar, lemon juice, and salt and pepper. Whisk in the oil until emulsified and smooth.

2. Put the arugula and radicchio in a salad bowl. Pour the dressing over the salad and toss well. Serve immediately.

Insalata di Arugola e Radicchio

Arugula and Radicchio Salad

❧

Leaves of peppery arugula and mildly bitter radicchio create a lively tasting salad when tossed with this anchovy dressing.

❧

Serves 6 to 8

Insalata d' Acetosella ed Indivia

Sorrel and Endive Salad

❦

Lemon-flavored sorrel is an herb
that is used sparingly in Italian
cooking. In this recipe, its dark
green leaves are combined with
Belgian endive to provide a
pleasing color contrast as well as
a refreshing taste enhanced by a
lemon and mustard dressing.
Sorrel, from the spinach family,
is available in the spring.

❦

Serves 8 to 10

3 tablespoons fresh lemon juice

1 teaspoon grainy mustard

1 teaspoon fine sea salt

$^1/_3$ cup extra-virgin olive oil

4 heads Belgian endive, leaves separated, washed, and dried

3 ribs celery, thinly sliced

2 cups shredded sorrel leaves

1. In a small bowl, whisk the lemon juice, mustard, and salt together. Gradually whisk in the olive oil, drop by drop, until emulsified and smooth.

2. In a salad bowl, toss the endive, celery, and sorrel together. Pour the dressing over the salad and toss. Serve immediately.

SALAD

²/₃ cup extra-virgin olive oil

¹/₄ cup red wine vinegar

1 tablespoon sugar

3 cloves garlic, minced

9 large fresh basil leaves, minced

¹/₂ cup tightly packed flat-leaf parsley, minced

Fine sea salt to taste

8 to 9 large meaty plum tomatoes, diced

8 Frisedde (page 104)

1. In a glass bowl, combine all the salad ingredients and gently toss. Cover the bowl and let marinate at room temperature for several hours.

2. Spoon the salad over the frisedde and let stand for about 20 minutes, cut before serving.

Insalata di Pomodori con Frisedde

Tomato Salad Pugliese Style

From Puglia comes this delightful summer salad that sits atop frisedde, a hard ring-shaped roll that is quickly softened in water. This salad can also be served as an antipasto.

Serves 8

Vegetarian Summer Buffet

Tomato Salad Pugliese Style

Fresh Vegetable Lasagne
(page 63)

Vegetable Pizza (page 74)

Rice and Spinach Mold
(page 68)

Watermelon in Sparkling Wine
(page 207)

Insalata di Fagiolini e Finocchio

Green Bean and Fennel Salad

❧

This salad of slender young green beans and crunchy fennel strips gets its lively flavor from fresh mint. How do you tell when beans are fresh? They should make a snapping sound when broken in half.

❧

Serves 4 to 8

2 cloves garlic, minced

$^{1}/_{3}$ cup extra-virgin olive oil

3 tablespoons red wine vinegar

1 teaspoon sugar

Fine sea salt to taste

3 tablespoons finely chopped fresh mint

1 pound young green beans, trimmed

1 small bulb fennel, cut into thin strips

1. In a shallow serving dish, mix together the garlic, olive oil, vinegar, sugar, and salt. Stir in the mint. Set aside.

2. Bring a medium saucepan of salted water to a boil. Add the beans and cook until al dente. Drain well.

3. Add the beans to the dressing along with the fennel and toss well. Cover and let marinate for several hours at room temperature before serving.

1 large yellow bell pepper

2 pounds carrots, peeled and cut into 3-inch-long matchstick pieces

¼ cup minced shallots

¼ cup minced fresh mint

¼ cup plus 2 tablespoons extra-virgin olive oil

3 tablespoons Raspberry-Mint Vinegar (page 304) or other fruit-flavored vinegar

1½ teaspoons sugar

1 head red leaf or curly green lettuce, leaves separated, washed, and dried

1. Preheat the broiler. Place the pepper on the broiler pan and broil it, turning, until the skin is blackened all over. Place the pepper in a paper bag and let cool.

2. Peel, core, and seed the pepper and cut into thin strips. Place the pepper strips in a glass dish large enough to hold the carrots.

3. Bring a medium saucepan of water to a boil. Add the carrots and cook until just tender. Drain well and add to the peppers.

4. Add the shallots and mint, then add the olive oil, vinegar, and sugar and toss gently to coat the carrots and peppers with the dressing. Cover the dish and let marinate for several hours at room temperature, or overnight in the refrigerator (bring to room temperature before serving).

5. To serve, line a platter with the lettuce leaves. Arrange the carrot salad on top.

Insalata di Carote

Carrot Salad

❧

Crisp-tender carrots marinated with shallots, roasted sweet yellow peppers, and raspberry-mint vinegar make an eye-appealing salad for a picnic or spring luncheon.

❧

Serves 8 to 10

Insalata di Fagiolini, Ceci, e Pomodori

Green Bean, Chickpea, and Tomato Salad

❧

There is a nice balance of colors and flavors in this salad of green beans, chickpeas, and tomatoes.

Save time by using canned chickpeas. The longer this salad marinates, the tastier it will be.

As a summer lunch, serve the salad with Libretti di Olive (page 76), small pizzas that are folded in half and eaten out of hand.

❧

Serves 6 to 8

2 pounds green beans, trimmed

½ cup extra-virgin olive oil

3 tablespoons balsamic vinegar

2 cloves garlic, minced

3 tablespoons minced fresh basil

4 medium ripe plum tomatoes, sliced

1½ cups canned chickpeas, drained and well rinsed

Fine sea salt to taste

2 small heads radicchio, leaves separated, washed, and dried

1. Cook the beans, uncovered, in a large pot of boiling salted water until tender, about 8 minutes. Drain well.

2. In a shallow glass dish, combine the oil, vinegar, garlic, and basil. Add the beans and toss to coat. Add the tomatoes, chickpeas, and salt and toss again. Cover the dish and let marinate at room temperature for several hours, stirring the salad occasionally.

3. To serve, line individual salad dishes with the radicchio leaves. Spoon the salad onto the lettuce.

Frutte e Dolci

Fruit and Desserts

Pere con Menta

Pears with Mint

❧

Pears with Pecorino cheese are often served after an Italian meal, but pears poached in a light sugar syrup with vanilla bean and marinated with mint leaves, is an even more elegant end to any meal. Anjou, Bartlett, or Bosc pears all work well; make sure that the pears are not overripe, or they will not hold their shape during poaching. Prepare these early in the day to allow the fruit to marinate.

❧

Serves 4

4 ripe but firm pears

$\frac{1}{4}$ cup sugar

$1\frac{1}{2}$ cups water

1 teaspoon fresh lemon juice

One 3-inch piece vanilla bean

$\frac{1}{8}$ teaspoon salt

10 to 12 fresh mint leaves, cut into thin strips, plus 4 mint sprigs for garnish

Sweetened whipped cream, optional

1. Peel the pears, cut them lengthwise in half, and remove the seeds and cores.

2. Place the pears cut sides down in a skillet large enough to hold them in a single layer. Sprinkle the sugar over them and add the water, lemon juice, vanilla bean, and salt. Cover the skillet and bring to a simmer. Simmer for about 20 minutes, or until a knife can easily be inserted into the pears.

3. With a slotted spoon, remove the pears to a bowl large enough to hold them in a single layer. Pour the poaching liquid over them, and sprinkle with the mint. Let cool. Cover the dish with plastic wrap and refrigerate until chilled.

4. To serve, place 2 pear halves in each goblet or custard dish and pour some of the poaching liquid over them. Garnish with sweetened whipped cream if desired and mint sprigs.

4 medium bananas

Juice of 2 lemons

¹/₂ cup turbinado (coarse brown) sugar

4 to 6 blood oranges, peeled, pith removed, and sliced into
¹/₄-inch-thick rounds

²/₃ cup Amaretto liqueur

1. Peel the bananas, slice lengthwise, and cut into 3-inch strips about ¼ inch thick. Place in a large glass dish in a single layer. Pour the lemon juice over the bananas and set aside.

2. Spread the sugar on a plate. Dip each orange slice into the sugar, coating both sides. Set aside.

3. Pour the Amaretto into a large serving dish. Drain the banana slices and arrange them, slightly overlapping, around the outside edge of the serving dish. Arrange a ring of orange slices, slightly overlapping, inside the ring of bananas, and fill in the center with the remaining oranges. Cover and let marinate for several hours at room temperature before serving.

4. To serve, place the oranges and bananas on dessert plates and spoon over the juices.

Arance e Banane in Amaretto

Oranges and Bananas in Amaretto

❧

Simple but elegant is the best description for this soothing banana and orange dessert laced with Amaretto. I first had it at Trattoria Cicio in Bagheria, Sicily. Red-fleshed blood oranges are not only beautiful but also intensely flavorful. If not available, use Mineola, mandarin or navel oranges. This is a great do-ahead dessert for a buffet.

❧

Serves 8 to 10

Melone e Banane con Ricotta

Cantaloupe and Bananas with Ricotta

❧

In Sicily, fresh sheep's milk ricotta cheese is often served with a citrus marmalade for dessert. I have taken my inspiration from that classic dessert. The recipe can easily be doubled for a buffet.

❧

Serves 8

1 ripe cantaloupe, cut in half and seeded

2 cups skim-milk ricotta cheese, preferably fresh, well drained

²/₃ cup sugar

³/₄ teaspoon ground cinnamon

2 small bananas, sliced

¹/₄ cup fresh orange juice

Fresh mint sprigs for garnish

1. Cut a small slice off the bottom of each cantaloupe half to prevent from tilting. Place them on a plate.

2. In a small bowl, mix the ricotta cheese, sugar, and cinnamon. Gently fold in the bananas and orange juice. With a spoon, pack the mixture into the cavities of the cantaloupe halves, mounding it slightly. Cover loosely with plastic wrap and refrigerate for several hours.

3. To serve, cut the cantaloupe into wedges with a sharp knife, place the wedges on a serving tray, and decorate each one with a mint sprig.

One 4-pound watermelon

¹/₂ cup sugar

Juice of 1 lemon

30 seedless white grapes

¹/₃ cup rum

1 bottle Asti Spumante, well chilled

1 lemon, thinly sliced, for garnish

Fresh mint leaves for garnish

1. Set the watermelon on a work surface and cut off the top to create a lid. Set aside. Scoop out the flesh, and cut it into cubes. Place the cubes in the watermelon, add the sugar, lemon juice, grapes, rum, and Asti Spumante, and mix gently. Replace the watermelon lid and freeze the watermelon for 1 hour. (Alternatively, chill the watermelon in the refrigerator.)

2. To serve, scoop the watermelon filling into goblets, and garnish with lemon slices and mint leaves.

Anguiria allo Spumante

Watermelon in Sparkling Wine

❧

Watermelon, a beloved summer fruit in Italy, is often served in sparkling wine, for a refreshing dessert that is perfect for a hot summer day.

❧

Serves 10 to 12

Gelatina d'Arancia

Orange-Marsala Gelatin

❧

Gelatina *is a shimmering, smooth dessert made from the juice of citrus fruits and unflavored gelatin that no packaged sweetened gelatin could ever match. The best gelatina is made in Sicily from intensely sweet fruits such as lemons, oranges, tangerines, and grapefruits. Mineola or mandarin oranges are suggested to approximate the flavor of Sicilian orange gelatina.*

❧

Serves 8

3 packages unflavored gelatin

1½ cups water

¾ cup sugar

2 cups fresh orange juice (from 7 to 8 medium Mineola or mandarin oranges, 8 "half-shells" reserved)

¼ cup sweet Marsala wine

Fresh mint leaves for garnish

1. In a small saucepan, soften the gelatin in ½ cup of the water. Heat over low heat, stirring until the gelatin dissolves completely. Set aside.

2. In a small saucepan, combine the remaining 1 cup water and the sugar and bring to a boil, stirring constantly until the sugar is dissolved. Remove from the heat and stir in the gelatin with a wooden spoon. Stir in the orange juice and wine. Pour the mixture into a rectangular or square dish and chill for at least several hours, or until the gelatin is set.

3. To serve, scoop the gelatin from the dish with a spoon, or cut it into cubes with a knife, and fill the reserved orange shell halves. Garnish each one with a mint leaf.

Variation: The gelatina can also be poured into a decorative mold and then unmolded on a serving platter.

Do-Ahead Informal Christmas Eve Supper

Beans, Mussels, and Pasta Soup (page 24)

Pane Rustico (page 96)

Orange-Marsala Gelatin

Apple and Pear Cake (page 268)

5 large pomegranates

1 tablespoon fresh lemon juice

3 packages unflavored gelatin

1 1/2 cups water

3/4 cup sugar

1. Cut the pomegranates in half. Working over a bowl, scoop out the seeds with a spoon. Remove 1 cup of seeds and set aside.

2. Place a fine-mesh strainer over another bowl, and pour the remaining seeds and juice into the strainer. With the back of a wooden spoon, press on the seeds to extract as much juice as possible. (A weighted meat pounder or an electric juicer can also be used to extract the juice.) If using a juicer, scoop out 1 cup seeds and reserve, then juice the remaining fruit as you would an orange. You should have 2 cups of juice. Add the lemon juice, and set aside.

3. In a large bowl, soften the gelatin in 1/2 cup of the water.

4. In a medium saucepan, bring the remaining 1 cup water to a boil. Add the sugar and stir constantly until the mixture returns to a boil and the sugar dissolves. Slowly add the sugar mixture to the gelatin, stirring until completely blended. Stir in the pomegranate juice, then stir in the reserved pomegranate seeds.

5. Pour the mixture into a square or rectangular pan. Cover with plastic wrap and refrigerate for at least 5 to 6 hours, or until the gelatin is set.

6. Scoop the gelatin with a spoon, or cut into cubes with a knife, and mound in individual serving dishes.

Variation: Pour the gelatin mixture into a decorative mold or individual molds, then unmold onto a serving platter or dessert plates.

Gelatina di Melagrana

Pomegranate Gelatin

❧

Lovely pomegranates, hanging from their branches like precious Christmas ornaments, are one of my favorite images of the Italian countryside. The ruby-red seeds of this fruit are eaten raw, or the juice is extracted for a refreshing drink. The juice also makes a refreshing and beautiful gelatina. To make this gelatina all year round, buy pomegranates when they are in season and squeeze and freeze the juice.

❧

Serves 8

Budino di Tre Frutte

Three-Fruit Pudding

❧

Budini, *or gelatin-based molded fruit desserts, are ideal do-ahead sweets. In this version, pears and apples are cooked and pureed, then served with a fresh strawberry sauce.*

❧

Serves 4

2 medium Golden Delicious apples, peeled, cored, and thinly sliced

2 Bosc pears, peeled, cored, and thinly sliced

1 teaspoon fresh lemon juice

¼ cup sugar

1 teaspoon ground cinnamon

Grated zest of 1 lemon

2 large eggs, lightly beaten

1 teaspoon unbleached all-purpose flour

1 package unflavored gelatin

¼ cup water

STRAWBERRY SAUCE

1 pint strawberries, hulled and sliced

3 tablespoons sugar

1 tablespoon fresh lemon juice

1. In a medium saucepan, combine the apples, pears, lemon juice, sugar, cinnamon, and zest. Cook, covered, over medium-low heat until the fruits are very soft but not mushy.

2. Meanwhile, in a small bowl, whisk together the eggs and flour until smooth.

3. Stir the egg mixture into the fruit and cook, stirring continually, for about 1 minute. Transfer the mixture to a food processor and process until the fruits are pureed.

4. In a small saucepan, soften the gelatin in the water. Heat over low heat, stirring until the gelatin dissolves completely. With the motor running, pour the gelatin through the feed tube of the food processor. Pour the mixture into a one-quart mold. Cover with plastic wrap and refrigerate until the pudding is set, about 3 to 4 hours.

5. In a blender or food processor, puree the strawberries with the sugar. Transfer the sauce to a small dish and stir in the lemon juice. Refrigerate, covered, until serving time.

6. To serve, run a knife around the outside edges of the mold. Place a serving plate over the top of the mold and invert the pudding onto it. Surround the base of the pudding with some of the strawberry sauce, and pass the rest separately.

1 package unflavored gelatin

¹/₄ cup water

8 to 9 large oranges, preferably blood oranges

¹/₄ cup sugar

3 tablespoons Orange Liqueur (page 320)

²/₃ cup heavy cream

Fresh mint leaves for garnish

1. Place a 5- to 6-cup straight-sided mold or bowl in the refrigerator to chill.

2. In a medium saucepan, sprinkle the gelatin over the water and let soften.

3. Squeeze 2 cups of juice from 7 or 8 of the oranges, and reserve the remaining orange(s) for garnish. Pour the orange juice into a saucepan, stir in the sugar, and bring to a boil. Set aside.

4. Add the orange liqueur to the gelatin and cook over very low heat until smooth and liquid. Remove from the heat. Slowly pour the orange juice through a strainer into the gelatin and stir until smooth. Discard the pulp. Pour the gelatin mixture into a bowl and refrigerate until cooled and just starting to set.

5. Whip the cream until soft peaks form. Carefully fold it into the orange gelatin. Pour the gelatin into the chilled mold, cover with plastic wrap, and refrigerate for at least 2 hours, or until set.

6. Peel the reserved orange(s), remove the pith, and separate into segments.

7. To serve, dip the bottom of the mold in hot water for a few minutes. Place a serving dish over the top of the mold and invert the mold. Shake the mold to release the gelatin. Garnish the Bavarian with orange segments and mint leaves. Serve at once.

Bavarese d'Arance

Orange Cream Bavarian

❧

This dessert starts out as a gelatina, but heavy cream is folded into the mixture before it is completely set, turning it into a creamy-textured bavarese. Blood oranges lend a particularly beautiful pink color to the dessert, but mandarin oranges or tangerines make good substitutes. Leave the oranges out at room temperature for at least a day before squeezing; they will yield more juice than if cold.

❧

Serves 6 to 8

Budino al Cioccolato

Chocolate Pudding

❧

My son, Christopher, is not a fan of cakes, or desserts for that matter, but he did like this Pugliese chocolate pudding dessert, served for his twenty-first birthday.

❧

Serves 6 to 8

⅔ cup sugar

¼ cup unsweetened cocoa

¼ cup plus 1 tablespoon unbleached all-purpose flour

4 cups milk

2 tablespoons unsalted butter, softened

1 ¾ cups heavy cream

Candied cherries for garnish

1. In a medium saucepan, mix together the sugar, cocoa, and flour. With a wooden spoon, slowly stir in the milk until smooth. Cook, stirring constantly, over medium heat until the mixture has thickened and coats the spoon. Remove from the heat and stir in the butter. Pour the pudding into a bowl, cover with a sheet of buttered wax paper, and refrigerate for several hours, until chilled. Do not let it set completely.

2. In another bowl, whip 1¼ cups of the heavy cream until stiff peaks form. Carefully fold the cream into the pudding. Spoon into dessert cups or a decorative bowl. Refrigerate, covered, for several hours.

3. To serve, whip the remaining ½ cup cream until stiff peaks form. Cover the pudding with puffs of cream and decorate with candied cherries.

Biscotti

Cookies

Torta di Biscotto di Nozze

Wedding Cookie Cake

꙰

Traditions surrounding Italian weddings vary from region to region and town to town. One that has descended from my southern Italian heritage is the wedding cookie cake, thought to have originated around Naples. A wedding cookie cake (shown on the jacket) consists of layer upon layer of a variety of cookies arranged in a pyramid, held together with icing, and decorated with candy, ribbons, and flowers. Making one is not difficult, if certain procedures are followed to ensure success.

You will want to make a variety of cookies so that the cake has many different layers, although layers can be repeated. I have suggested cookies that have worked well for me. Most of these cookies can be made up to a month ahead and frozen until the day before the wedding, when the cake is assembled. If you make the cookies ahead, freeze them carefully in single layers between wax paper or plastic wrap, and place them in airtight containers, not plastic bags. If the recipe is for a frosted cookie, frost as directed after baking and let the frosting dry completely before storing the cookies between layers of wax paper for freezing.

The Pasta Ciotti (Custard Tarts) cannot be frozen, but should be made the day before assembling the cake. Keep the tarts covered in the refrigerator after they cool.

In addition to the cookies, you will need white and green sugar-coated almonds (confetti, see page 227), the traditional color for the bride and groom, narrow pastel-colored ribbons for streamers, and a nosegay or bridal top ornament. To hold the cookies in place, you will need to use "icing glue," which is just confectioners' sugar and a little milk mixed to a thick frosting consistency.

Build the cake on a decorative round dish or tray. I often use one sixteen inches in diameter, but smaller or larger trays can be used. The larger the tray, the more a flat pyramid effect will be produced. How large you make the cookie cake is a matter of choice, depending on the number of wedding guests. For a sixteen-inch tray, make the eight different types of cookies on the menu for a wedding cookie cake (page 219). (I usually put about eleven layers of cookies on a sixteen-inch tray.)

Use firm cookies, such as biscotti, for the bottom layers. The more delicate cookies should be used for the top layers. Arrange the biscotti on their sides on the tray, making sure the entire surface is covered. I like to have the ends of the biscotti protrude just a bit over the edge of the tray.

Build the second layer using a different kind of cookie, or a mixture of cookies, and continue building until you have a pyramid. For a sixteen-inch tray, the cake should be at least twelve inches high, without the bridal ornament or flower nosegay at the top.

As you build the layers, use the icing glue to anchor the cookies in place by dabbing just a bit of frosting on the bottom of each one. This is important, especially if the cake is to be moved any distance.

For the finishing touches, insert white and green almonds between the cookies all around the cake. Make ribbon streamers for the cake and place a nosegay of wedding flowers at the top. I leave an indentation at the top of the cake for the flower stems.

At the wedding reception, position the cookie cake next to the wedding cake, and post a graceful sign that asks guests to make their selections starting at the top, not the bottom of the cake—although with the icing holding the cookies in place, there is little fear that it will fall like the tower of Babel!

At a traditional southern Italian wedding, the wedding party surrounds the cake table in a circle and dances the tarantella before the guests begin eating the cookies. Many times the cookie cake gets more attention than the wedding cake itself. The best thing, of course, is that the tradition lives on.

Biscotti al Cioccolato con Pepe Nero

Chocolate and Black Pepper Cookies

❧

Walnut-studded chocolate drop cookies are always found on a wedding cookie cake because they are firm and provide a good color contrast to the lighter cookies. This recipe has changed hands and ingredients many times in my family, but the one thing that remains constant is the black pepper in the dough. These freeze beautifully.

❧

Makes 3 ½ dozen

3 ¼ cups unbleached all-purpose flour

1 ½ cups sugar

1 tablespoon baking powder

¼ cup unsweetened cocoa

1 ¼ teaspoons freshly ground black pepper

1 ¼ teaspoons ground cloves

1 ½ teaspoons ground cinnamon

½ teaspoon salt

¾ cup solid vegetable shortening

½ to ⅔ cup milk

⅔ cup chopped walnuts

FROSTING

1 ½ cups confectioners' sugar, sifted

3 to 3 ½ tablespoons milk

1 teaspoon rum extract

Colored sprinkles

1. Preheat the oven to 350°F. Lightly grease two cookie sheets. Sift all the dry ingredients together into a large bowl. Work in the shortening with your hands until the mixture resembles coarse cornmeal. Add ½ cup milk and the nuts and mix with your hands until well blended. If the mixture seems too dry and does not hold together, add just enough additional milk so the dough holds together.

2. Pinch off 1-inch pieces of dough and roll them into balls. Place 1 inch apart on the cookie sheets. Bake for 15 to 20 minutes, or until firm.

3. While the cookies bake, make the frosting: In a bowl, combine the confectioners' sugar, 3 tablespoons milk, and the rum extract and beat until smooth. Add additional milk if necessary to make a thin frosting.

4. Let the cookies cool on racks only until warm. Dip the tops into the icing, place on the racks, and sprinkle with colored sprinkles. Let the frosting dry completely before layering the cookies between wax paper. These will keep in an airtight container for up to 1 week or can be frozen for up to 2 months.

3 1/2 cups unbleached all-purpose flour

1 tablespoon baking powder

1/2 teaspoon baking soda

1 teaspoon salt

4 large eggs

2 cups sugar

1 cup solid vegetable shortening, melted and cooled

2 tablespoons fresh lemon juice

1 tablespoon vanilla

1. Preheat the oven to 350°F. Sift together the flour, baking powder, baking soda, and salt into a bowl.

2. In another bowl, whisk the eggs with the sugar until light and lemon-colored. Whisk in the shortening, lemon juice, and vanilla. Gradually stir in the flour mixture, mixing well to blend the ingredients. Let the batter sit, covered, for 5 minutes.

3. Fill a tipless pastry bag two thirds full of the batter to form 3-inch-long Ss or 8s on cookie sheets or drop heaping teaspoonfuls of dough onto ungreased cookie sheets, spacing them about 1½ inches apart, and shape each one into a 3-inch-long S, using the back of the spoon.

4. Bake the cookies for 10 to 12 minutes, or until pale golden in color. Watch carefully and rotate the sheets to prevent burning. Let the cookies cool slightly on the cookie sheets before removing them to cooling racks.

Note: These are wonderful with coffee or tea and make a great after-school snack. They can be frozen, but will be softer in texture.

Esse

S Cookies

S cookies were originally made using a funnel attached to an old-fashioned meat grinder, but they can be formed with a pastry bag. Sometimes they are shaped like a figure eight. This cookie is soft when it first comes out of the oven, but crisps up like a sugar cookie as it cools. They are a cookie jar favorite, but also look stylish on a wedding cookie cake.

Makes about 3 ½ dozen

Biscotti d' Anici

Anise Cookies

❦

Biscotti *is the generic Italian word for "cookie." The literal translation is "twice cooked," and in this case the cookies are baked in long flat loaves, then sliced and baked again until dry. You can vary the flavorings for biscotti. Orange and almond extracts are popular. Because these cookies are dry, they will keep a long time.*

❦

Makes 3 dozen

1 cup unblanched whole almonds

3 1/4 cups unbleached all-purpose flour, sifted

2 1/2 tablespoons baking powder

1/2 teaspoon salt

5 1/3 tablespoons (1/3 cup) unsalted butter or solid vegetable shortening

6 large eggs

1 cup sugar

2 tablespoons anise extract

1. Preheat the oven to 350°F. Spread the almonds on a cookie sheet and, stirring once, toast for about 7 minutes, until golden. Remove the nuts to a bowl and let cool. (Leave the oven on.)

2. In a large bowl, combine the flour, baking powder, and salt. Add the butter and rub the mixture between your palms until it is the texture of coarse cornmeal.

3. In a large bowl, with a sturdy whisk or electric mixer, beat the eggs well. Beat in the sugar, then beat in the anise extract. Gradually add the flour mixture and mix until a dough is formed. Add the almonds and work them into the dough, using your hands or a wooden spoon.

4. Lightly grease a cookie sheet. Turn the dough out onto a floured surface. Divide the dough in half and place on the cookie sheet. Shape into two 12 by 3-inch loaves.

5. Bake the loaves for 25 minutes, or until puffed and firm to the touch. Remove the loaves from the oven and let cool for 5 minutes.

6. Cut each loaf on the diagonal into 1/2-inch slices. Place the slices on their sides on the cookie sheets and bake for an additional 7 minutes on each side, or until toasted.

7. Cool the biscotti completely on racks. The cookies will keep in an airtight container for several weeks.

2 1/2 cups unbleached all-purpose flour

1 1/4 cups fine semolina flour or pastry flour

1 tablespoon baking powder

2/3 cup sugar

1/2 cup lard or 1/4 cup lard plus 1/4 cup margarine

2 large eggs, beaten

Grated zest of 1 lemon

2/3 cup milk

1 egg beaten with 1 tablespoon water, for egg wash

2 cups sesame seeds

1. Preheat the oven to 350°F. Lightly grease two cookie sheets. In a bowl, mix the flours and baking powder together. Add the sugar and mix again. Work in the lard or lard and margarine until the mixture resembles coarse cornmeal. Add the beaten eggs and lemon zest, then add the milk a little at a time until a ball of dough forms.

2. Divide the dough into 4 pieces. On a floured surface, roll each piece into a rope about 12 inches long and the thickness of your middle finger. Cut the ropes into 2-inch pieces. Dip each piece into the egg wash, roll in the sesame seeds to coat on all sides, and place 1 inch apart on the cookie sheets.

3. Bake for 20 to 25 minutes, or until nicely browned. Cool on wire racks. Store in an airtight container.

Biscotti Regina

Sesame Cookies

❦

Sesame seed cookies get their crisp, dry texture from lard. They have a distinctive nutty flavor and are good keepers. These were made by the bushelful for my own wedding, and each wedding guest received a package of these cookies to take home.

❦

Makes 2 1/2 to 3 dozen

Menu for a Wedding Cookie Cake

....

Chocolate and Black Pepper Cookies (page 216)

S Cookies (page 217)

Rita Ricci's Cookies (page 224)

Anise Cookies (page 218)

Sesame Cookies

Marriage Cookies (page 220)

Almond Cookies (page 221)

Sicilian Fig Cookies (page 222)

Little Custard Tarts (page 225)

....

Biscotti Sposalizi

Marriage Cookies

❦

The name of this cookie speaks for itself. To make ahead, freeze unfrosted. After defrosting completely, frost as directed and let dry.

❦

Makes 3 to 4 dozen

1 ³/₄ cups unbleached all-purpose flour, sifted

8 tablespoons (1 stick) unsalted butter, softened, or ¹/₂ cup solid vegetable shortening

³/₄ cup sugar

¹/₂ teaspoon grated nutmeg

1 teaspoon ground cinnamon

¹/₂ teaspoon baking powder

³/₄ teaspoon baking soda

¹/₄ cup unsweetened cocoa

¹/₄ cup coarsely ground walnuts

1 cup raisins, coarsely chopped

¹/₂ cup milk

FROSTING

1 ¹/₂ cups confectioners' sugar

2 ¹/₂ tablespoons heavy cream

1 teaspoon unsalted butter or margarine, softened

1 teaspoon rum extract

Colored sprinkles

1. Preheat the oven to 350°F. Lightly grease two cookie sheets. In a bowl, beat the flour and butter or shortening until well blended. Add the sugar, spices, baking powder, baking soda, cocoa, nuts, and raisins and mix well. Add the milk and mix well to make a soft dough.

2. Drop teaspoonfuls of the dough onto the cookie sheets, spacing them about 1 inch apart. Bake for 10 minutes, or until firm. Cool on wire racks before frosting.

3. In a bowl, mix all the frosting ingredients until smooth. Dip the tops of the cookies into the frosting, place on wire racks, and sprinkle the tops with colored sprinkles. Let the frosting dry completely before layering the cookies between wax paper.

1 pound unblanched whole almonds

2 ¼ cups confectioners' sugar

1 teaspoon baking powder

4 large egg whites, at room temperature

Parchment paper

1. Preheat the oven to 350°F. Line two cookie sheets with parchment paper. In a food processor, finely chop the almonds. Place them in a large bowl.

2. In another bowl, mix the confectioners' sugar and baking powder together. Add to the almonds and mix well.

3. In a large bowl, beat the egg whites with an electric mixer until stiff peaks form. With a rubber spatula, gently fold the egg whites into the almond mixture a little at a time.

4. Using two soup spoons, shape the batter into balls about 2 inches in diameter and place at least 2 inches apart on the cookie sheets. Bake for 10 to 12 minutes, or until firm to the touch and golden brown.

5. Let the cookies cool completely on the parchment paper before removing or they will break. Store in an airtight container or freeze for up to 3 months.

Amaretti

ALMOND COOKIES

These amaretti are just one of the many versions to be found all over Italy. They are elegant enough to be one of the cookies to be found on a wedding cookie cake. In Italy, amaretti (the name means "bitter") are made with both sweet and bitter almonds, but since bitter almonds are not available here, this recipes uses all sweet almonds.

Makes 2 ½ dozen

Cucidati

Sicilian Fig Cookies

❧

Sicilian fig-filled cookies are traditional for a wedding cookie cake. These can be made ahead, layered in airtight tins, and frozen until needed. Arrange them at the bottom of the cookie cake, since they are a little heavier than some of the other cookies.

❧

Makes 4 dozen

DOUGH

4 cups unbleached all-purpose flour

1 1/2 tablespoons baking powder

1/4 teaspoon salt

1/2 cup sugar

1 cup solid vegetable shortening

1 large egg

1/2 cup milk

1 tablespoon vanilla

FILLING

2 cups dried figs

2 cups dried dates, pitted

1 1/2 cups raisins

1/2 cup honey

1 teaspoon ground cinnamon

1/2 cup orange marmalade

1 1/4 cups (10 ounces) walnuts or almonds, coarsely chopped

1 egg white beaten with 1 tablespoon water, for egg wash

Colored sprinkles

1. Sift the flour, baking powder, and salt together into a large bowl. Add the sugar and mix well. Cut in the shortening with a fork and work the mixture until it looks like coarse cornmeal.

2. In a bowl, beat the egg, milk, and vanilla together. Add to the flour and work the ingredients with your hands until a rough dough forms. Turn the dough out onto a floured surface and knead for 5 minutes, or until smooth. The dough will be soft. Cut the dough into 4 pieces, wrap each piece in plastic wrap, and chill for 45 minutes.

3. Meanwhile, preheat the oven to 375°F. Lightly grease two cookie sheets. Grind the figs, dates, and raisins in a meat grinder or in a food processor until coarse. Or coarsely chop with a large knife. Place the mixture in a bowl, add the remaining filling ingredients, and mix well. The mixture will be thick. Set aside.

4. On a floured surface, roll out one piece of dough at a time into a 12-inch square. Cut the dough into 4 by 3-inch rectangles. Spoon 2 tablespoons of the filling mixture down the center of each rectangle. Carefully fold the long edges of each rectangle over to meet in the center, then pinch the seam to close securely. Turn the cookies seam side down and seal the short ends by folding the dough under. Shape the cookies into crescents and place on the cookie sheets.

5. Make 2 or 3 diagonal slits in the top of each crescent with scissors. Brush with the egg wash and sprinkle on the colored sprinkles. Bake for 25 minutes, or until golden brown. Cool on racks.

Note: I wrap the crescents individually in plastic wrap, twist the ends, and tie them with ribbons. They make a wonderful Christmas present. They can be made ahead and frozen.

Biscotti di Margherita Ricci

Rita Ricci's Cookies

This recipe is an heirloom. The cookie shape, a figure eight or a knot, is symbolic of the marriage of two people. There are many versions of this cookie. This one bears the name of an old Italian woman who made these cookies for my wedding almost thirty years ago.

Makes 4 ½ dozen

4 large eggs

1 ½ cups sugar

2 teaspoons vanilla

1 cup solid vegetable shortening, melted

½ cup milk

6 cups unbleached all-purpose flour

2 tablespoons baking powder

2 tablespoons grated lemon zest

1 tablespoon fresh lemon juice

GLAZE

2 cups confectioners' sugar, sifted

¼ cup milk

1 tablespoon vanilla

1 to 2 drops pink or green food coloring, optional

1. Preheat the oven to 350°F. Lightly grease two cookie sheets. In a bowl, beat the eggs until pale yellow. Add the sugar and vanilla and beat until light-colored. Beat in the melted shortening and milk.

2. Sift the flour and baking powder together, and add to the egg mixture. Add the lemon zest and juice, mixing well. The dough will be soft. Wrap it in wax paper and refrigerate for 1 hour to make it easier to handle.

3. Break off egg-size pieces of dough and roll each one under the palms of your hands into an 8-inch rope. Bring the ends together, pinch to seal, and twist to form a figure eight, or loosely knot the dough, and place the cookies 1 inch apart on the cookie sheets. Bake for 20 minutes, or until lightly colored and firm to the touch.

4. While the cookies bake, make the glaze: In a bowl, mix all the ingredients until smooth.

5. Let the cookies cool only until warm. Dip the top of each cookie in the frosting and place the cookies on wire racks. Let the glaze dry completely.

DOUGH

2 cups unbleached all-purpose flour

1/2 cup sugar

3/4 teaspoon baking powder

1/8 teaspoon salt

1/2 cup solid vegetable shortening

1/4 cup milk

3/4 teaspoon vanilla

1 large egg, well beaten

FILLING

3 tablespoons cornstarch

2/3 cup sugar

1 1/2 cups milk

1 1/2 tablespoons unsalted butter

1 large egg yolk, slightly beaten

1 teaspoon almond extract

1 egg beaten with 2 tablespoons milk, for the egg wash

1. Sift together the flour, sugar, baking powder, and salt into a large bowl. Cut in the shortening with a pastry blender until the mixture resembles coarse cornmeal. Add the milk, vanilla, and egg and use your hands to mix the ingredients into a smooth ball of dough. Wrap the dough in plastic wrap and set aside.

2. In a medium saucepan, whisk together the cornstarch and sugar, making sure there are no lumps. Gradually whisk in the milk. Add the butter, place the saucepan over medium heat, and cook, stirring constantly with a wooden spoon, until thickened. Remove from the heat and stir in the egg yolk and almond extract. Set the custard aside.

3. Divide the dough in half. On a lightly floured surface, roll one piece into an 11-inch circle, about 1/4 inch thick. Using a 3-inch fluted biscuit cutter, cut out circles of dough and press each one into the bottom and up the sides of 3 by 1 1/4-inch tart pans. Reroll the scraps and cut out additional circles. You should have 12 tart shells.

continued

Pasta Ciotti

LITTLE CUSTARD TARTS

These little custard-filled tarts can be used on a wedding cookie cake, but should be made no earlier than the day before assembling the cake since they do not store or freeze well. The tarts can be made any size from three inches (as here) to one inch. I think the miniatures look nicer on a wedding cookie cake. Place them at the top of the cake, so they won't be crushed by the heavier cookies.

Makes 12

4. Place the tart pans on a cookie sheet. Spoon about 2 table-spoons of filling into each tart shell.

5. Roll out the second piece of dough and cut out 3-inch circles. Place a circle over each tart and pinch the edges closed.

6. With a pastry brush, paint the top of each tart with the egg wash. Refrigerate the tarts for 30 minutes.

7. Preheat the oven to 425°F. Bake the tarts on the middle oven rack for 12 to 15 minutes, or until the tops are golden brown. Remove the tarts to racks and let cool completely.

8. Carefully remove the tarts from the pans. Store in an airtight container in the refrigerator.

Note: If you make miniature tarts, bake for only 8 to 10 minutes. This recipe makes about 2½ dozen miniature tarts.

Far Mangiare i Confetti

To Celebrate a Wedding

❦

We think of confetti as small dots of colored paper floating from the sky in celebration of something special, but to Italians confetti are pastel-colored candy-coated almonds. They are made from whole almonds dipped in a thin, hard, colored sugar coating. Colors range from very vibrant to the palest pastel.

Originally, confetti were any sweetmeats or small candies thrown during parades and carnivals. Eventually this custom proved to be a costly one, and gave way to paper confetti.

At an Italian wedding, it still is customary to give every wedding guest a *bomboniera* (candy box) to take home. The bomboniera itself can be modest (paper) or very elaborate (silver), and is filled with candy-coated almond confetti. In America, bomboniere are usually squares of pastel netting, tied with ribbons.

Confetti colors are traditional and symbolic. White denotes virginity, green signals an engagement, pink or blue announces the birth of a girl or boy, and silver and gold sparkle for wedding anniversaries.

Sulmona, a town of twenty-five thousand people in the region of Abruzzi, is famous for its elaborate confetti confections, and it is said that the nuns of the convent of Santa Chiara were the first to make confetti flowers. Walking down the main street of Sulmona is like being in a huge field, surrounded by vibrantly colored flowers that never wither or fade. Wherever you look there are confetti bouquets, confetti baskets, and all sorts of arrangements, all made from candied almonds.

The almond confetti are glued and wired onto florists' wire stems to create flowers, and paper leaves are attached to give the flowers a finished look. These flowers can be purchased individually or as a grouping to form a bouquet. The groupings are endless; deep purple almonds bunched together to form violet bouquets, pink and white almonds wired together to form delicate sprays of almond blossoms, and bright yellow daisy bouquets. My favorite are the exquisite realistic-looking bridal bouquets, made in the selected colors of the bride. The beauty of these is that they will last almost forever.

Biscotti al Cioccolato e Pistacchio

Chocolate-Pistachio Biscotti

❧

I have made all the traditional types of biscotti, but when I created chocolate biscotti studded with pistachio nuts, raves came from my family. These are not too sweet and have a nice airy texture.

❧

Makes about 2 ½ dozen

1 cup shelled natural pistachio nuts

8 tablespoons (1 stick) unsalted butter, softened

1 cup sugar

1 large egg

½ cup fresh tangerine juice

2 cups unbleached all-purpose flour

¼ cup unsweetened cocoa

1 teaspoon baking soda

1 teaspoon ground cinnamon

¼ teaspoon salt

1. Preheat the oven to 350°F. Spread the nuts on a cookie sheet and toast until fragrant, about 12 minutes. Cool, then coarsely chop and set aside. (Leave the oven on.)

2. In a bowl, using an electric mixer, cream the butter and sugar until well blended. Beat in the egg and tangerine juice.

3. Sift the flour, cocoa, baking soda, cinnamon, and salt together onto wax paper. Gradually beat the dry ingredients into the butter mixture. Fold in the nuts. Cover the dough and let stand for 10 minutes at room temperature.

4. Lightly butter two cookie sheets. Place half the dough on each cookie sheet. With a spatula, spread each half into an 11 by 4½-inch loaf.

5. Bake the loaves for 20 to 25 minutes, or until firm to the touch. Remove from the oven and let cool on the cookie sheets for 20 minutes.

6. With a spatula carefully transfer each loaf to a cutting board. With a sharp knife, cut on the diagonal into ½-inch slices. Place the slices on their sides on the cookie sheets and bake for 5 to 7 minutes on each side, until toasted. Remove the biscotti to racks to cool completely. Store at room temperature in an airtight container for up to 1 week, or freeze for up to 2 months in airtight plastic containers.

5 ounces dried Calimyrna figs, (about 12), coarsely chopped

¹/₄ cup plus 1 tablespoon Orange Liqueur (page 320) or fresh orange juice

1 cup walnuts

3¹/₂ cups unbleached all-purpose flour

2 tablespoons baking powder

¹/₂ teaspoon salt

6 large eggs

1 cup plus 2 tablespoons sugar

¹/₃ cup vegetable oil

1. Place the figs in a bowl with the orange liqueur or orange juice, cover, and let marinate overnight in the refrigerator.

2. Preheat the oven to 350°F. Spread the walnuts on a cookie sheet and toast in the oven for about 10 minutes. Set aside.

3. Sift together the flour, baking powder, and salt into a large bowl.

4. In another bowl, whisk together the eggs, sugar, and oil. Add to the flour mixture and mix well with a spoon. Add the figs, with their liquid, and the walnuts and mix until well blended. The dough will be sticky. Cover and refrigerate for 1 hour.

5. Lightly butter two cookie sheets. Place half the dough on each cookie sheet. With a spatula, spread each half into a 13 by 7-inch loaf.

6. Bake the loaves for 15 to 20 minutes, or until they are light golden and just firm to the touch. Remove from the oven and let the loaves cool on the sheets for 10 minutes.

7. Carefully remove each loaf to a cutting board and cut on the diagonal into ¹/₂-inch-thick slices. Place the slices on their sides on the cookie sheets and bake for about 7 minutes on each side, or until toasted and golden brown. Transfer to wire racks to cool.

Variation: Hazelnuts can be used in place of walnuts. A combination of nuts is good too.

Biscotti di Fichi Secchi e Noci

Dried Fig and Walnut Biscotti

❧

A departure from classic anise-flavored biscotti, these are studded with chunks of dried Calimyrna figs and toasted walnuts. Steeping the figs in homemade orange liqueur imparts a wonderful flavor. Or use orange juice if you prefer. These biscotti are about seven inches long and look impressive standing tall in a footed glass dish.

❧

Makes about 3 dozen

Biscotti Bianchi e Neri

White-and-Black Biscotti

I call these "white-and-black" biscotti because they are made from two doughs shaped side by side on the cookie sheets. One dough has the cocoa added, the other remains light, and they fuse together while baking. The mingled flavors of amaretto and homemade orange liqueur and the crunchy texture of almonds and hazelnuts complement each other. These make an unusual gift.

Makes 3 dozen

WHITE DOUGH

1 1/2 cups whole almonds

8 tablespoons (1 stick) unsalted butter, softened

1 cup sugar

1 large egg

3 1/2 tablespoons Orange Liqueur (page 320)

1 tablespoon grated orange zest

2 cups unbleached all-purpose flour

1 teaspoon baking soda

1/4 teaspoon salt

DARK DOUGH

1 1/2 cups hazelnuts

8 tablespoons (1 stick) unsalted butter, softened

1 cup plus 2 tablespoons sugar

1 large egg

3 1/2 tablespoons amaretto liqueur

2 cups unbleached all-purpose flour

1/4 cup unsweetened cocoa

1 teaspoon baking soda

1/4 teaspoon salt

1. Preheat the oven to 350°F. Place the almonds for the white dough on one cookie sheet and the hazelnuts for the dark dough on another cookie sheet, and toast for 6 to 7 minutes. Set aside to cool. (Leave the oven on.)

2. To make the white dough, in a large bowl, with an electric mixer, cream the butter and sugar. Beat the egg, orange liqueur, and orange zest.

3. Sift together the flour, baking soda, and salt onto wax paper. On low speed, beat the dry ingredients into the butter mixture. Stir in the almonds. Set the dough aside.

4. To make the dark dough, in a large bowl, with an electric mixer, cream the butter and sugar. Beat in the egg and liqueur.

5. Sift together the flour, cocoa, baking soda, and salt onto wax paper. On low speed, beat the dry ingredients into the butter mixture. Stir in the hazelnuts.

6. Lightly butter two cookie sheets. Scoop half the white dough onto one cookie sheet, and form it into a 12 by 2½-inch log. Scoop half the chocolate dough onto the sheet, and form it into a log of the same size, positioning it next to the white log. It is important that the two sides meet. Form the remaining dough into a second double log.

7. Bake for 20 to 25 minutes, or until the tops of the loaves are firm to the touch. Remove from the oven and let cool on the cookie sheets for 10 minutes.

8. Carefully transfer each loaf to a cutting board. With a sharp knife, cut each loaf on the diagonal into ½-inch slices. Lay the slices on their sides on the cookie sheets, and bake for 8 to 10 minutes on each side, until toasted. Cool the biscotti on wire racks.

Note: These can be frozen for up to 2 months in airtight containers.

Variation: To make smaller biscotti, divide each batter into quarters and make four 10 by 1½-inch logs.

Biscotti al Limone

Lemon Wafer Cookies

These simple wafer cookies, a good accompaniment to fresh fruit, ice creams, or ices, need no embellishment, but they can be sandwiched together with jam or a cream filling for a fancier presentation if you wish.

Makes about 5 dozen

4 large eggs
1 cup less 1 tablespoon sugar
1 1/2 cups unbleached all-purpose flour
Grated zest of 1 lemon

1. Preheat the oven to 350°F. Lightly butter two cookie sheets. In a bowl, whisk together the eggs and sugar until light-colored and thick. Sprinkle one third of the flour over the egg mixture and fold in with a rubber spatula. Gradually fold in the remaining flour and then the lemon zest. The dough will be stiff.

2. Drop the batter by teaspoonfuls onto the cookie sheets, spacing them about 1 1/2 inches apart. Bake the cookies for about 15 minutes, or until the edges are lightly browned. Carefully remove the cookies to a cooling rack.

12 tablespoons (1½ sticks) unsalted butter, softened

1 cup Vanilla Sugar (page 329)

2 large eggs

1 tablespoon Homemade Vanilla Extract (page 328)

2 cups unbleached all-purpose flour

¼ teaspoon baking soda

¼ teaspoon salt

4 ounces bittersweet chocolate, coarsely chopped

½ cup whole natural almonds, coarsely chopped

1. Preheat the oven to 350°F. Line two cookie sheets with parchment paper, or lightly butter and flour them. In a bowl, using an electric mixer, cream the butter and sugar until light and pale in color. Beat in the eggs one at a time, then beat in the vanilla.

2. Sift the flour, baking soda, and salt together onto wax paper. On low speed, beat the flour mixture into the butter mixture. Stir in the chocolate and nuts.

3. Drop scant teaspoonfuls of the batter onto the cookie sheets, spacing them about 1 inch apart. Bake for 12 to 15 minutes, or until the cookies are lightly browned. Cool slightly on the pans, then remove the cookies with a spatula to racks to cool completely.

Note: These cookies can be frozen for up to 2 months in airtight plastic containers.

Cialde al Cioccolato

Chocolate Wafer Cookies

❧

These chocolate-and-almond-studded cookies make use of homemade vanilla flavoring and vanilla sugar, which can be used in other cookie recipes too. For best flavor, use a good bittersweet chocolate, such as Ghirardelli, and drop scant teaspoonfuls of the batter to make thin wafer cookies.

❧

Makes about 5 dozen

Biscotti di Noci

Nut Cookies

Rich-tasting and delicate, these butter and nut cookies are nice for a special occasion. To use on a wedding cookie cake, put each cookie in a small white paper candy cup and place them at the top of the cake so they do not get crushed.

Makes about 2 ½ dozen

8 tablespoons (1 stick) unsalted butter or margarine, softened
2 tablespoons sugar
1 teaspoon vanilla
1 cup unbleached all-purpose flour
1 cup finely chopped walnuts
Confectioners' sugar for coating

1. In a bowl, with an electric mixer, cream the butter or margarine and the sugar until light-colored. Beat in the vanilla. Gradually beat in the flour. Stir in the nuts. Wrap the dough in wax paper and chill for about an hour for easier handling.

2. Preheat the oven to 375°F. With floured hands, break off 1-inch pieces of dough and roll into balls. Place the balls on ungreased cookie sheets, spacing them about ½ inch to 1 inch apart. Bake for about 15 minutes, or until lightly browned. Let cool slightly on the pans.

3. Place the confectioners' sugar in a shallow dish. Remove the cookies carefully with a spatula, and gently roll the warm cookies in the sugar to coat. Allow to cool completely on wire racks. You may need to coat them a second time.

1 pound (3 1/3 cups) whole almonds

1 1/4 cups sugar

2 large eggs

1 tablespoon cold water

Grated zest of 1 large lemon

Confectioners' sugar for sprinkling, optional

1. Preheat the oven to 350°F. Line two cookie sheets with parchment paper, or lightly butter and flour them. In a food processor, finely grind the almonds with the sugar. With the motor running, add the eggs and water through the feed tube and process to form a loose dough. Transfer the dough to a bowl and mix in the zest with your hands.

2. With wet hands, form generous tablespoonfuls of the dough into S or U shapes about 2 1/4 inches long. Place the cookies 1 inch apart on the cookie sheets.

3. Bake for about 20 to 25 minutes, or until the cookies are firm to the touch and lightly browned. Remove the cookies to wire racks to cool completely.

4. Sprinkle the cooled cookies with confectioners' sugar if you wish.

Riccolini a Mandorle

Little Almond Curls

This old Sicilian recipe makes use of two basic Sicilian ingredients, almonds and lemons. The cookies are easy to make and, as the name implies, are shaped like curls.

Makes about 3 1/2 dozen

Tarallini con Brinato e Confettini

Confetti-Sprinkled Butter Cookies

❦

This spiral-shaped holiday cookie from Benevento, in southern Italy, descended through a long line of bakers in the Giuseppina Tavino family.

❦

Makes 4 dozen

DOUGH

½ pound (2 sticks) unsalted butter, softened

1 cup sugar

6 large eggs

1 tablespoon almond extract

6 cups unbleached all-purpose flour

2 tablespoons baking powder

¼ teaspoon salt

FROSTING

2 cups confectioners' sugar

2 tablespoons plus 1 teaspoon half-and-half or light cream

Colored sprinkles

1. In a large bowl, with an electric mixer, cream the butter and sugar until well blended. Beat in the eggs one at a time. Beat in the almond extract.

2. Sift the flour, baking powder, and salt together onto wax paper. Add to the butter mixture and mix with your hands until blended. Turn the dough out onto a lightly floured work surface and knead until the dough holds together and is smooth. Cover the dough with a bowl and allow to rest for 15 minutes.

3. Preheat the oven to 350°F. Lightly butter two cookie sheets. Divide the dough in half, then into quarters, and so on, until you have 48 pieces.

4. On a floured surface, roll each piece under the palms of your hands into a 7-inch rope. Form each rope into a spiral about 1½ inches in diameter, leaving a tail pointing up in the center of each one. Space the cookies 1 inch apart on the cookie sheets.

5. Meanwhile, in a bowl, stir together the confectioners' sugar and half-and-half until smooth. Cover and set aside.

6. Bake for 10 to 12 minutes, until firm to the touch but only lightly colored.

7. Cool the cookies on the pans for 5 minutes. Then frost and sprinkle with colored sprinkles. Place on wire racks and let the frosting dry completely before storing between layers of wax paper in airtight containers.

½ cup plus 1½ tablespoons unbleached all-purpose flour

½ teaspoon baking powder

¼ teaspoon salt

2 large eggs

½ cup sugar

1 tablespoon vanilla

2 cups diced dates (10 ounces)

1 cup chopped walnuts

Confectioners' sugar for sprinkling

1. Preheat the oven to 350°F. Butter a 10-inch square pan and dust it with flour, shaking out the excess. Sift ½ cup of flour, the baking powder, and salt together into a bowl.

2. In another bowl, beat the eggs until foamy. Gradually add the sugar and vanilla, beating until well blended. Fold in the flour mixture, blending well.

3. In a small bowl, toss the dates and nuts with the remaining 1½ tablespoons flour. Fold the date and nut mixture into the batter.

4. Spread the batter evenly in the pan. Bake for 20 to 25 minutes, or until golden brown on top and firm to the touch. Cool completely in the pan on a wire rack.

5. Sprinkle the top with confectioners' sugar and cut the cookies into bars.

Biscotti di Datteri e Noci

Date and Nut Cookies

✒

My mother's light-textured date and nut cookies were always a part of her holiday baking and giving. I bake them as part of mine too, and when I eat them, I am home again. The recipe can be doubled easily and the cookies can be made up to a month ahead and frozen, layered between wax paper in an airtight container. Sprinkle the confectioners' sugar over the top after defrosting.

✒

Makes 25

Biscotti d' Albicocca di Mamma

Mom's Apricot Bar Cookies

✦

As Christmas approaches, the memory of my mother preparing her sweet-tart dried apricot filling for apricot bars, and then sandwiching it between flaky lemon-scented dough, leads me to the kitchen to carry on the tradition. These can be made ahead and frozen before glazing them. A combination of dried fruits can be substituted for the apricots.

✦

Makes 40

DOUGH

3 1/2 cups unbleached all-purpose flour
1/4 teaspoon salt
3/4 cup confectioners' sugar
14 tablespoons (1 3/4 sticks) unsalted cold butter, cut into pieces
2 large egg yolks
1/4 cup cold water, or more as necessary
1 tablespoon grated lemon zest

FILLING

1 pound dried apricots
1/2 cup sugar

GLAZE

1 1/2 cups confectioners' sugar
3 tablespoons fresh orange juice

1. In a food processor or in a bowl combine the flour, salt, and confectioners' sugar and pulse or mix together. Add the butter and pulse or blend in with a pastry blender until the mixture resembles coarse cornmeal. Add the yolks, water, and lemon zest and pulse or mix with your hands until the dough comes together. Add a little more water if the dough seems dry. Wrap the dough in plastic wrap and refrigerate for 1 hour.

2. Put the apricots in a saucepan, cover with water, and bring to a boil. Simmer until tender, about 20 minutes. Drain the apricots and place in a food processor or blender. Add the sugar and puree until smooth. Set aside.

3. Preheat the oven to 350°F. Butter a 15 by 11-inch baking pan. Divide the dough in half. On a floured surface, roll out one piece to a 15 by 11-inch rectangle. Carefully fold the dough in half, then in half again. Lift the dough onto the cookie sheet, unfold it, and fit it into the pan. Do not worry if there are any tears; simply pat any holes closed. If necessary, stretch and press the dough to the edges.

4. Spread the filling evenly over the dough.

5. Roll the remaining piece of dough out to a 15 by 11-inch rectangle. Carefully lift the dough and place it over the apricot filling. Press gently around the edges to even the dough.

6. Bake for about 30 minutes, or until the crust is golden brown. Remove the pan to a rack and let cool slightly.

7. In a small bowl, mix the confectioners' sugar and orange juice together until smooth. With a rubber spatula, spread the glaze evenly over the warm crust. Let dry completely, then cut into bars.

Note: To make ahead and freeze, bake the cookies as directed. After cooling, cut the sheet of cookies crosswise in half. Wrap each half in aluminum foil and freeze. To serve, let thaw at room temperature, glaze, and let dry before cutting into bars.

Biscotti per Natale
Cookies for Christmas

❧

Cookies are one of my staple Christmas gifts, and a few years ago, I started a baking tradition by inviting some friends to a Buon Natale cookie exchange. Here's how it works: Invite some friends (eight to twelve seems to work well) to your home just before the holidays for a cookie swap. Use recipe cards as your invitations, and ask each person to bring six dozen of her or his favorite Italian cookies, with copies of the recipe for each guest. This may seem like a lot of cookies to make, but remember, it's only one kind and one time that each person will be making cookies. As the host, make an Italian dessert to serve with espresso. I like to make Zuppa Inglese (page 296) because it can be done ahead, but other popular Italian desserts such as tiramisù or cannoli work well too. If they are available, I also serve strawberries and or raspberries in Asti Spumante.

When your guests arrive, put a dozen of each type of cookie on a large serving tray; display the rest with the recipes on a table or kitchen counter. Provide an inexpensive Christmas box or basket for each guest to fill with some of each kind of cookie, plus the recipes. Each person will go home with almost six dozen assorted cookies and the recipes to make them. This is a great way to save time, work, and energy in the kitchen, and an easy way to have festive Italian cookies for the holidays.

1 3/4 cups unbleached all-purpose flour

1/2 cup potato starch

1/2 pound (2 sticks) unsalted butter, melted

3/4 cup sugar

1 tablespoon vanilla

5 hard-boiled large egg yolks sieved or mashed with a fork

1 egg white, lightly beaten

Turbinado (coarse brown) sugar, colored sprinkles, or sesame seeds
   for sprinkling

1. Preheat the oven to 350°F. Sift the flour and potato starch together onto wax paper.

2. Using a whisk or electric mixer, beat the butter and sugar until well blended. With a wooden spoon, stir in the vanilla. Stir in the flour mixture and egg yolks and mix with the spoon or your hands until a ball of dough is formed. The dough will be soft.

3. Divide the dough in half working with one piece of dough at a time, place the dough between two sheets of wax paper and roll out to a rectangle approximately 14 inches by 8 inches. Remove the top sheet of wax paper. Using a pastry wheel, cut lengthwise into eight 1-inch-wide strips, cut each strip into pieces. Carefully lift the pieces off the wax paper and place about 1/2 inch apart on ungreased cookie sheets. Brush the tops of the cookies with the beaten egg white and sprinkle with the turbinado sugar, colored sprinkles, or sesame seeds.

4. Bake the cookies for about 12 minutes, or until golden brown. Remove them to wire racks and let cool completely.

Note: These may be frozen in airtight plastic containers for up to 3 months.

Variation: Use cookie cutters to make Christmas, Easter, or Valentine's cookies.

Frollini

Frollini are scrumptious cookies with a rich, buttery taste. In fact, the word frollini means "soft" or "tender." I see them in pastry shops throughout Italy. Some are topped with coarse sugar, others with sesame seeds or brightly colored tiny sprinkles. Their delicate texture is the result of adding potato starch to the dough. Because the dough is soft, it's best to roll it out between sheets of waxed paper.

Makes about 9 dozen

Biscotti Morbidi di Signora Pilla

Mrs. Pilla's Soft Cookies

❧

Signora Libera Pilla sent me the recipe for this heirloom cookie, which she begins making right after Thanksgiving and continues until Christmas. The dough is very soft, so it's best to refrigerate it for several hours before forming the cookies. Their delicate cake-like texture and not-too-sweet taste make these cookies a perfect accompaniment to fresh strawberries, raspberries, and peaches.

❧

Makes about 4 1/2 dozen

4 cups unbleached all-purpose flour

1 teaspoon baking powder

1 teaspoon baking soda

2 cups sugar

1 cup solid vegetable shortening

4 large eggs, at room temperature

1/2 cup milk

1 1/4 tablespoons almond extract

3/4 cup confectioners' sugar

1. Sift the flour, baking powder, and baking soda together into a bowl.

2. In another bowl, with an electric mixer, beat the sugar and shortening together until light and fluffy. Beat in the eggs one at a time. Beat in the milk and almond extract, beating until smooth. On low speed, slowly beat in the flour mixture until well combined. Cover the dough and refrigerate for 2 to 3 hours.

3. Preheat the oven to 350°F. Lightly grease two cookie sheets. Place the confectioners' sugar in a dish.

4. Using two teaspoons, form balls of dough the size of a walnut, drop the balls into the confectioners' sugar, and gently roll them to coat completely. Place the balls on the cookie sheets, spacing them 1 inch apart.

5. Bake the cookies for about 15 minutes, or until firm to the touch and just lightly browned. Transfer to cooling racks.

Note: These can be made ahead and frozen for up to 1 month. When ready to serve, sprinkle additional confectioners' sugar over the tops.

4-13-05
Too much work
not worth the
effort.

½ pound (2 sticks) unsalted butter, softened

¼ cup sugar

2 cups unbleached all-purpose flour

2 teaspoons vanilla

4 hard-boiled extra-large egg yolks, sieved or mashed with a fork

About ¾ cup jam (apricot, raspberry, or orange marmalade)

Confectioners' sugar for sprinkling

1. In a bowl, with an electric mixer, cream the butter and sugar. Beat in flour and then the vanilla and beat until a soft dough is formed. Beat in the egg yolks just until blended. Wrap the dough in wax paper and chill for at least 1 hour.

2. Preheat the oven to 350°F. Lightly grease two cookie sheets. Divide the dough in half.

3. On a well-floured surface, roll out each half ¼ inch thick. Use an assortment of cookie cutters to cut out the dough, making sure to cut out an even number of each shape, and place the cookies about 1 inch apart on the cookie sheets.

4. Spread a thin coating of jam over half the cookies, and top each one with another cookie to form a sandwich. Seal the edges by pressing on all sides with the tines of a fork.

5. Bake for 15 to 18 minutes, or until the cookies are lightly browned. Let cool on the cookie sheets for a few minutes before removing them to cooling racks.

6. When cool, sprinkle the cookies with confectioners' sugar.

Biscotti con Marmellata

JAM-FILLED COOKIES

❧

These jam-filled cookies have a shortbread-like texture. Sieved hard-boiled egg yolks in the dough give it added richness. This dough can be rolled and cut into various shapes to fit the occasion.

❧

Makes 2 dozen

Bocconotti Dolci

Sweet Mouthfuls

❧

Bocconotti *translates to "mouthfuls" or "bites." This traditional half-moon–shaped cookie with a cake-like texture is filled with grape jam and chocolate. The recipe comes from my friend Domenica Baglioni Flamminj, a chef who lives in Teramo in the region of Abruzzi.*

❧

Makes about 5 dozen

DOUGH

10 1/2 tablespoons unsalted butter, softened
2/3 cup plus 1 tablespoon sugar
1 large egg
3 large egg yolks
Grated zest of 1 lemon
3 2/3 cups unbleached all-purpose flour
1 1/2 teaspoons baking soda

FILLING

2/3 cup grape jam
1/2 cup finely chopped toasted almonds (3 ounces)

2 ounces semisweet chocolate, finely chopped
1 teaspoon unsweetened cocoa
Confectioners' sugar for dusting

1. In a bowl, using an electric mixer, cream the butter and sugar until light-colored. Beat in the egg and then the egg yolks one at a time. Beat in the lemon zest.

2. Sift the flour with the baking soda over the egg mixture, stirring it in with a wooden spoon. The dough will be very soft. Wrap in plastic wrap and refrigerate for several hours.

3. Preheat the oven to 375°F. Lightly grease two cookie sheets. In a bowl, combine the filling ingredients and mix well. Set aside.

4. Divide the dough in half. On a floured surface, roll out each half to a thickness of 1/4 inch. Using a 2 1/4-inch round cookie cutter, cut out circles from the dough. Place a generous teaspoon of the filling on one half of each circle and fold the other half over to enclose the filling. Press the edges closed with a fork dipped in flour, and place the cookies 1 inch apart on the cookie sheets. Reroll the scraps to make more cookies.

5. Bake for 12 to 15 minutes, or until the edges of the cookies are lightly browned. Remove to cooling racks to cool completely.

6. Dust the cooled cookies with confectioners' sugar.

DOUGH

3/4 cup unbleached all-purpose flour

3 tablespoons unsalted butter, softened

2 tablespoons cold water

FILLING

1/2 cup finely ground walnuts

1/2 cup plus 3 tablespoons sugar

1 teaspoon ground cinnamon

1 tablespoon unsalted butter, melted

Vegetable oil for deep-frying

1. In a bowl, mix the flour and butter together with your hands or a fork until it resembles coarse crumbs. Slowly add the water and mix until a ball of dough is formed. Do not overmix. (Alternatively, combine all the ingredients in a food processor and pulse until a ball of dough is formed.) Wrap the dough in plastic wrap and refrigerate for 2 hours.

2. In a small bowl, mix together the walnuts and 3 tablespoons of the sugar. Set aside. In another bowl, mix the remaining 1/2 cup sugar and cinnamon. Set aside.

3. On a lightly floured surface, roll the dough into a square, and trim it to an even 10-inch square, reserving the scraps. With a pastry wheel, cut the dough lengthwise into 5 strips, and cut each strip into 5 squares.

4. Lightly brush each square with the melted butter. Place about 1 teaspoon of the walnut filling in the center of each square, and roll each one up like a small jelly roll. Pinch the seam closed and twist each end. Place the caramelle on a clean towel. Gather the dough scraps together and reroll to make more caramelle.

5. In a deep-fryer or a deep heavy pan, heat the oil to 375°F. Fry the caramelle, a few at a time, until golden brown. With a slotted spoon, transfer to brown paper to drain.

6. While they are still warm, roll each caramella several times in the sugar and cinnamon mixture.

Caramelle di Noci

Walnut Twists

These twisted and fried cookies, which look like wrapped pieces of candy, are a favorite Christmas giveaway. I developed it using leftover pieces of dough and a few teaspoons of ground walnuts that were on hand after making a sweet *rotolo*. Everyone loves these, and the dough is very easy to work with.

Makes about 2 1/2 dozen

Treccine

Little Braids

❧

I found these little braided cookies in a pasticceria in the very baroque city of Lecce in Puglia. The dough, which has just a hint of sweetness, is made with flour, olive oil, and wine. I like these with a glass of chilled Moscato dessert wine.

❧

Makes 1 1/2 dozen

2 1/2 cups unbleached all-purpose flour

1/4 cup plus 1 tablespoon sugar

1/4 teaspoon salt

1/2 cup dry white wine

1/4 cup plus 2 tablespoons extra-virgin olive oil

2 tablespoons water

About 2/3 cups whole natural almonds

1 egg, slightly beaten

2 tablespoons turbinado (coarse brown) sugar

1. Preheat the oven to 350°F. Lightly grease two cookie sheets. In a bowl, mix together the flour, sugar, and salt. Add the wine, oil, and water, and mix with a fork, until a ball of dough begins to form. Alternatively, make the dough in a food processor; combine the flour, sugar, and salt in the bowl of the processor. Add the wine, oil, and water through the feed tube, pulsing until a dough begins to form.

2. Turn the dough out onto a work surface and knead a few times, until smooth. (You should not need to add any flour.) The dough will be soft.

3. Pinch off 1-inch pieces of dough and roll each one under the palms of your hands into a 6-inch rope. To shape each cookie, braid two ropes together to form a twist, and place on the cookie sheets.

4. Insert 3 almonds in the folds of each twist, spacing them evenly. Brush the tops of the braids with the beaten egg, and sprinkle with the turbinado sugar.

5. Bake for 20 to 25 minutes, or until the braids are lightly browned. Remove the braids to wire racks to cool completely.

Note: These can be made larger or smaller as you wish. They can be frozen for up to 2 months in an airtight container.

DOUGH

2 cups unbleached all-purpose flour

2 tablespoons sugar

¹/₄ teaspoon salt

2 tablespoons unsalted butter, softened

1 extra-large egg

1 tablespoon milk

1 tablespoon fresh lemon juice

2 tablespoons brandy or rum

Vegetable oil for deep-frying

Confectioners' sugar for sprinkling

1. To make the dough using a food processor, combine all the ingredients in the bowl and process until a ball of dough starts to form. Add a little water if the mixture seems dry. The dough should be soft but not sticky, with the consistency of pasta dough. Turn the dough out onto a lightly floured surface and knead a few times.

To make the dough by hand, in a bowl, mix the flour, sugar, and salt. Work in the butter with your hands or a fork until the mixture resembles coarse meal. Add the egg, milk, lemon juice, and brandy or rum, and knead until a ball of dough forms.

2. Divide the dough into 4 pieces. Work with one piece at a time. Run each piece of dough through the rollers of a pasta machine to the thinnest setting. Alternatively, using a rolling pin, roll each piece out on a floured surface until it is about ⅛ inch thick.

3. With a pastry wheel, cut each piece into 5 by 1-inch strips. Twist each strip loosely and place on clean cloths.

4. In a deep-fryer or deep heavy pan, heat the vegetable oil to 375°F. Fry the strips about 12 at a time until golden brown. Drain on brown paper.

5. When cool, sprinkle the strips with confectioners' sugar.

Chiacchiere

Chatters

❧

Somewhere between a pastry and a cookie, these flaky, twisted strips of dough are usually made during Carnevale, the period just before Lent. Chiacchiere means "chit-chat," or "gossip," and like chatter that does not stop, you will not be able to stop eating these. The dough has the consistency of pasta dough, and if you have a hand-crank pasta machine, you can turn these out in no time at all. Mound these on a pretty plate for a party presentation.

❧

Makes 9 to 10 dozen

Occhi di Santa Lucia

Eyes of Saint Lucy

❧

Expressions of devotion on the Feast of Saint Lucy are not always in the form of prayer; the making of these cookies, formed in the shape of eyes, is a tradition in honor of this revered saint, the protector of eyesight. These fried cookies are best eaten warm as soon as they are made.

❧

Makes about 5 dozen

$4\,^2/_3$ to 5 cups unbleached all-purpose flour

1 cup sugar

$^1/_2$ teaspoon salt

2 large eggs, at room temperature

1 cup milk

Vegetable oil for deep-frying

Confectioners' sugar for sprinkling

1. In a bowl, mix together 4 cups of the flour, 2 tablespoons of the sugar, and the salt.

2. In a medium bowl, whisk the eggs and milk together. Stir the mixture into the flour mixture, adding enough additional flour to make a soft ball of dough.

3. On a floured surface, knead the dough until smooth and no longer sticky. Divide the dough in half. Roll out each piece into a rectangle about 15 by 12 inches. Sprinkle each rectangle evenly with half of the remaining sugar and roll up tightly like a jelly roll. Cut the rolls into $^1/_2$-inch-thick slices.

4. In a deep-fryer or deep heavy pot, heat the vegetable oil to 375°F. Fry the cookies, a few at a time, until golden brown. Remove with a slotted spoon to brown paper to drain. Sprinkle the cookies with confectioners' sugar and serve.

2¹/₂ cups unbleached all-purpose flour

1 tablespoon baking powder

1 tablespoon sugar

¹/₈ teaspoon salt

4 large eggs

2 large egg yolks

2 teaspoons olive oil

1 teaspoon fresh lemon juice

Grated zest of 1 lemon

Vegetable oil for deep-frying

Confectioners' sugar for coating

1. Sift the flour, baking powder, sugar, and salt, together into a bowl.

2. In another bowl, stir the eggs, egg yolks, olive oil, lemon juice, and zest together until well blended. Stir in the flour mixture to form a thick batter.

3. In a deep-fryer or deep heavy pot, heat the vegetable oil to 375°F. Drop tablespoons of the batter into the oil and fry until golden brown and puffed. Remove to brown paper to drain and cool.

4. Put the confectioners' sugar in a heavy paper bag. Add a few puffs at a time and shake them in the bag to coat with the sugar.

Crostoli

Fried Dough Puffs

Crostoli *means "crusty," and these fried puffs of dough remind me of fritters. They are made during Carnevale, just before Lent, and for Easter in the Naples area. This recipe is from my good friend Maria Castaldo Esposito.*

Makes about 2¹/₂ dozen

Eroi di Natale

Christmas Heroes

❧

At Christmastime in Italy, San Nicola (Saint Nicholas), Santa Lucia (Saint Lucy), and a lovable old witch known as Befana magically weave spells of anticipation and excitement, as they visit each child's house during the season of Christmas (Natale) and Epiphany (Epifania).

On December 5, the eve of the Feast of San Nicola, Italian children leave their shoes near their beds. If they have been good, the gentle saint leaves little boxes of sweet, chewy nougat studded with almonds, known as *torrone*, in their shoes. I remember hanging my stocking on December 5 in observance of Saint Nicholas, hoping that he would have a lapse of memory and not recall all the times that I had not lived up to my parents' expectations. On December 6, I would shake my stocking out to find one or two little blue boxes of torrone and plump, bright oranges. I knew then that I had a chance at Christmas, but I still had to pass muster with Saint Lucy, whose feast day came on December 13. Saint Lucy was a favorite with my Grandmother Saporito, who never let me forget how much this saint was revered in Sicily, as the patron saint of eyes and eyesight.

The story as told to me by Grandma had Saint Lucy riding through the snowy streets of the world on a kind and wise donkey's back. Her face was always veiled in heavy, snowy lace because she was blind, having sacrificed her eyesight to God. By magic, the donkey always knew exactly where good children lived. The children left their windows ajar before going to sleep, so that the donkey could come in. It was to those children that Saint Lucy paid a visit, leaving little gifts of sweetmeats and small toys.

Babbo Natale, Father Christmas, needs no explanation. He is celebrated in Italy as much as here. But here, on the day after Christmas, the magical figure is dismissed with lightning speed. In Italy bonfires and fairs in *piazze* both large and small continue the celebration until January 6, the Feast of The Three Kings. This is the day to expect a visit from Befana, a haggard, toothless old witch who lives in chimney tops. She is really a symbol of missed opportunity, but children love her because she too travels around Italy with a bagful of presents, in search of good children. She leaves toys and sweet treats, and there is also the occasional lump of coal—made from sugar—and garlic, for those who have been *un pò cattivo* (a little bit bad).

Christmas heroes are a part of tradition, reflecting a small part of the fabric of the Italian character, a character that observes in every season of the year the celebration of life and each person's connection to the spiritual.

Ravioli Dolci Fritti

Sweet Fried Ravioli

❧

Made from a spice-flavored dough, filled with ricotta cheese, cut like ravioli, fried, and showered with confectioners' sugar, these are the favorite Christmas cookies of my good friend Louis Terramagra. His Sicilian grandmother, Stella La Marca, was from Caltinasetta, and this cookie was her hallmark. The dough is very soft, so chilling it is recommended for easier handling. To make the job even easier, use a ravioli form, which yields a dozen squares at a time.

❧

Makes 5 1/2 to 6 dozen

DOUGH

1/2 cup sugar

1 large egg

1/2 cup milk

1 tablespoon lard or solid vegetable shortening, melted

1 teaspoon vanilla

2 1/4 to 2 1/2 cups unbleached all-purpose flour

1 1/2 teaspoons baking powder

1/4 teaspoon ground cinnamon

1/4 teaspoon ground ginger

1/4 teaspoon grated nutmeg

1/2 teaspoon salt

FILLING

1 pound skim-milk ricotta cheese, well drained

1/2 cup confectioners' sugar

2 tablespoons unbleached all-purpose flour

1 tablespoon grated orange zest

Vegetable oil for deep-frying
Confectioners' sugar for sprinkling

1. In a bowl, mix together the sugar, egg, milk, lard or shortening, and vanilla.

2. Sift together 2 1/4 cups flour, the baking powder, spices, and salt to another bowl. Add the egg mixture and mix with your hands until a ball of dough is formed, adding additional flour if the dough seems very sticky; this is a soft dough. Wrap the dough in wax paper and refrigerate for at least several hours, or overnight.

3. In a bowl, combine the ricotta cheese, confectioners' sugar, flour, and orange zest. Refrigerate, covered, until ready to use.

4. Divide the dough into 4 pieces. Work with one piece at a time, keeping the rest covered and refrigerated.

5. To make the ravioli using a ravioli form, divide each piece of dough in half. On a floured surface, roll out each piece into a 12 by 5-inch strip. Place one strip over the bottom section of the form. Make slight impressions in the dough with the top part of the form. Place a scant teaspoonful of the filling in the center of each impression, and cover with a second strip of dough. Roll over the top of the form with a rolling pin until the teeth of the form show through the dough. Turn the form over and shake out the ravioli. Place the ravioli on kitchen towel–lined cookie sheets and refrigerate for 15 minutes before frying.

To shape the ravioli by hand, on a floured surface, roll each piece of dough out to about ¼ inch thick. Using a pastry wheel, cut into squares of the desired size. Place a spoonful of filling in the center of half the squares and top each one with a second square. Seal the edges of the ravioli with a fork dipped in flour, place on towel–lined cookie sheets and refrigerate as above.

6. In a deep-fryer or deep heavy pot, heat the vegetable oil to 375°F. Fry the ravioli, a few at a time, until golden brown. Drain on brown paper and let cool slightly, then sprinkle with confectioners' sugar.

Meringhe

Meringues

❧

Wispy meringues, pink puffs of melt-in-your-mouth lightness, with a scattering of colored confetti over their tops make a holiday statement when they come out of the oven. Although they are found all over Italy, I am partial to the huge pink ones of Assisi. Meringues require nothing more than egg whites and sugar, with a little flavoring. In this version, I have used Alchermes as a flavoring and coloring agent. This syrupy-red clove and cinnamon liqueur, made from cochineal, can be found in Italian specialty stores (for Mail-Order Sources, see page 331). Red food coloring or cranberry juice are other options, or just leave the meringues uncolored.

❧

Makes 4 dozen

4 large egg whites, at room temperature
3³/₄ cups sifted confectioners' sugar
2 teaspoons Alchermes liqueur or other flavoring (see headnote)
Colored sprinkles

Parchment paper

1. Preheat the oven to 300°F. Line two cookie sheets with parchment paper, or lightly butter and flour them. In a clean glass or copper bowl, with an electric mixer, beat the egg whites and 2 cups of the confectioners' sugar together until smooth. Beat in the remaining 1³/₄ cups sugar and the Alkermes or other flavoring and continue beating until stiff glossy peaks form.

2. Fill a large pastry bag fitted with a large star tip with the meringue. Pipe 1¹/₂-inch meringues onto the cookie sheets, spacing them about 1 inch apart. Sprinkle the tops of the meringues with colored sprinkles.

3. Bake, rotating the sheets once or twice, for about 1 hour, or until the meringues are firm and completely dry. Remove from the parchment paper and let cool completely on wire racks.

Variation: Sandwich the meringues together with sweetened whipped cream and serve with sliced strawberries for an elegant dessert.

14 tablespoons (1³⁄₄ sticks) unsalted butter, softened

1 cup confectioners' sugar

1 tablespoon vanilla

2 cups unbleached all-purpose flour, sifted

3 large egg whites, at room temperature

GLAZE (OPTIONAL)

4 ounces bittersweet chocolate, coarsely chopped

Parchment paper

1. Preheat the oven to 450°F and position the racks in the center and upper part of the oven. Line two cookie sheets with parchment paper, or lightly butter and flour them. In a bowl, with an electric mixer, beat the butter, sugar, and vanilla until creamy. Gradually beat in the flour, a few spoonfuls at a time.

2. In a clean bowl, with clean beaters, beat the egg whites until stiff but not dry peaks form. Fold the whites into the butter mixture, taking care not to deflate the whites.

3. Fill a pastry bag fitted with a ¹⁄₂-inch plain tip with the batter and pipe out 3-inch-long cookies on the cookie sheets, spacing them 1 inch apart.

4. Bake for 5 to 7 minutes, rotating the sheets once, until the cookies are firm to the touch but still pale and only very lightly browned around the edges. Remove them to cooling racks.

5. If making the glaze, bring 2 cups of water to a simmer in the base of a double boiler. Turn off the heat. Place the chocolate in the top of the double boiler and let sit, stirring occasionally, until it melts.

6. Spread the tops of the cookies with a thin layer of glaze, and let it set. Or use the glaze to sandwich the cookies.

Lingue di Gatto

Cats' Tongues

❧

There are many versions of lingue di gatto (cats' tongues), but this remains my favorite. It is a very versatile cookie that looks like a ladyfinger or, by a short stretch of the imagination, a tongue. Serve them as is, or frost the tops with a thin glaze of bittersweet chocolate. Or sandwich them together with chocolate and a smidge of jam, or just with jam alone.

❧

Makes 3¹⁄₂ dozen

Pizzelle Bicolori

Two-Colored Waffle Cookies

Like the White-and-Black Biscotti on page 230, these waffle cookies are a departure from the traditional plain ones, made with two flavors of batter. Sweet baking cocoa is added to half the batter, while the remaining half is left plain. Spoonfuls of each one are placed side by side in a pizzelle iron so the batter fuses, creating a half-and-half waffle cookie. If you like, roll the warm cookies around cannoli forms, then let cool before sliding the forms out.

Fill the rolled pizzelle with sweetened whipped cream or pastry cream. Pizzelle, called brigidini *in some parts of Italy, are a treat at street fairs.*

Makes about 4 dozen

3 1/2 cups unbleached all-purpose flour

1 tablespoon baking powder

1/8 teaspoon salt

12 tablespoons (1 1/2 sticks) unsalted butter, softened

1 1/4 cups sugar

5 extra-large eggs, at room temperature

1 tablespoon almond extract or vanilla

1/4 cup sweet cocoa, such as Ghirardelli, or 1/4 cup unsweetened cocoa plus 2 tablespoons sugar

1. In a medium bowl, sift together the flour, baking powder, and salt.

2. In another bowl, beat the butter and sugar together with a sturdy wire whisk or an electric mixer. Whisk or beat in the eggs one at a time until well blended. Add the almond extract or vanilla. Using a wooden spoon or the mixer, add the flour mixture, mixing until well blended.

3. Remove half the batter to another bowl and stir in the cocoa, blending well.

4. Heat a pizzelle maker according to the manufacturer's directions. If it is not nonstick, you may want to spray the iron first with baking spray or lightly brush with vegetable oil.

5. Place a scant teaspoon of plain batter slightly off-center in the pizzelle maker. Add a scant teaspoon of the chocolate batter slightly off-center, just touching the plain batter. Close the lid and cook until golden brown, about 1 minute, depending on the pizzelle maker.

6. With the end of a small fork, carefully remove the pizzelle to a wire rack to cool completely. Repeat with the remaining batter.

7. Alternatively, remove the pizzelle from the form and immediately roll them around cannoli forms. Place them seam side down on wire racks to cool. When cool, slip the pizzelle off the form.

Note: The plain cookies can be frozen in airtight containers for up to two months.

Crostate e Torte

Tarts and Cakes

Crostata di Fichi Secchi, Pere, e Pignoli

Dried Fig, Pear, and Pine Nut Pie

❦

A crostata is a two-crusted pie. This one is a favorite of my husband, Guy, because it reminds him of another holiday favorite, mincemeat. Pasta frolla (pastry dough) encases a dense filling of dried figs, fresh pears, pine nuts, and candied orange peel. I use tiny Seckel pears in this recipe, but ripe Bosc pears will work too.

❦

Serves 8

PASTRY DOUGH

2 cups unbleached all-purpose flour

¼ teaspoon salt

½ cup sugar

6 tablespoons unsalted butter, softened

2 large egg yolks, slightly beaten

2 tablespoons cold water, or more as needed

FILLING

½ cup pine nuts

½ pound dried Calimyrna figs

1 pound pears, cored and thinly sliced lengthwise

1 tablespoon fresh lemon juice

⅓ cup diced candied orange peel

2 tablespoons sugar

1 tablespoon milk

1 tablespoon turbinado (coarse brown) sugar

1. In a bowl or in a food processor, mix the flour, salt, and sugar together. Work in the butter with a pastry blender, or pulse several times, until the mixture resembles coarse meal. Blend in the yolks and water, or add through the feed tube and pulse to blend, until a ball of dough is formed. If the dough seems dry, add a little more water. Divide the dough into two pieces, one slightly larger than the other, and wrap in plastic wrap. Refrigerate for 1 hour.

2. Preheat the oven to 350°F. Place the pine nuts on a cookie sheet and lightly toast them, about 7 minutes. Watch carefully so they do not burn. Place the pine nuts in a small bowl, and set aside. Increase the oven temperature to 425°F.

3. Put the figs in a saucepan, cover with water, and bring to a gentle boil. Simmer for about 10 minutes, until softened. Drain and let cool.

4. Remove the stems, cut the figs into small pieces, and place in a large bowl. Add the pears, lemon juice, orange peel, and sugar and toss well. Cover and let marinate while you roll out the dough.

5. Lightly butter an 11-inch tart pan with a removable bottom. On a floured surface, roll out the larger piece of dough to a 14-inch circle. Fit the dough into the tart pan, and trim off the excess dough. (If the dough tears, simply patch it with the scraps.)

6. Spread the filling evenly in the tart pan.

7. Roll the remaining dough into a 12-inch circle. Using a pastry wheel, cut twelve ½-inch-wide strips. Make a crisscross or lattice top on the filling with the strips, trim the ends, and pinch the ends to seal. Brush the strips with the milk and sprinkle the turbinado sugar evenly over the top.

8. Bake for 30 to 35 minutes, or until the crust is golden brown. Cool completely on a wire rack, and cut into wedges to serve.

Crostata di Rabarbaro e Ficchi Secchi

Rhubarb and Fig Pie

❦

Tart rhubarb and sweet dried figs create a delicious filling for an unusual lattice-crust pie. I make it in celebration of spring, but I also harvest and freeze some of the deep ruby-colored stalks so I can make this jewel-like pie any time of the year.

❦

Serves 6 to 8

DOUGH

2 ½ cups unbleached all-purpose flour

½ cup sugar

¼ teaspoon salt

8 tablespoons (1 stick) unsalted butter, cut into pieces

1 large egg

1 large egg yolk

Grated zest of 1 lemon

2 ½ tablespoons fresh lemon juice

FILLING

1 ¼ pounds rhubarb, trimmed and cut into 1-inch chunks

¾ cup sugar

½ cup water

¾ cup chopped Calimyrna figs (¼ pound)

1 tablespoon vanilla

½ cup slivered almonds

1 tablespoon turbinado (coarse brown) sugar

1. In a food processor or in a bowl, mix together the flour, sugar, and salt. Add the butter and pulse, or cut in with a pastry blender, until the mixture resembles coarse cornmeal. Add the egg, egg yolk, lemon zest, and juice through the feed tube, or stir in, and pulse or mix just until a dough starts to form. Gather the dough into a ball and wrap in wax paper. Refrigerate for 30 minutes.

2. Meanwhile, make the filling: In a medium saucepan, combine the rhubarb, sugar, and water. Cook, stirring, over low heat until the mixture thickens. Remove from the heat and stir in the figs and vanilla. Cover and refrigerate.

3. Preheat the oven to 375°F. Divide the dough in half. On a lightly floured board surface, roll out one piece to a 13-inch circle. Fit it into a 10-inch tart pan with a removable bottom, and trim off the excess dough.

4. Spoon the filling into the pan. Sprinkle the almonds evenly over the top.

5. Roll out the second piece of dough to an 11-inch circle. With a pastry wheel, cut the dough into ½-inch-wide strips. Make a lattice top for the tart. Pinch the ends of the strips into the bottom pastry. Scatter the turbinado sugar over the top of the tart.

6. Bake for 40 to 45 minutes, or until the lattice top is nicely browned. Remove from the oven and let cool completely on a rack. Cut into wedges to serve.

Note: If you wish, use any leftover dough to make miniature tarts and fill them with jam.

Crostata Fragolina

Strawberry Tart

❧

Only sweet ripe strawberries will do for this wonderful tart. Make the dough ahead and chill it; the filling can be made the day before too. This tart can also be made without the pastry cream filling, using only the strawberries and the strawberry orange glaze. Raspberries, blueberries, and nectarines can also be used in season. Mascarpone cheese is a sweet creamy cheese used in many Italian desserts. If it is unavailable, substitute a good cream cheese.

❧

Serves 8

FILLING

4 large egg yolks

1/4 cup sugar

2 tablespoons plus 1 teaspoon unbleached all-purpose flour

1 cup milk

1/4 cup mascarpone cheese, at room temperature

DOUGH

1 1/4 cups unbleached all-purpose flour

2 tablespoons sugar

1/8 teaspoon salt

8 tablespoons (1 stick) cold unsalted butter, cut into pieces

1/4 cup cold water

1 tablespoon strawberry or apple jelly, melted

GLAZE

3 pints strawberries

1/2 cup water

2/3 cup sugar

2 tablespoons cornstarch

2 1/2 tablespoons Orange Liqueur (page 320)

1. In the top of a double boiler, off the heat, whisk together the egg yolks and sugar. Whisk in the flour until well blended. Whisk in the milk. Cook over medium heat, whisking, until the filling begins to thicken and coats the whisk. Pour the filling into a bowl. Cover with a piece of buttered wax paper, pressing it against the surface of the filling, and refrigerate for several hours, or overnight.

2. In a food processor, combine the flour, sugar, and salt, and process to blend. Add the butter and process until the mixture resembles coarse cornmeal. With the motor running, add the water through the feed tube and process just until a ball of dough begins to form. Do not overprocess the dough, or it will be tough. Alternatively, in a bowl, mix the flour, sugar, and salt. With a fork or pastry blender, work in the butter until the mixture resembles coarse cornmeal. Add the water and stir to form a dough.

3. Gather the dough into a ball and wrap in plastic wrap. Refrigerate for 1 hour, or overnight.

4. Preheat the oven to 425°F, and place a rack in the center of the oven. On a lightly floured surface, roll the dough out into a 14-inch circle. Fit the dough into an 11-inch tart pan with a removable bottom, and trim the excess dough. Prick the dough all over with a fork.

5. Bake the tart shell for about 15 minutes, or until golden brown. Remove to a cooling rack and immediately brush it with the jam. Let cool completely.

6. Hull the strawberries and wipe them clean with a damp towel; do not wash the berries, or the tart will be soggy. Chop enough of the berries to make ½ cup. Put the chopped berries in a saucepan, add the water, and bring to a boil, crushing the berries with a wooden spoon to release their juices. Pour the mixture into a fine strainer set over a bowl, and set the saucepan aside. Press on the berries to release as much juice as possible, then discard the strawberry pulp. You should have about ⅔ cup juice.

7. In the saucepan, stir together the sugar and cornstarch, making sure there are no lumps. Slowly stir in the strawberry juice and blend well. Cook over medium heat, stirring, until the glaze thickens to the consistency of honey. Remove the from the heat and stir in the orange liqueur. Cover to keep warm.

8. Stir the mascarpone cheese into the cream filling. Spread the filling over the cooled tart shell. Arrange the remaining whole strawberries decoratively over the filling. With a pastry brush, paint the strawberries with the glaze, letting it run down between the berries.

9. Place the tart on a serving plate and refrigerate for several hours before serving. To serve, cut into wedges. (This is best eaten the day it is made.)

Torta di Lampone e Ricotta

Raspberry and Ricotta Tart

❧

Sometimes taking liberties with culinary traditions can bring a nice surprise, as is the case with this delicate ricotta cream and fruit tart in a lemon-flavored poppy seed (papavero) pasta frolla crust. Make this in the summer, when fresh berries are at their best. Use raspberries, blackberries, or blueberries, or a combination. The dough makes enough for two nine- or ten-inch tart shells. Freeze one unbaked for later use (if you have only one tart pan, simply freeze half the dough and roll it out later).

❧

Serves 8

DOUGH

1½ cups unbleached all-purpose flour

2 tablespoons sugar

¼ teaspoon salt

8 tablespoons (1 stick) cold unsalted butter, cut into small pieces

1 large egg

1 tablespoon ice water

2 tablespoons grated lemon zest

2 tablespoons poppy seeds

1 tablespoon apricot jam

FILLING

½ cup sugar

1½ tablespoons cornstarch

2 large eggs

⅛ teaspoon salt

1 cup heavy cream

1 tablespoon unsalted butter, softened

1 cup ricotta cheese, well drained

2 cups raspberries

1. In a bowl or food processor, combine the flour, sugar, and salt. Add the butter and cut in with a pastry blender, or until the mixture is the consistency of coarse cornmeal. Add the egg, water, lemon zest, and poppy seeds and stir or process until a ball of dough is formed. Divide the dough in half. Wrap each piece in plastic wrap and refrigerate for 30 minutes.

2. Preheat the oven to 425°F. Roll one piece between two sheets of wax paper to an 11-inch circle and fit it into a 9-inch tart pan with a removable bottom. (Roll out the remaining dough, and freeze for future use.) Prick the dough all over with a fork. Line the dough with parchment paper or foil and fill the paper with dried beans or rice. Bake the shell for 12 minutes, or until golden brown.

3. Set the tart pan on a wire rack. Carefully remove the beans and wax paper. Immediately brush the shell with the jam. Let cool completely.

4. Sift together ¼ cup of the sugar and the cornstarch into a large bowl.

5. In a medium bowl, whisk the eggs with the salt until frothy. Gradually whisk the eggs into the cornstarch mixture.

6. In a double boiler, heat the cream with 2 tablespoons of the sugar, stirring with a wooden spoon until the sugar dissolves. Add half the cream to the cornstarch mixture, stirring constantly. Pour the cornstarch mixture into the double boiler and cook over medium heat, stirring constantly, until the custard thickens enough to coat the back of a spoon. Remove from the heat and stir in the butter. Transfer the custard to a bowl and let cool slightly.

7. In a small bowl, beat the ricotta cheese and the remaining 2 tablespoons sugar until smooth. Gently stir the ricotta into the custard. Refrigerate, covered, until chilled, about 1½ hours.

8. To assemble the tart, spread the filling evenly in the tart shell. Arrange the berries on top of the filling. Refrigerate for 3 hours. To serve, cut into wedges.

Torta Ripiena di Ricotta

Ricotta Pie

❧

This rich sheep's-milk ricotta pie was served to my husband and me by my friend Maria Iapichino, whose home in Cefalù on the northern coast of Sicily overlooks the sea. Shepherds and their flocks are all you see for miles in the interior of Sicily. Sheep's-milk ricotta cheese, a by-product of Pecorino cheese, is much stronger in flavor than the cow's-milk ricotta found in our supermarkets. I used skim-milk ricotta in the recipe with excellent results.

❧

Serves 6

FILLING

3 cups skim-milk ricotta cheese, well drained

$^1/_2$ cup sugar

1 tablespoon vanilla

One $3^1/_2$-ounce bar milk chocolate, chopped

1 tablespoon grated orange zest

DOUGH

3 cups (12 ounces) unbleached all-purpose flour

$^1/_2$ teaspoon salt

8 tablespoons (1 stick) unsalted butter, cut into pieces

2 large eggs, lightly beaten

2 to $2^1/_2$ tablespoons ice water

1 egg, beaten

1. Preheat the oven to 375°F. In a bowl, combine all the filling ingredients. Cover and refrigerate while you make the crust.

2. In a bowl, mix the flour and salt together. Add the butter and, with a pastry blender, work the butter into the flour until the mixture resembles coarse crumbs. Add the eggs and ice water and mix with your hands until a ball of dough is formed. Wrap the dough in wax paper and chill for 10 to 15 minutes.

3. Divide the dough in half. On a floured surface, roll out one piece of the dough to a 12-inch round. Fit it into a 9-inch pie dish. Scoop the filling into the crust.

4. Roll out the second piece of dough to an 11-inch round and place it on top of the filling. Trim the excess dough and pinch the edges to seal them. With a skewer, make tiny holes all over the crust. Brush the top crust with the beaten egg.

5. Bake for 35 to 40 minutes, or until the crust is nicely browned. Let the pie cool completely before cutting into wedges.

3 tablespoons toasted bread crumbs

2 Golden Delicious apples, peeled and thinly sliced

¼ cup fresh lemon juice

2 large eggs, at room temperature

¾ cup sugar

6 tablespoons unsalted butter, melted

½ cup cold milk

1 tablespoon vanilla

2 cups unbleached all-purpose flour

1¼ tablespoons baking powder

1. Preheat the oven to 350°F. Butter a 9-inch round cake pan and coat it with the bread crumbs. Refrigerate.

2. Place the apples in a bowl, pour the lemon juice over them, and toss to coat. Set aside.

3. In a large bowl, with an electric mixer, beat the eggs with the sugar until light-colored. Beat in the butter. Beat in the milk and then the vanilla.

4. Sift the flour and the baking powder together. Add to the egg mixture a little at a time, beating well after each addition. Fold in the apples. Spoon the batter into the pan.

5. Bake for about 45 minutes, or until the cake is firm to the touch and nicely browned on top and a cake tester inserted in the center comes out clean. Cool the cake in the pan on a rack. Turn out onto a plate and cut into wedges to serve.

Torta di Mele alla Raffaella

Raffaella's Apple Cake

☙

This is a good winter cake that goes well with afternoon tea or coffee. The recipe comes from my friend Raffaella Neviani, who lives in Reggio Emilia. Use Golden Delicious apples in the batter, which, in Raffaella's words, make this cake "squisita!"

☙

Serves 6 to 8

Torta di Mele e Pere

Apple and Pear Cake

❦

Thinly sliced apples and pears nestled in a rich batter produce a light and moist cake that is a perfect winter dessert. For a Christmas touch, use red pears, which provide a hint of color.

❦

Serves 8

2 cups unbleached all-purpose flour

1 teaspoon baking powder

1/4 teaspoon salt

3/4 cup sugar

2 large eggs

1/4 cup milk

6 tablespoons unsalted butter, softened

1 tablespoon fresh lemon juice

2 medium apples, peeled and thinly sliced

2 medium pears, unpeeled, thinly sliced

1 teaspoon ground cinnamon

1. Preheat the oven to 350°F. Brush a 10-inch tart pan with a removable bottom with butter. Sift the flour, baking powder, and salt together into a bowl.

2. In another bowl, beat 1/2 cup of the sugar and the eggs until smooth and light-colored. Beat in the milk. Then beat in the butter and lemon juice. Gradually beat in the flour mixture until smooth.

3. Spread the batter evenly in the tart pan. Arrange the apple and pear slices in circles on top of the batter, alternating them and overlapping slightly.

4. In a small bowl, mix the remaining 1/4 cup sugar and the cinnamon together. Sprinkle the mixture evenly over the top of the tart. Bake for 45 minutes, or until a cake tester inserted into the middle comes out clean.

5. Cool the tart on a rack. Remove the sides of the pan, place the tart on a serving plate, and cut into wedges.

2 cups unbleached all-purpose flour

1 1/3 cups finely ground cornmeal

1 cup whole almonds, finely chopped

1 cup sugar

8 tablespoons (1 stick) unsalted butter, at room temperature

1/2 cup lard

3 large eggs

1 tablespoon vanilla

Grated zest of 1 lemon

Confectioners' sugar for sprinkling

1. Preheat the oven to 350°F. Lightly grease a 10 by 2-inch round cake pan. In a bowl, mix the flour, cornmeal, almonds, and sugar together. With a pastry blender or your hands, work in the butter and lard until the mixture is the consistency of coarse cornmeal.

2. In a medium bowl, beat the eggs, vanilla, and lemon zest together. Add to the flour and blend with your hands. The batter will be very stiff.

3. Pat the batter into the pan, smoothing the top. Bake for 35 to 40 minutes, or until the top is nicely browned.

4. Let the cake cool completely in the pan on a rack, then dust the top with confectioners' sugar. Cut into wedges to serve.

Variation: Serve the cake as a shortcake, either split in half or whole, with sliced and sugared fresh strawberries or other fruits. It is also good with ice cream.

Torta Sbrisolona

Crumbly Cake

❧

This flat, crumbly cake comes from Mantua in the region of Lombardy. My friend Terri Rozzi, who comes from that region, gave me her recipe, which I have altered slightly. Use finely ground cornmeal; if you have only coarse cornmeal, grind it fine in a food processor. This batter is more the consistency of a dough; don't be surprised by its compactness and dryness, which give it its crumbly texture and its name. This is a good cake to have on hand for company.

❧

Serves 8

Torta di Agnello

Easter Lamb Cake

❧

Pass by pastry shop windows in Italy at Eastertime and you will see an array of Easter lamb cakes, some filled with almond paste, others with candied fruits and nuts in the batter. People buy them as the centerpiece for their Easter table and to give as an appropriate gift of the season. To make this cake, you will need a lamb cake mold, available in cake decorating or kitchenware stores.

❧

Serves 8 to 10

CAKE

2 cups cake flour

³/₄ teaspoon baking powder

¹/₈ teaspoon grated nutmeg

¹/₄ teaspoon salt

¹/₂ pound (2 sticks) unsalted butter or margarine

1 cup sugar

2 teaspoons grated lemon zest

1 teaspoon grated orange zest

1 tablespoon vanilla

1 teaspoon almond extract

4 large eggs

¹/₂ cup finely ground hazelnuts

FROSTING

¹/₂ cup solid vegetable shortening

8 tablespoons (1 stick) unsalted butter, softened

8 cups confectioners' sugar

1 tablespoon almond extract

Currants for the lamb's eyes
Almond confetti
Colored ribbon

1. Preheat the oven to 350°F. Grease a 10 by 4-inch two-piece lamb cake mold well with butter and dust it with flour. Sift the flour, baking powder, nutmeg, and salt together into a bowl.

2. In another bowl, with an electric mixer, beat the butter and sugar until pale yellow. Beat in the zests, vanilla, and almond extracts. Beat in the eggs one a time, then gradually beat in the flour mixture. Fold in the nuts.

3. Spoon the batter into the bottom half of the mold. Place the top piece of the mold over the bottom, making sure the fit is even.

Bake for 40 to 45 minutes. Carefully lift off the top of the mold and test the cake for doneness; if it is still soft in the middle, bake about 10 to 15 minutes longer, until firm, without replacing the mold top. A cake tester inserted in the middle should come out clean. Remove the mold to a rack to cool completely.

4. In a bowl, beat the shortening and butter until smooth. Gradually beat in the sugar. Beat in the almond extract. The frosting should be firm enough to pipe through a pastry bag. Chill if necessary.

5. Run a knife around the edges of the mold and carefully remove the cake. Stand the cake upright on a cake stand or decorative platter. You may need to glue the base of the cake to the serving dish by spreading some frosting on it.

6. Fill a pastry bag fitted with a medium star tip with frosting and squiggle the frosting over the cake to simulate wool. Use the currants for eyes and sprinkle almond confetti along the lamb's back and at the base of the cake to give it a festive look. Tie a ribbon carefully around the neck. To serve, cut the cake into thin slices.

Pandoro

This traditional Christmas cake from Verona is named pandoro, *"golden bread," because of its pleasing yellow color. Light and airy in texture, the cake is baked in a special star-shaped mold, but it can also be baked in coffee cans or other deep molds. Start the process early in the day: The cake requires making a sponge first and then letting the dough rise several times. I make these ahead and freeze them well wrapped in foil. They make a beautiful gift from your kitchen and a delight for breakfast on Christmas morning.*

Makes 2; serves 16

SPONGE

$^1/_4$ cup warm (110° to 115°F) water

1 package active dry yeast

1 teaspoon sugar

1 large egg yolk, at room temperature

$^1/_2$ cup unbleached all-purpose flour

DOUGH

$4^1/_2$ to 5 cups unbleached all-purpose flour

7 large egg yolks

$^3/_4$ cup sugar

3 tablespoons unsalted butter, softened

$^1/_2$ cup water

1 large egg

Grated zest of 1 large lemon

$^1/_4$ cup apricot jam

Confectioners' sugar for sprinkling

1. Pour the water into a small bowl and stir in the yeast, sugar, egg yolk, and flour. Blend well. Cover with plastic wrap and place the sponge in a warm place to rise until doubled in size, about 2 hours.

2. Mound 3 cups of the flour on a work surface and make a well in the center.

3. Beat together in a bowl 4 of the egg yolks, $^1/_2$ cup of the sugar, the butter, and water. Add the sponge and mix well. Pour the mixture into the well in the flour. With your hands, work the flour from the inside walls of the well into the sponge until a soft and somewhat sticky ball of dough is formed. Sprinkle a little additional flour on the work surface and knead the dough for 5 to 10 minutes. Resist adding too much flour—the dough should remain tacky to the touch.

4. Lightly grease a large bowl with butter, add the dough, and turn to coat. Cover the bowl tightly with plastic wrap and then a towel, and place it in a warm place to rise for 2 hours.

5. Punch down the dough, leaving it in the bowl. Add 1½ cups more flour, the remaining 3 egg yolks, the whole egg, the remaining ¼ cup sugar, and the lemon zest, and knead until blended.

6. Turn the dough out onto a floured surface and knead for 10 to 12 minutes, or until smooth and soft, adding additional flour if necessary. Put the dough into a lightly buttered bowl, turn to coat, and cover with plastic wrap and a towel. Let rise for 2 hours.

7. Butter and flour two 6 by 9-inch pandoro molds or coffee cans. Punch down the dough, and divide it in half. On a lightly floured surface board, knead each piece briefly and form into a ball. Place each ball in a mold, cover with a clean cloth, and let rise for about 1½ hours, or until the dough has risen two thirds of the way up the molds.

8. Preheat the oven to 375°F. Bake the cakes for 35 to 40 minutes, or until the tops are browned and a cake skewer inserted in the middle comes out clean. Let the cakes cool in the pans for 10 minutes, then unmold and let cool completely on wire racks.

9. Heat the apricot jam in a small saucepan, stirring until melted. Brush the tops of the cakes with the jam, then sprinkle heavily with confectioners' sugar. Slice into wedges to serve.

Note: If freezing the cakes, do not brush with jam or sprinkle with confectioners' sugar until defrosted.

Pandorato di Verona

Quick Veronese Christmas Cake

In addition to its renowned Christmas cake (see page 272), Verona is also famous for its large confection houses such as Bauli, which makes a quick version of pandoro called pandorato. This cake does not begin with a yeast starter; instead the batter is lightened with baking powder and stiffly beaten egg whites.

Using a pandoro mold is optional—any deep one-and-a-half-quart mold will do. The cake has an interesting biscuit-like texture and is very good with fresh fruit.

Serves 8

1 cup unbleached all-purpose flour

1 cup potato starch

1 teaspoon baking powder

9 tablespoons butter, softened

³/₄ cup sugar

4 large eggs, separated

1 tablespoon Cognac

1¹/₂ tablespoons fresh lemon juice

1 tablespoon vanilla

¹/₄ teaspoon cream of tartar

Confectioners' sugar for sprinkling

1. Preheat the oven to 350°F. Generously butter and flour a pandoro or other deep 1¹/₂-quart mold. Sift the flour, potato starch, and baking powder together into a bowl.

2. In a large bowl, with an electric mixer, beat the butter until smooth. Beat in the sugar, then beat in the egg yolks one at a time. Beat in the Cognac, lemon juice, and vanilla. Spoon the flour mixture over the egg yolk mixture a little at a time, beating well after each addition.

3. In another bowl, with clean beaters, beat the egg whites with the cream of tartar until stiff peaks form. With a rubber spatula, fold the whites into the egg yolk mixture. Fill the mold with the batter.

4. Bake for 45 to 50 minutes, or until a cake tester inserted in the middle of the cake comes out clean. Let the cake cool in the mold on a rack for 30 minutes.

5. Gently run a knife around the edges of the mold, turn the mold upside down, and gently shake the cake loose. Let the cake cool completely, then dust the top with confectioners' sugar. Cut into wedges to serve.

1 cup hazelnuts

1/2 cup candied orange peel, finely chopped

1/3 cup candied lemon peel, finely chopped

1/2 cup plus 1 tablespoon unbleached all-purpose flour

1/4 cup unsweetened cocoa

1 teaspoon ground cinnamon

1/2 teaspoon ground cloves

1/2 teaspoon ground white pepper

1/4 teaspoon mace or ground nutmeg

1/2 cup sugar

1/2 cup honey

Confectioners' sugar for sprinkling

1. Preheat the oven to 400°F. Grease an 8 or 9-inch pie pan or round cake pan with butter. Line the bottom of the pan with parchment paper and grease the paper. Place the hazelnuts on a baking sheet and toast in the oven for 5 to 8 minutes. Let cool. Reduce the oven temperature to 325°F.

2. Coarsely chop the hazelnuts. Put them in a bowl, add the candied citrus peel, flour, cocoa, and spices, and mix well. Set aside.

3. In a saucepan, combine the sugar and honey and bring to a boil, stirring until the sugar is dissolved. Cook, stirring constantly, for 5 minutes or until a spoonful of the mixture forms a ball when dropped into a small bowl of cold water.

4. Add the sugar syrup to the flour and nut mixture and stir to mix well. Pour into the pan and pat the top smooth.

5. Bake for 30 to 35 minutes, until firm to the touch and a cake tester inserted in the middle comes out clean. Carefully turn the cake out onto a rack and remove the parchment paper. Invert the cake onto another rack and let cool completely.

6. Sprinkle the cake liberally with confectioners' sugar. Cut into small wedges to serve.

Panforte di Siena

Fruitcake from Siena

❧

Although panforte *literally means "strong bread," this is more like a spicy, dense flat cake. It is a specialty of Siena, but its origins date back to the Renaissance, when it was characteristic to use an abundance of spices in many foods for both flavor and preservation. Panforte is enjoyed year-round, but it is especially welcome at Christmastime, wrapped in its artistic Renaissance-inspired paper.*

❧

Serves 10 to 12

Cartocci ca Crema di Ricotta

Ricotta-Filled Pastry Cones

❧

The yeast dough for these cones is soft and elastic. Shaping the dough into cones makes me think of the paper cones that Sicilians snack from on the streets of Palermo. This recipe makes a lot of dough; I use it when I want to serve a nifty Sicilian dessert to a crowd. The cones can be frozen for up to one month and used as needed. The filling, which makes enough for about two dozen cones, can be made a day ahead. Fill the cones just before serving. The stainless steel cone forms can be found at kitchenware stores (or see Mail-Order Sources, page 331).

❧

Makes 5 dozen cones; makes 4 cups filling, enough to fill 2 dozen cones

DOUGH

1 small cake fresh yeast (0.6 ounce) or 1 tablespoon active dry yeast

1¼ cups warm (110° to 115°F) water

12 tablespoons (1½ sticks) unsalted butter, softened

5 large eggs, at room temperature

1 cup sugar

⅛ teaspoon salt

8 to 8½ cups unbleached all-purpose flour

FILLING

Two 16-ounce containers ricotta cheese, well drained

1½ cups sugar

½ cup diced candied orange peel

½ cup diced candied lemon peel

1½ tablespoons ground cinnamon

One 12-ounce bar milk chocolate with almonds, chopped

Vegetable oil for deep-frying
Confectioners' sugar for sprinkling

1. In a large bowl, crumble or sprinkle the yeast over ¼ cup of the warm water. Stir to dissolve. Let proof, covered, for about 10 minutes, until foamy. Add the remaining water and stir to blend.

2. In another bowl, using an electric mixer, cream the butter with the sugar and salt. Stir into the yeast, then beat in the eggs. Add 5 cups of the flour and mix in with your hands. (Or use a mixer with a dough hook to make the dough.) Gradually add additional flour until a smooth ball of dough is formed.

3. Turn the dough out onto a floured surface and knead for about 5 minutes. Grease a deep bowl with olive oil, place the dough in the bowl, and turn to coat. Tightly cover the bowl with plastic wrap and let rise in a warm place until doubled in size, about 1½ hours.

4. In a bowl, with an electric mixer, beat the ricotta cheese until smooth. Beat in the remaining filling ingredients. Cover and refrigerate until ready to use.

5. Punch down the dough and knead it for a few minutes. Divide the dough into 15 equal pieces. Divide each piece in quarters and place on clean towels. Keep the pieces covered as you work.

6. On a floured surface, roll each piece into a narrow rectangle about 10 inches long and 2 inches wide. Wrap each strip around a 4-inch-long stainless steel pastry cone, starting at the bottom of the cone and overlapping the dough as you wrap it to the top. Seal the end with a little cold water. Place on clean towels and let rise, covered, for about 15 minutes.

7. In a deep-fryer or deep heavy pot, heat the vegetable oil to 375°F. Fry the cones, a few at a time, until golden brown. Carefully remove them with a slotted spoon and let drain on brown paper.

8. When ready to serve, fill a tipless pastry bag with the filling and fill the cones. (Or use a spoon to fill them.) Sprinkle with confectioners' sugar and serve.

Torta di Ricotta con Salsa di Melagrana

Ricotta Cheesecake with Pomegranate Sauce

❦

Christmas cooking would not be complete without pomegranates. The fruit is often depicted in Italian works of religious art. It is said that the multitude of seeds, nestled together so neatly in one fruit, is like the union of people who make up one church. For eating, the seeds are squeezed to make a drink called granatina, or they are sprinkled into salads of bitter chicories. This recipe is a modern departure for another use of the fruit, as a sauce for ricotta cheesecake. The cake, as well as the sauce, can be made two days ahead. Skim-milk ricotta best approximates the texture of Italian ricotta.

❦

Serves 8

CHEESECAKE

1 tablespoon unsalted butter, softened

One 16-ounce container skim-milk ricotta cheese, well drained

1 pound mascarpone cheese or cream cheese, softened

1 cup sugar

4 large eggs, separated

1/3 cup unbleached all-purpose flour

1 teaspoon salt

Pomegranate Sauce (recipe follows)

1. Preheat the oven to 325°F. Grease a 9-inch springform pan with the the butter. Line the bottom of the pan with parchment paper and grease the paper with the remaining butter. Generously dust the pan with flour and shake out the excess.

2. In a bowl, with an electric mixer, beat the cheeses until smooth. Beat in the sugar. Beat in the egg yolks one at a time, until well blended. Fold in the flour.

3. In another bowl, with clean beaters, beat the egg whites with the salt until stiff peaks form. Fold the egg whites into the cheese mixture. Pour the batter into the pan, and smooth the top with a spatula.

4. Bake for 1 hour and 10 minutes, or until a knife inserted in the center comes out clean.

5. Turn off the oven and leave the cake in the oven with the door ajar for 30 minutes. Remove the cake to a rack and let cool completely, then cover and refrigerate the cake for at least 2 hours.

6. To serve, run a knife around the edges of the cake to loosen it. Release the spring on the side of the pan and remove the spring-form ring. Put a serving dish over the top of the cake and invert it onto the plate. Remove the parchment paper.

7. Spread the pomegranate sauce evenly over the top of the cake. Cut the cake into wedges. (The sauce may be also be placed in a bowl and passed on the side.)

POMEGRANATE SAUCE

4 large pomegranates (about 3 pounds)

3 tablespoons cornstarch, sifted

³/₄ cup sugar

1. Cut the pomegranates in half. Place a fine mesh sieve over a large bowl. Using a spoon or your fingers, scrape the seeds into the sieve.

2. With a wooden spoon or a flat meat pounder, press on the seeds to extract 2 cups of juice. Discard the seeds and set the juice aside.

3. In a medium saucepan, mix the cornstarch with the sugar. Slowly stir in the pomegranate juice and mix well. Cook the sauce over medium heat, stirring constantly, until the sauce begins to thicken and darkens to a deep wine color, and the sauce coats the back of the spoon. Remove from the heat and let cool. The sauce may be made ahead and stored in a jar in the refrigerator. It will thicken somewhat if stored. When ready to use, thin with a little warm water if necessary.

Torta della Befana

Befana Cake

✦

This cake, which is more of a fruit-studded sweet bread, is traditionally made for the Feast of Epiphany, or Three Kings, the day when Befana, la vecchia (the old woman), brings gifts to children, hoping that one of them is the child king she refused to acknowledge centuries ago. Before the cake is baked, a large dried bean is kneaded into the dough. The cake is presented on a silver crown, and whoever receives the slice with the bean is king or queen for the day. This is a very old recipe that begins with a sponge, or starter, that sits in water to rise. Because this is a stiff and sticky dough, it is best to make it in a food processor.

Make it ahead for the holidays and freeze.

✦

Serves 8 to 10

DOUGH

1¼ cups raisins
½ cup diced candied lemon peel
½ cup diced candied orange peel
¼ cup brandy
1 tablespoon active dry yeast
½ cup warm (110° to 115°F) water
5 cups plus 2 tablespoons unbleached all-purpose flour
½ cup sugar
½ teaspoon salt
1 tablespoon grated lemon zest
8 tablespoons (1 stick) unsalted butter, cut into pieces, softened
2 large eggs
½ cup warm milk
½ cup chopped almonds
1 dried fava or other large bean

egg yolk
2 tablespoons turbinado (coarse brown) sugar

1. Put the raisins in a bowl, cover with warm water, and set aside to plump.

2. In a bowl, mix the citrus peels with the brandy. Set aside.

3. In a medium bowl, dissolve the yeast in the warm water. Add 1 cup of the flour and mix until a ball of dough is formed. Fill a large bowl two-thirds full with warm water. Place the ball of dough in the water, cover with plastic wrap, and let the sponge rise in a warm place until doubled, about 20 minutes.

4. In a food processor, combine 4 cups of the flour, sugar, salt, and lemon zest. Add the butter, eggs, and milk and process to a slightly stiff dough. With a slotted spoon, scoop the risen sponge from the water and add it to the dough. Process until thoroughly incorporated into the dough. If the dough seems too stiff, add a little tepid water.

5. Turn the dough out onto a lightly floured surface and knead for a few minutes. Butter a large bowl, place the dough in the bowl, and turn to coat. Cover with plastic wrap, then a towel, and let rise in a warm spot for 1 hour, or until doubled in size.

6. Butter a 10 by 3½-inch-deep round cake pan, ceramic pan, or tube pan. Dust with flour and shake out the excess. Drain the raisins, pat dry with paper towels, and toss with 1 tablespoon of the flour. Drain the candied citrus peels, reserving the brandy. Toss the peels with the remaining 1 tablespoon flour.

7. Punch down the dough. Turn the dough out onto a floured surface. With your hands, work the raisins, candied peels, almonds, and dried bean into the dough, and knead until you have a uniform ball of dough. It should feel slightly tacky.

8. Place the dough in the pan, cover with a towel, and let rise in a warm place for 1 hour, until doubled in size.

9. Preheat the oven to 350°F. In a small bowl, beat the egg yolk and reserved brandy together. Brush the top of the cake with this mixture and sprinkle with the coarse sugar.

10. Bake for 45 minutes, or until nicely browned. Let the cake cool for 10 minutes in the pan. Carefully run a knife around the sides of the pan to loosen the cake, and turn the cake out onto a cooling rack to cool completely. To serve, cut into wedges.

Note: To freeze, wrap the cake well in aluminum foil. Freeze for up to 1 month.

Befana, La Vecchia

The Old Woman Befana

No one ever went near the house of *la vecchia* ("the old woman"), whose name was Befana. Some thought that she was a witch with mysterious powers. Her body was twisted, and she leaned on an old broom in order to move about. Her hands were withered and crooked from working the land and tending her few animals. She had stringy gray hair that was pulled back from her face and tied with rags, and her clothes were patched and worn.

The old woman kept to herself. She busily spent every day keeping the fire going in her small cottage and sweeping the floor all day long.

Befana lived near Bethlehem. One cold winter's night while preparing her supper of beans and bread, she heard a knock at the door. Leaning on her broom, she slowly hobbled to the door and called out, "Who is it?"

A deep, soothing voice answered, "Please help us, we are lost."

Befana opened the door just a crack, but the light that shone through nearly blinded her. Before her towered three kings dressed in brilliant colorful cloaks of purple, blue, and green. Each king wore a crown of gold and a large jeweled necklace. Befana kept squinting to see them because they were so dazzling.

"We have come to worship at the feet of the Child King, born in Bethlehem," said the tallest king. "We have been following His star as the angel prophesied, but have lost the way. Can you tell us where He is?"

Befana was astonished by their words. "I know of no king born in these parts," she said and proceeded to shut the door.

"Wait," begged one of the kings, "come with us and we will find Him together."

Befana shook her head from side to side. "I cannot go. I have animals to tend, vegetables to water, and a house to clean. Besides, what would this king want with an old woman like me?"

The kings said good-bye to the unwilling Befana and continued on their journey. The old woman sat down to eat her now-cold beans, but she was not hungry. She kept thinking about the strangers and their invitation. Something inside her said that she should go. Without wasting a minute, Befana picked up her broom, put a few pieces of bread in a sack, and set out to find the strangers. She followed their footsteps and those of their camels for as long as she could. But then a great wind came and blew away all traces of their path. Befana walked and walked, and in each town that she came to, she asked if the three men in brilliant clothes had passed through, but no one had seen or heard of them. Discouraged, she lay down near a rock and fell asleep.

The next day, she began her journey again, never ceasing to ask the same question. Every time she saw a baby boy, she broke off a crust of bread and gave it to the child, thinking that he might be the Child King who would recognize her.

To this day, Befana is still wandering through towns and villages looking for the Child King. Every year on the Feast of Epiphany, or Three Kings, the children of Italy eagerly await the arrival of la vecchia, who still leaves each child a small gift.

Tortine di Natale

Little Christmas Cakes

✦

This old recipe for Christmas cakes was sent to me by Mariann Sterling, whose ancestors came from Calabria. To make them, a pastry dough is spread with a raisin and nut filling, rolled up jelly-roll fashion, and cut into rounds. These can also be shaped to resemble little gondolas, the traditional water transport of Venice.

✦

Makes 2 dozen

DOUGH

3 cups unbleached all-purpose flour

¹/₂ teaspoon salt

1 cup solid vegetable shortening

2 tablespoons warm water

FILLING

¹/₄ cup warm honey

³/₄ cup diced raisins or currants

¹/₄ cup chopped walnuts or almonds

1 cup sugar

1¹/₂ teaspoons ground cinnamon

1. In a bowl, mix the flour, salt, and shortening together with your hands or a fork until well blended. Add the water a little at time until a ball of dough forms. Wrap the dough in plastic wrap and chill for at least 1 hour.

2. Preheat the oven to 375°F. Line two cookie sheets with parchment paper. Divide the dough in half. On a well-floured surface, roll one piece into a 12 by 9-inch rectangle. With a pastry brush, spread half the honey over the dough, spreading it to the edges. Sprinkle on half the raisins or currants and nuts.

3. Mix the sugar with the cinnamon and sprinkle half of it evenly over the dough. Carefully roll the dough up from a long side like a jelly roll. Cut the roll into 1-inch pieces and place on the cookie sheet. Repeat with the remaining dough and filling.

4. Bake for 25 to 30 minutes, or until the pastry is golden brown. Carefully remove the cakes to a cooling rack.

Note: To shape gondolas, cut each rectangle of dough into six 6 by 3-inch strips. Pinch the strips together at each end. Fill the centers with the filling. Twist the ends like a candy wrapper to form gondolas.

6 large eggs, separated, at room temperature

1 cup sugar

2 tablespoons unsalted butter, softened

2 tablespoons Orange Liqueur (page 320)

2 large carrots, peeled and grated

1/2 cup unbleached all-purpose flour

1/8 teaspoon salt

1 1/4 cups finely chopped walnuts

Confectioners' sugar for sprinkling

18 aluminum foil cupcake cups, 3 inches wide and 1 1/2 inches deep

1. Preheat the oven to 350°F. Lightly butter the aluminum foil cupcake cups. In a large bowl, with an electric mixer, beat the egg yolks and sugar until lemon-colored and doubled in volume. Gradually beat in the butter and orange liqueur. Fold in the carrots, flour, and salt. Fold in the nuts.

2. In another bowl, with clean beaters, beat the egg whites until stiff but not dry. Gently fold the egg whites into the egg yolk mixture.

3. Divide the batter among the cupcake cups, filling them about two-thirds full. Place the cups on two cookie sheets. Bake for about 10 minutes, or until the cakes are golden brown and firm to the touch. Remove the cups to racks and let cool completely.

4. Run a knife around the outside edge of each cup, and unmold the cakes onto a serving dish. Sprinkle the tops with confectioners' sugar.

Note: The cakes can be baked a day ahead. Let cool, wrap each foil cup in plastic wrap, and store at room temperature.

Tortine di Carote

Small Carrot Cakes

For a large gathering, I like to serve several desserts, choosing those I can prepare ahead. These light-textured small carrot cakes can be baked a day ahead.

Makes 1 1/2 dozen

Tortina al Cioccolato della Campagna

Small Country Chocolate Cake

Not too sweet, with a dense texture like pound cake, this simple chocolate cake is a good choice for an afternoon merenda (snack). Care and patience must be taken in making it, and a light hand is needed for folding the beaten egg whites into the batter. The bittersweet chocolate must be of good quality, such as Perugina, Lindt, or Callebaut. A six by five-and-a-half-inch tube pan turns out a perfect cake. An eight-inch one will also do, as will a ring mold, but the cake will not rise to towering heights.

Serves 8

CAKE

6 tablespoons unsalted butter

4 ounces bittersweet chocolate, coarsely chopped

4 large eggs, separated, at room temperature

1/2 cup plus 2 tablespoons Vanilla Sugar (page 329)

1 teaspoon vanilla

1/4 teaspoon salt

3/4 cup cake flour

Confectioners' sugar for sprinkling (if not using the glazes)

CHOCOLATE GLAZE (OPTIONAL)

3 tablespoons unsalted butter

2 1/2 tablespoons light corn syrup

2 ounces bittersweet chocolate, coarsely chopped

1 tablespoon Orange Liqueur (page 320) or brandy

WHITE GLAZE (OPTIONAL)

1/2 cup confectioners' sugar

1 1/2 tablespoons milk or half-and-half

1. Preheat the oven to 350°F. Generously butter a 6 by 5½-inch tube pan, or an 8 by 2½-inch tube pan or ring mold, dust with unsweetened cocoa, and shake out the excess. In a saucepan, melt the butter and chocolate over low heat, stirring until smooth. Set aside to cool slightly.

2. In a large bowl, with an electric mixer on high speed, beat the egg yolks until pale yellow. Beat in the sugar a little at a time. Beat in the vanilla. Add the chocolate mixture and beat until well blended. Beat in the flour a little at a time until well blended.

3. In another bowl, with clean beaters, beat the egg whites with the salt just until soft peaks form. Do not overbeat. Fold the whites into the chocolate batter a third at a time, taking care not to deflate the whites. Carefully spread the batter in the prepared pan.

4. Bake for 20 to 25 minutes if using an 8-inch tube pan or ring mold, for 35 to 40 minutes, if using a 6-inch tube pan, or until a

cake tester inserted in the middle comes out clean. Remove the pan to a rack and let cool completely.

5. Carefully run a knife around the edges of the cake and invert the cake onto a serving dish. Sprinkle with confectioners' sugar, or glaze with the two glazes.

6. In a small saucepan, melt the butter over medium-low heat. Add the corn syrup and cook for 1 minute, stirring constantly. Add the chocolate and stir until the chocolate is melted and the mixture is smooth. Remove from the heat, stir in the liqueur, and set aside to cool.

7. In a small bowl, blend the confectioners' sugar with the milk or half-and-half until smooth. Set aside.

8. Brush any crumbs from the cake with a pastry brush. Tape strips of wax paper around the edges of the cake to catch the glaze drippings. With a pastry brush, paint the cake with chocolate glaze. Brush a second time with the remaining glaze, making sure the entire cake is covered. Let the glaze set for 1 hour.

9. Use a teaspoon to drizzle the white glaze over the cake in a decorative pattern. Remove the wax paper. Serve the cake cut into slices.

Zuccotto Casanova

Zuccotto

❧

Zuccotto, which means "skullcap," is the name given to a richly layered pastry creamy fruit- and chocolate-filled cake that is said to resemble the dome of Florence's cathedral. This recipe is a variation on the zuccotto theme. Purchase good-quality firm ladyfingers, not the soft spongy type found in grocery stores.

❧

Serves 10

PASTRY CREAM

2 cups milk

1 tablespoon vanilla

4 large egg yolks

¼ cup unbleached all-purpose flour

½ cup sugar

2 tablespoons Orange Liqueur (page 320) or Grand Marnier

1 teaspoon water

1 tablespoon sugar

About 30 ladyfingers (¾ pound)

1¾ cups heavy cream, whipped to firm peaks

¾ cup sliced strawberries

8 ounces bittersweet chocolate, chopped medium-fine

Confectioners' sugar for sprinkling

1. In a saucepan, bring the milk to a boil over medium heat. Remove from the heat, add the vanilla, and cool slightly.

2. In the top of a double boiler, off the heat, whisk the egg yolks. Slowly whisk in the flour. Whisk in the warm milk. Cook, stirring constantly with a wooden spoon, until the cream thickens and coats the back of the spoon. Add the sugar and stir to incorporate. Pour the pastry cream into a bowl and cover with a piece of buttered wax paper, pressing it against the surface of the cream. Refrigerate.

3. Line an 8¾ by 4¼-inch glass bowl with plastic wrap, letting the edges overhang the bowl by several inches. Fill a clean spritzer with the orange liqueur or Grand Marnier, water, and sugar, and use it to spritz the ladyfingers as you assemble the cake. (Alternatively, combine the Grand Marnier, water, and sugar in a bowl and dip the ladyfingers briefly in the mixture as you work. You may need slightly more liqueur if you choose this method.)

4. Line the sides of the bowl with spritzed ladyfingers, standing them on end and making sure the tops of the ladyfingers are even with the rim of the bowl (you will need about 14). Break up 2 or 3 more ladyfingers and fill in the bottom of the bowl.

5. Spread a layer of pastry cream over the ladyfingers in the bottom of the bowl. Spread about 3 tablespoons of the whipped cream over the pastry cream. Arrange a layer of ladyfingers over the heavy cream and spritz with the orange liqueur mixture. Spread about ⅔ cup of pastry cream over the ladyfingers. Arrange the strawberries over the pastry cream, pressing them gently into the cream. Sprinkle half of the chocolate over the strawberries.

6. Cover the chocolate with another layer of ladyfingers and spritz with the orange liqueur mixture. Spread the remaining pastry cream over the ladyfingers and sprinkle the remaining chocolate over the pastry cream. Spread the remaining heavy cream over the chocolate.

7. Add a final layer of ladyfingers, covering the filling completely, and spritz with the orange liqueur mixture. Bring the overhanging edges of the plastic wrap up over the top of the cake, pressing down on the cake gently. Refrigerate overnight.

8. To unmold, unwrap the top of the cake. Place a serving dish over the top and invert the mold. Remove the plastic wrap carefully from the cake. Sprinkle the top of the cake with confectioners' sugar. Cut into wedges to serve.

Torta di Peppina

Peppina's Cake

❧

Bits of bittersweet chocolate and crushed amaretti cookies add a wonderful taste and texture to this cake. The recipe, which comes from my friend Raffaella, was given to her mother by an old woman called Peppina from Reggio Emilia. It is a simple cake, but one of my very favorites.

❧

Serves 6 to 8

1 cup unbleached all-purpose flour

1 teaspoon baking powder

8 tablespoons (1 stick) unsalted butter, softened

1/2 cup sugar

4 large eggs, separated, at room temperature

2 ounces bittersweet chocolate, coarsely chopped

3/4 cup crushed amaretti cookies

Pinch of salt

Confectioners' sugar for dusting

1. Preheat the oven to 350°F. Butter a 9-inch cake pan. Line it with parchment paper and butter the paper. Sift the flour and baking powder together onto wax paper.

2. In a large bowl, with an electric mixer, cream the butter and sugar until light and fluffy. Beat in the egg yolks one at a time. With a rubber spatula, fold in the flour mixture. Stir in the chocolate and crushed cookies.

3. In another bowl, with clean beaters, beat the egg whites with the salt until stiff peaks form. With a rubber spatula, fold the egg whites into the egg yolk mixture one at a time.

4. Pour the batter into the prepared pan. Bake for 30 minutes, or until a cake tester inserted in the middle comes out clean. Let the cake cool in the pan for 2 to 3 minutes, then invert it onto a cooling rack. Carefully remove the parchment paper, set another rack on top of the cake, and turn right side up. Cool the cake completely.

5. Dust the cake with confectioners' sugar and cut into wedges to serve.

²/₃ cup cornstarch

¹/₄ teaspoon baking powder

4 large eggs, separated, at room temperature

¹/₂ cup plus 2 tablespoons Vanilla Sugar (page 329)

1 tablespoon Homemade Vanilla Extract (page 328) or vanilla

1 tablespoon grated lemon zest

1 tablespoon fresh lemon juice

¹/₄ teaspoon salt

Confectioners' sugar for sprinkling

1. Preheat the oven to 350°F. Butter an 8 by 2¹/₂-inch spring-form tube pan or two 8 by 1¹/₂-inch round cake pans. Sift the cornstarch and baking powder together onto wax paper.

2. In a large bowl, using an electric mixer, beat the egg yolks until pale in color. Slowly beat in the sugar. Beat in the vanilla, lemon zest, and juice. Fold in the cornstarch mixture.

3. In a clean bowl, with clean beaters, beat the egg whites with the salt until stiff but not dry. With a rubber spatula, fold the whites into the egg yolk mixture a little at a time, taking care not to deflate the whites. Spread the batter evenly in the pan(s).

4. Bake for 20 minutes, or until the top is golden brown and springs back when pressed with your finger. Remove the cake(s) from the oven. If using a tube pan, invert the pan over a long-necked funnel or bottle and cool completely before removing from the pan. If using cake pans, let the cakes cool for just 10 minutes, then run a knife around the edges of the cake pans and carefully turn the cakes out onto a cooling rack. Let cool completely.

5. To serve, sprinkle with confectioners' sugar and cut into wedges with a serrated knife. (This cake can be frozen for up to 1 month.)

Torta Margherita

Queen Margaret's Cake

❧

Torta margherita, one of several Italian specialties named after the Neapolitan Queen Margaret, is a simple cake, similar in texture to a chiffon cake. In summer, serve the cake plain with slightly sweetened fresh fruits. I make the cake in a tube pan, to serve eight, but baking it in two eight-inch cake pans gives you two cakes that will serve six or more if cut into thin slices, with the option of freezing one for later use.

❧

Serves 8

Una Torta per la Marchesa

A Cake for the Marchesa

※

Anna Tasca Lanza said that the *scirocco*, winds from Africa, were responsible for the cold April weather. There was snow on the ground in central Sicily on this of all days, her birthday.

I had come to her family's venerable wine estate, Regaleali, to learn more about aristocratic Sicilian cooking, the cooking of the aristocrats, that is described in great detail in Giuseppe Lampedusa's novel of nineteenth-century upper-class Sicilian life, *Il Gattopardo (The Leopard)*. The estate seemed especially quiet today; the only noise fracturing the stillness was an occasional rooster call.

We ate our breakfast of her homemade tangerine *marmalata*, crusty, dense semolina bread, and tea. Sipping my tea, I wondered how Anna, a Sicilian marchesa, a woman of nobility, would celebrate her birthday.

As if reading my mind, she said, "Let us go to the town of Vallelunga. It's market day and you will find some nice wooden spoons and local cheeses. Since it is the week before Easter, we are sure to see some special breads being made in the *panificio*, including *pane di cena* (Good Friday bread)."

On the way, Anna told me that there was no school on market day in Vallelunga, and that people came from all around central Sicily to set up stalls and sell and buy everything from shoes to wild fennel. Central Sicily is isolated, its boundaries defined by spectacular views of the Madonie Mountains and steep rolling hills dotted with sheep. One small *stazione* (train station) was Vallelunga's lifeline to Palermo, the capital, and other parts of Sicily.

We parked the car and walked down the hill to the outdoor market. A sea of women dressed in black, including young girls, walked arm in arm from stall to stall, looking at and arguing about the price of everything. Anna pointed out the intricately woven palm branches that were for sale for Palm Sunday, then left me on my own while she looked for wooden spoons.

At the flower stall, giant stemmed white, yellow, and pink daisy mums were for sale. I bought a yellow bunch to give to

Anna for her birthday, feeling very Italian carrying the bouquet upside down, as is the custom. The snowy white table linens glistening in the bright sunshine caught my eye. Taking my purchase, I squirmed my way through the ever-thickening crowd looking for Anna. She was waiting at the top of the hill.

"*Buon compleanno,*" I said, handing her the flowers and the linens. She seemed surprised and touched.

On the way back to Regaleali, I asked her if she would like me to make her a birthday cake.

"Of course, Mary Ann" was her immediate reply.

"I will make you an American cake. Have you ever had angel food cake?"

She gave me a quizzical glance before asking, "What is it?"

I described a light-textured cake, made with egg whites, sugar, and almond extract. The thought of it intrigued her, but she surprised me even more with her next question.

"You will make the dinner too?"

I said yes, already planning the menu in my head. Since there was so much fresh sheep's-milk ricotta cheese made at Regaleali, I suggested *gnocchi di ricotta*, dumplings made from the cheese, for our *primo piatto*. Anna had never had them, which surprised me, since my Grandmother Saporito, who was born not far from Regaleali, in Caltanisetta, made them all the time. The *secondo piatto* would be *farsumagru*, stuffed and rolled beef filled with eggs, olives, parsley, and cheese, all simmered in tomato sauce. My grandmother called it *braciole*. We would finish with a salad of *cicoria*, bitter greens from Anna's garden, and then the cake.

In the kitchen I showed Anna how to use the cheese for making ricotta gnocchi. After mixing the flour and cheese, we began rolling little pieces of the dough off a fork to create the classic line of the gnocco. On the stove, the meat simmered in tomato sauce made from just-picked plum tomatoes. We would use the sauce over the cooked gnocchi.

The cake was next. I asked Anna for a tube pan, and was met with a blank stare. I improvised.

"This cake will be my best one," I shouted over the noise of the mixer, as I beat the egg whites. "It is a treat to have fresh eggs right off the farm."

Anna watched the egg whites stiffen into fluffy peaks, looking like a miniature version of the steep mountain range that rings

Sicily. When I added finely ground almonds, picked right from her own almond trees, she said, "Now the cake will be authentic because of the almonds."

After the cake went into the oven, we set the table. None of Anna's family could join us for the birthday dinner. Her husband was away on business, her parents, the count and countess, could not come, and her daughter Fabrizia lived in Verona.

We sipped Regaleali wine as we cooked the gnocchi. Finally all was ready. Before sitting down, I took the angel food cake from the oven, and turned it upside down to let it cool.

I asked Anna how she liked the gnocchi.

"They are so light," she said. "Now I know what to do with all the extra ricotta cheese we make."

The farsumagru made a beautiful sight and was delicious with its stuffing of Pecorino cheese, olives, eggs, and bread crumbs. Our *digestivo* was the insalata di cicoria. It just does not get any better than this, I thought.

When all was finished, I brought over the cake, dusted it with a heavy layer of confectioners' sugar, and put it in front of Anna. Then I cleared my throat and sang "Tanti Auguri."

Anna smiled and cut the first piece. I reminded her to make a wish. The cake was snowy white, and eating it was like biting into almond-flavored air.

"*Ti piace?*" I asked Anna.

She nodded her approval, her lips outlined in a fine coating of confectioners' sugar.

12 large egg whites (1¼ cups), at room temperature

½ teaspoon cream of tartar

¼ teaspoon salt

1⅓ cups sugar

¾ cup sifted cake flour

⅔ cup finely ground blanched almonds

1 tablespoon almond extract

Confectioners' sugar for sprinkling (if not making the filling)

FILLING (OPTIONAL)

3 cups mascarpone cheese, softened

¼ cup sugar

1½ cups fresh or unsweetened frozen raspberries

1. Preheat the oven to 325°F. In a large bowl, with an electric mixer, beat the egg whites, cream of tarter, and salt, until soft peaks form. Beat in the sugar 1 tablespoon at a time. With a rubber spatula, fold in the flour a little at a time, being careful not to deflate the egg whites. Fold in the almonds and almond extract.

2. Spoon the batter evenly into an ungreased 10-inch tube pan. Bake until the cake is golden brown and firm to the touch, about 40 minutes. Remove the cake from the oven, invert the opening over a long-necked bottle or funnel, and let the cake cool completely.

3. Run a knife around the outside edges of the cake and around the center tube to loosen it. Invert the pan and gently remove the cake. Place the cake on a serving dish, sprinkle the top with confectioners' sugar, and cut into wedges for serving. Or make the filling and fill the cake.

4. In a bowl, combine the mascarpone cheese and sugar and blend well. Gently fold in the raspberries.

5. Cut the cake into 3 horizontal layers with a serrated knife. Place the bottom layer on a serving dish and spread one third of the filling over it. Place the second layer on top, and spread with half the remaining filling. Place the top layer on top and spread the remaining filling over it. Refrigerate for at least 2 hours before serving.

Torta di Anna

Anna's Cake

This is the angel food cake I made for the Marchesa's birthday. Its light and airy texture is complemented by finely ground almonds in the batter. Serve it with a simple dusting of confectioners' sugar, or split the cake into layers and sandwich them with a sweetened mascarpone cheese and raspberry filling.

Serves 10 to 12

Birthday Dinner for the Marchesa

Two-Cheese Gnocchi
(page 53)

Stuffed Beef Rolls
(page 144)

Endive, Radicchio, and
Escarole Salad
(page 196)

Anna's Cake

Zuppa Inglese

English Trifle Cake

❧

Zuppa inglese is similar to English trifle. The name derives from the word inzuppare, *which means "to moisten" or "to soak." In this recipe, the cake, which is similar to a sponge cake, is split and sprinkled with Alchermes, a spicy red liqueur made from cochineal and used in many Italian desserts. If Alchermes is difficult to find, substitute brandy or raspberry liqueur. The cake is best made a day ahead; add the whipped cream topping just before serving.*

❧

Serves 8

³/₄ cup plus 1 tablespoon cake flour
Pinch of salt
3 large eggs, separated, at room temperature
³/₄ cup sugar

FILLING
1 cup milk
4 large egg yolks
¹/₄ cup sugar
2 tablespoons unbleached all-purpose flour
1 teaspoon unsalted butter
1 tablespoon grated lemon zest
1 tablespoon vanilla
³/₄ cup diced mixed dried fruits (such as apricots, pears, and apples)

1 tablespoon Alchermes, rum, or raspberry brandy
1¹/₄ cups heavy cream
2 tablespoons confectioners' sugar
Dried apricots, pears, and/or apples for garnish, optional

1. Preheat the oven to 350°F. Lightly butter and flour a 9-inch round cake pan. Sift the flour and salt onto wax paper.

2. In a bowl, beat the egg yolks until lemon-colored. Gradually beat in the sugar.

3. In another bowl, with clean beaters, beat the egg whites, until stiff but not dry. Gradually fold the whites into the egg yolk mixture until well blended. Spoon the flour over the batter a little at a time, and fold in until no streaks of flour remain.

4. Pour the batter into the pan. Bake for 25 minutes, or until the cake is delicately browned and a cake skewer inserted in the middle comes out clean.

5. Let the cake cool completely in the pan on a rack, then use a knife to loosen the cake from the edges of the pan and invert it onto a rack.

6. Meanwhile, make the filling: In a small saucepan, scald the milk (bring to just under a boil). Let cool to warm.

7. In the top of a double boiler, off the heat, whisk the yolks with the sugar until smooth. Gradually whisk in the flour. Slowly whisk in the warm milk. Place the double boiler over medium-low heat and cook, whisking constantly, until the filling thickens and coats the whisk. Remove the top of the double boiler from the heat and stir in the butter, zest, vanilla, and diced fruits. Set the pan in a pan of ice cubes and water to cool.

8. When cool, transfer the filling to a bowl, cover with a piece of buttered wax paper, pressing it against the surface of the filling, and refrigerate for several hours, or overnight.

9. To assemble the cake, use a serrated knife to split the cake into 2 layers. Place one layer on a serving plate. Sprinkle with the Alchermes, rum, or raspberry brandy. Spread the filling evenly over the layer. Top with the second layer. Refrigerate until chilled. (The cake can be loosely covered with plastic wrap and refrigerated overnight.)

10. In a bowl, beat the cream with the confectioners' sugar until stiff peaks form. Fill a pastry bag fitted with a star tip with the cream. Pipe a decorative border around the top and bottom edges of the cake. If you wish, arrange dried fruits in the cream. Cut the cake into wedges with a serrated knife.

Torta Nuziale

Wedding Cake

≈

According to Diane Ackerman, author of *A Natural History of Love*, the ancient Romans celebrated marriage with a coarse, heavy cake made from wheat or barley flour, which was crumbled over the bride's head to encourage fertility. Wheat crumbs were also thrown at the bride and groom after the marriage ceremony, as a symbol of fertility and prosperity.

During the seventeenth century, French pastry chefs created the forerunners of today's elaborately styled tiered wedding cakes. The traditional heavy spice-scented cake was transformed into an edible palace covered in a white sugar icing. It became an English custom to build a tower of sorts by layering cake upon cake, held together with sugar icing.

In Italy, wedding cakes are made according to local tradition and custom. In Monrupino, in northern Italy, wedding guests eat *kuhani strukeli*, not a cake at all but a sweet bread studded with dried fruits. In Tuscany's Siena, *panforte*, a dense flat cake made with dried fruit, nuts, and spices, is served. In Sicily, it is *pan di spagna*, layers of sponge cake sandwiched with almond paste.

My own wedding cake was a deliciously moist, homemade tiered almond cake that served eight hundred guests.

The wedding cake I now make for family and friends is not a traditional Italian one, but a white almond-flavored cake I have perfected over the years. The cake serves about fifty people, ideal for a small wedding. Because this cake is almost three inches high, small squares provide quite ample servings. If you prefer to cut it into larger pieces, it will serve around thirty-six guests. The cake is moist, is easily made in an hour's time, and, best of all, can be made a month ahead and frozen. The mascarpone buttercream frosting can be made up to three days in advance and stored in the refrigerator. The cake can be iced and decorated the day before the wedding and stored in the refrigerator. The cake should be kept away from heat, displayed at the wedding in a cool area.

You will need a large serving platter or a sturdy board for the cake. This can be a masonite board, available in cake decorating stores. Cover the board with white freezer paper or aluminum foil.

Making a wedding cake requires organization, time, the right equipment, and the highest-quality ingredients. But you don't have to be an artist to decorate it. I personally do not like gritty sugar flowers on a wedding cake, preferring a simple nosegay of fresh flowers.

Serves 50

2 cups buttermilk

2 teaspoons baking soda

4 cups unbleached all-purpose flour

1/2 teaspoon salt

1/2 pound (2 sticks) unsalted butter, softened

1/2 cup solid vegetable shortening

3 cups sugar

10 large eggs, separated, at room temperature

2 tablespoons almond extract

1/2 cup finely ground hazelnuts

1/2 cup finely ground walnuts

1 cup shredded sweetened coconut

FROSTING

1 pound unsalted butter, softened

3/4 cup mascarpone (or good-quality cream cheese, softened)

12 to 13 cups sifted confectioners' sugar

2 1/2 tablespoons rum or almond extract

1. Preheat the oven to 350°F. Butter and flour a 12 by 12 by 3-inch cake pan. Combine the buttermilk and baking soda in a bowl. Set aside.

2. Sift the flour and salt onto wax paper.

3. In a large bowl, with an electric mixer, cream the butter, shortening, and sugar until well blended. Beat in the egg yolks one at a time, making sure that each one is well incorporated before adding the next. Beat in the almond extract. Beat in the flour mixture alternately with the buttermilk mixture, blending well. Stir in the nuts and coconut.

continued

4. In another bowl, with clean beaters, beat the egg whites until stiff but not dry. With a large spatula, fold the egg whites into the batter. Pour the batter into the pan. Bake for 50 to 60 minutes, or until a cake tester inserted in the middle comes out clean.

5. Cool the cake completely in the pan on a cooling rack. (At this point, the cake can be wrapped in heavy freezer paper, then in aluminum foil, and frozen for up to 1 month. It can be frosted still-frozen.)

6. In a heavy-duty mixer or a food processor, beat or process the butter and cheese until smooth. Add the confectioners' sugar a cupful at a time, beating or processing to achieve a frosting that is easily spreadable but firm enough to pipe through a pastry bag. Add the extract. (The frosting can be made up to 3 days ahead. Store in an airtight container in the refrigerator. Let come to room temperature before using.)

7. When ready to frost the cake, assemble a cake frosting knife, or icing spatula, a rubber spatula, and a pastry bag and assorted tips. Prepare a bowl of ice water.

8. Using a pastry brush, gently brush any loose crumbs from the top and sides of the cake. Spread a small amount of the frosting on the cake platter or board to help anchor the cake and prevent it from shifting. Carefully position the cake on the platter or board. Slip a border of wax paper around the bottom edges of the cake to keep the platter or board clean.

9. Apply a base coat of frosting to the cake, covering the top first then the sides. Dip the frosting knife in the ice water frequently and wipe clean to help to keep the frosting smooth as it is spread and to prevent loose crumbs from making unsightly flecks in the frosting.

10. Using the pastry bag and an assortment of decorative tips, pipe the frosting to make a design on the cake: swags, swirls, a basket-weave design, columns, free-form designs, or whatever you desire. Finish with a decorative border around the bottom of the cake. Carefully pull away the wax paper. Refrigerate the cake until ready to serve.

11. To give the cake a final elegant touch, place a small spray of fresh flowers on the top.

Regali dalla Cucina

Gifts from the Kitchen

*I*talian hospitality is centered around the eating and giving of food. Whether it's a loaf of *pane casalingo* (homemade bread), *pasta fatta in casa* (homemade pasta), or *vino di casa* (homemade wine), nothing makes an Italian happier than to offer something he or she created *a mano* (by hand).

Inspiration for the recipes in this chapter has come from perusing specialty shops all over Italy. One of my favorites is in Rome, Caffè Castroni on Via Cola di Rienzo. I learned from a friend that this is *the* street where Romans do their serious shopping.

At Caffè Castroni, there is everything from fresh creamy cheeses to batter-fried cardoons to go, as well as fluffy frittatas and marinated fish that can be ordered and eaten standing up right on the spot. Much of the store space is devoted to beautifully packaged food gifts. I admired everything from colossal capers in brine to herb-infused grappas, while at the same time gingerly looking for the sticker prices that usually prompted me to say to myself, "I can make that much cheaper at home."

The variety of Italian foods and condiments in this chapter could easily fill a large basket. Most of these can be made months before they are needed, for any occasion, and for considerably less than their counterparts in gourmet food stores.

Included are flavored vinegars, both herbal and fruit ones, which can be used to perk up a salad or dessert or to deglaze a pan to add an extra depth of flavor to meat, poultry, and fish dishes. There are ready-to-use sauces for pasta or vegetables, perfect for giving with Italian pasta, for a quick meal. Or fill a basket with a fruit sauce, a spicy mustard, herb and prosciutto *grissini* (breadsticks), orange liqueur, caponata, vanilla sugar, dried zucchini chips, and even confections, like crunchy almond croccante. Give a jar of almond paste with a recipe for a favorite tart, or for your bread-baking friends, present a jar of bread starter. Most people love it when a recipe is included to show how to use your food gifts.

Package your gifts in inexpensive bottles, jars, baskets, or boxes. You can find interesting selections in discount, craft, and hardware stores. Or see the Mail-Order Sources on page 331.

The best part of preparing and giving a gift of food from your kitchen is that the receiver of your efforts will have something *fatto a mano e con amore* (made by hand with love).

3 to 4 large basil sprigs per bottle

1 clove garlic, peeled, per bottle

Red wine vinegar

Sterilized glass bottles and caps or corks

1. Carefully wash and dry the basil sprigs. Place 3 or 4 sprigs in each bottle. With a small knife, make a small slit in each garlic clove. Add 1 clove to each bottle. Insert a funnel into the mouth of each bottle and fill with vinegar. Cap or cork the bottles and place them in a sunny spot to "ripen" for 4 to 5 days.

2. Store the vinegar in a cool dark place for at least 6 weeks before using. The vinegar will keep indefinitely.

3. To give as a gift, cover the top of each bottle with gingham or other material and tie with a ribbon. Use a decorative label on the bottle and attach a recipe for using the vinegar.

Aceto Basilico

Basil Vinegar

The word basil *means "kingly," a fitting description for bottles of basil vinegar you can make in no time in your kitchen to give as a welcome addition to any cook's pantry. Start by gathering a collection of interestingly shaped clear glass bottles.*

Only fresh basil will work for this. The method for making basil vinegar can also be used with other herbs, such as parsley, thyme, rosemary, and tarragon.

Be creative and combine different herbs for new flavor combinations.

Use herb vinegars on green and vegetable salads, including potato salads, to deglaze pans when cooking meats, and in marinades.

Aceto di Lampone e Menta

Raspberry-Mint Vinegar

Fruit-flavored vinegars were served as refreshing hot-weather drinks by the ancient Romans. Fruit vinegars are best made with seasonal fruits. This recipe for raspberry vinegar is easily adaptable; try blackberries, blueberries, and strawberries, or a combination. Use a good-quality white vinegar.

Sometimes I create food still lifes with my vinegars, adding a sprig of mint, as here, or curled strips of orange or lime zest. Use the vinegar on potato or green salads, for deglazing pans when cooking pork chops or chicken, or on fresh fruit salads.

Makes about 2 ½ cups

2 ½ cups distilled white vinegar

¼ cup packed fresh raspberries plus ¼ cup loosely packed for skewering

3 tablespoons sugar

⅛ teaspoon fine sea salt

2 sprigs fresh mint

Thin wooden skewers
Sterilized 20-ounce bottle

1. In a saucepan, combine the vinegar, ¼ cup of the raspberries, the sugar, and salt and bring to a boil. Boil for 3 minutes. Strain through a sieve set over a bowl, pressing on the raspberries to extract as much juice as possible. Set aside to cool slightly.

2. Skewer the remaining raspberries and place them in the sterilized bottle. Add the mint sprigs.

3. Insert a funnel into the mouth of the bottle and pour in the raspberry vinegar. Cap or cork the bottle and place it in a sunny spot for 8 hours.

4. Place the vinegar in a dark place and let it age for about 6 weeks before using.

1 cup brown mustard seeds
1 cup yellow mustard seeds
2 cups red wine vinegar
½ cup honey
2 teaspoons fine sea salt
1 teaspoon allspice

6 sterilized ½-pint jars

1. Put the mustard seeds in a noncorrosive bowl and pour the vinegar over them. Cover the bowl and let the seeds soak for 2 days. As they do, they will absorb most of the vinegar.

2. Transfer the mustard seeds to a food processor, add the honey, salt, and allspice, and pulse until a grainy paste is formed.

3. Fill the sterilized jars with the mustard. Place a round of wax paper slightly larger than the jar opening over the top of each one, and cap. Store in a cool, dark place. Unopened, the mustard will keep indefinitely. Once opened, refrigerate it.

Senape Piccante

Spicy Mustard

☙

The ancient Romans pounded mustard seeds into a powder and mixed it with wine to add flavor to foods. In Italy today, mustard (senape) is used in cucina nuova recipes like Leeks with Mustard Sauce (page 180) and in marinades for meat and fish. Sometimes it is added to salad dressings. This recipe produces a grainy, spicy mustard, the result of soaking mustard seeds for two days in good red wine vinegar. Pack it in small glass jars with the recipe attached.

☙

Makes 3 pints

Il Presepio

The Crèche

❧

Legend has it that during the observance of Christmas Eve mass in 1223, Saint Francis of Assisi carefully placed a tiny child on a clump of straw, while an ox and a donkey stood nearby. This reenactment of the original nativity scene so moved all who saw it that it quickly became part of the Christmas tradition, inspiring the development of the art form of *il presepio*, the crèche.

In the thirteenth century, nativity figures, chiseled from stone or wood, were to be found only in churches. But by the 1600s, artisans were making realistic nativity figures on commission for patrons, using wire and hemp instead of stone or wood, allowing the figures to be twisted into a variety of poses and draped in clothing. As time passed and demand increased, adoring shepherds, heralding angels, and kings from faraway lands were made in addition to the Holy Family, along with figures representing people from all walks of life.

By the 1800s, in Naples, the artistry of creating these figures had reached the pinnacle of refinement and elaboration. Street scenes showing everyday life were created and could be found in the homes of aristocrats and in the court. Presepio figures demonstrated a colorful blend of human activities, everything from men in rough-hewn clothing gathering wheat and women in colorful aprons preparing food to richly clothed merchants and aristocrats conducting their affairs on the streets of Naples.

Today Neapolitan artisans continue the tradition begun centuries ago. The best place to see their work in Naples is along the cramped Via San Gregorio Armeno. Each Christmas season, Italians flock here to add to the crèche figures they already have. They buy the figures and display them in elaborate home settings, some of which take up as much room as a large dining table.

Throughout the churches of Italy, the presepio can be found modeled in the style of those from Naples in every imaginable medium, from carved wood to coral and various metals. One of my very favorites is the sixteenth-century presepio by the artists Altobello Persio and Jacopo Sannazaro, found above a side altar in the cathedral of Matera, in the region of Basilicata. This simple presepio is fashioned from polychrome stone to represent the *sassi* (caves) where early inhabitants first lived, still in existence today.

Probably the most elaborate presepio is the eighteenth-century one made for the king of Naples, housed in the Royal Palace at Caserta. The panoramic view of Neapolitan street life is almost mind-boggling. Wherever one looks, a story is unfolding: People eat at long tavern tables, while prosciutto hams cure in the background; women nurse babies; children feed chickens; animals wander here and there; and noble ladies in lavish jewels carry delicate baskets of fruit. All this takes place amid the very moment of the Christ Child's birth, when everyone unequivocally receives the gift of love.

Olio di Timo e Granella di Pepe

Thyme-Peppercorn Oil

❧

Flavored oils are versatile and a snap to make. Use them to flavor salads, to baste meats, poultry, fish, and vegetables for the grill, and to enhance the taste of soups, sauces, and fried foods. Make other flavored oils from different herbs, such as a tarragon and lemon oil or basil oil.

❧

2 tablespoons pink peppercorns

2 tablespoons black peppercorns, peferably Tellichery

1 teaspoon coarse sea salt

6 large sprigs fresh thyme, washed and dried

1 cup extra-virgin olive oil

1. Combine 1 tablespoon of the pink peppercorns and 1 tablespoon of the black peppercorns in a clean bottle.

2. Crush the remaining peppercorns with the salt, and add to the bottle. Add the thyme, and pour the olive oil into the bottle. Cap the bottle and place it in a cool, dark place to age for 6 weeks before using.

Variation: Slit a small dried hot red pepper and add it to the bottle for a hotter version of the recipe.

3 medium eggplants

Red wine vinegar

Coarse sea salt

¼ cup diced red bell peppers

¼ cup diced green bell peppers

¼ cup diced yellow bell peppers

Fresh basil leaves

Freshly ground black pepper to taste

Extra-virgin olive oil

3 to 4 sterilized pint jars

1. Wash and dry the eggplants, remove the stems, and cut the eggplants into ¼-inch rounds. Place in a deep nonmetal bowl and cover with vinegar. Place a double layer of wax paper over the eggplants and place a bowl filled with water on top to keep the eggplants submerged. Let marinate at room temperature for 2 days.

2. Squeeze the vinegar out of the eggplants with your hands and layer the slices in the sterilized jars, sprinkling each layer with ½ teaspoon coarse salt. Divide the bell peppers among the jars. Add 1 or 2 basil leaves and pepper to taste to each jar. When the jars are three-quarters full, add olive oil to cover the eggplant mixture, pushing down on it with a wooden spoon to submerge it. Top off each jar with oil before capping it. Let the jars sit overnight at room temperature.

3. If the eggplant has absorbed some of the oil and the slices are poking through the oil, add more oil to cover them completely. Cap again and let sit overnight.

4. Add more oil to the jars if necessary so that the eggplant is fully submerged under the oil. Cap the jars, put them in a very cool place, and let ripen for 6 weeks before using them. Refrigerate after opening.

Variation: To serve as an antipasto, cut thick slices of good country bread or Pane Rustico (page 96), place the slices on a baking sheet, and toast in a preheated 400°F oven for about 10 min-

Melanzane sott' Olio

Eggplant Preserved in Olive Oil

❧

Preserving raw eggplant in olive oil is a very old tradition. Make this any time of year, since eggplants are available year-round, or, if you have a garden, preserve the bumper crop. When guests drop in, I serve this over toasted slices of good bread. Make sure to top off the jars with olive oil to ensure the eggplants' long shelf life.

❧

Makes 3 to 4 pints

utes, or until light golden brown. Remove the slices to individual serving dishes, and rub the slices with whole peeled garlic cloves. Layer a few of the eggplant slices on each slice of bread and drizzle on a little of the oil from the eggplant jar.

Note: Do not cut corners with this recipe. Sterilized jars and caps are a must, as are the freshest ingredients.

Pomodori Secchi

DRIED TOMATOES

When plum tomatoes are in season, I know that winter is not far behind. So I gather up what we can't possibly eat and dry them. Some I put in olive oil (see page 312), others I toss into small freezer bags and use during the long winter months for stews, soups, sauces, and sformati *like the Rice and Spinach Mold on page 68.*

Unblemished ripe plum tomatoes

1. Wash and dry the tomatoes and cut them in half lengthwise. Place cut sides down on the racks of a dehydrator and dry according to the manufacturer's instructions. Or place them cut sides down on wire racks on cookie sheets, place in a 200°F oven, and dry until the tomatoes have the texture of dried apricots. Depending on the size of the tomatoes, this may take a day or even longer.

2. Place the dried tomatoes in Ziploc freezer bags and freeze. They will keep for up to a year.

Note: Cherry tomatoes can also be dried and frozen using the same method.

1 tablespoon dried oregano

1 teaspoon fine sea salt

1 teaspoon red pepper flakes

¼ teaspoon freshly ground black pepper

½ pound (2 balls) fresh mozzarella (fior di latte), drained and patted dry

1 teaspoon black peppercorns

1 large bay leaf

Extra-virgin olive oil

Sterilized 12-ounce jar

1. Mix the oregano, salt, red pepper flakes, and ground pepper together on a piece of wax paper.

2. Roll each mozzarella ball in the oregano mixture, patting the seasonings evenly onto the balls. Place the balls in the sterilized jar. Add the peppercorns and bay leaf. Fill the jar with olive oil, completely covering the cheese. Cap the jar and let marinate at room temperature for 2 days. Then store in the refrigerator for up to 1 week. Bring the cheese to room temperature before using.

Variation: Add ¼ cup diced sweet red or yellow bell peppers to the jar.

Mozzarella Marinata

Marinated Mozzarella

I always eye those marinated fior di latte (fresh mozzarella balls) in gallon-size glass jars in specialty food shops, thinking to myself how easy it would be to make them at home. Fresh mozzarella balls the size of small oranges are readily available, but the smaller bocconcini are ideal for this recipe. Try topping thick toasted slices of Carmelo's Sicilian Bread (page 99) with the cheese or team it with slices of ripe plum tomatoes. Give a jar as a special gift. Make sure the cheese is completely covered with oil, and replenish the oil when necessary. Use the oil in cooking and on salads.

Makes 1½ cups

Pomodori Secchi Sott' Olio

Dried Tomatoes in Olive Oil

❦

Be sure to put up some jars of these dried tomatoes in olive oil when ripe plum tomatoes are at their peak. In the dead of winter, you'll thank yourself. They make a most welcome culinary gift as well. You can use a dehydrator for the drying process or dry the tomatoes on cookie racks in a warm oven. Cherry tomatoes can also be dried in the same way. Use the tomatoes in salads, or serve atop slices of toasted Carmelo's Sicilian Bread (page 99) for a classic antipasto.

❦

Makes 3 cups

14 unblemished, meaty plum tomatoes

3 cups red wine vinegar

8 fresh basil leaves

3 tablespoons capers in brine, drained

2 tablespoons black peppercorns

2 teaspoons fine sea salt

2 to 2 1/2 cups extra-virgin olive oil

2 sterilized 12-ounce jars

1. Wash and dry the tomatoes. Core and cut them lengthwise in half.

2. Place the tomatoes cut sides down in a dehydrator and dry according to the manufacturer's instructions. Or place cut sides down on wire racks on baking sheets, place in a 225°F oven, and let dry until they have the texture of dried apricots. This may take a day or longer, depending on the size of the tomatoes.

3. Pour the wine vinegar into a large noncorrosive saucepan and bring to a boil. Add the tomatoes and blanch them for 1 minute. Remove the tomatoes with a slotted spoon, and drain well.

4. Layer the tomatoes into the sterilized jars, adding half the basil, capers, peppercorns, and salt to each jar. Slowly pour the olive oil into the jars, pressing down on the tomatoes slightly with a wooden spoon. Make sure the tomatoes are completely submerged under the oil at all times, or they will be exposed to the air and potential bacteria. Cap the jars and place them in a cool spot overnight.

5. Add more oil to the jars if the tomatoes are poking out of the oil. Check the jars 2 or 3 more times, adding more oil if necessary.

6. Cap the jars and store them in a cool place for 6 weeks before using. Refrigerate after opening, and bring the tomatoes to room temperature before serving.

Small zucchini and/or yellow squash, washed, dried,
   and thinly sliced

Dried oregano

Fine sea salt

Finely ground cayenne pepper

1. Place the zucchini and yellow squash slices on the racks of a dehydrator and dry according to the manufacturer's directions until the chips are crisp. Or place the slices on wire racks on cookie sheets, place in a 175°F oven, and dry, rotating the sheets occasionally, until crisp. Drying times vary, depending on the dehydrator or oven and the size of the slices, but may take anywhere from 1 to 2 days.

2. Layer the chips in clean jars, sprinkling the layers with salt, oregano, and cayenne to taste. Cap the jars and shake to distribute the seasonings. These will keep for several months in a cool dark place.

3. Eat them like potato chips!

Zucchine Secche

Dried Zucchini Chips

This recipe was hatched from desperation when my zucchini plants, which seemed to have nine lives, conquered my garden. This is a great way to use an overabundance, and it makes a healthful snack. Pick the zucchini when it is about six inches long. Take care to dry the slices well, until they are as crisp as potato chips, or they may mold.

Salsa di Pomodori Secchi

Dried Tomato Sauce

🌶

Use your homemade dried tomatoes or those sold in some supermarkets and specialty stores to make this simple sauce. This is my sauce of choice for a fast pasta dinner, accompanied by bread, a green salad, and poached Pears with Mint (page 204) for dessert.

The sauce is very concentrated and one cup is enough to dress a pound and a half of rigatoni or other short macaroni. Package it in a decorative jar along with a box of your favorite pasta for a memorable gift.

🌶

Makes about 1 cup

¼ cup olive oil, plus more as needed
1 large clove garlic, minced
4 anchovies in olive oil, drained and chopped
1 tablespoon capers packed in salt, rinsed
1 cup Dried Tomatoes in Olive Oil (page 312)
¼ cup dry red wine
Coarsely ground black pepper to taste

1. In a skillet, heat the olive oil. Add the garlic and anchovies and stir with a wooden spoon until the anchovies dissolve. Add the capers, tomatoes, and wine and simmer for about 2 minutes, stirring often, until slightly reduced.

2. Transfer to a food processor and pulse until the tomatoes are coarsely chopped. Add the pepper.

3. Let the sauce cool, then put it into a jar. Pour just enough extra-virgin olive oil over the surface of the sauce to cover it. Cap and refrigerate for up to 4 weeks.

4. To serve, heat the sauce in a saucepan over low heat. Toss with cooked rigatoni, shells, or other short pasta, and pass freshly grated Parmigiano-Reggiano cheese for sprinkling.

½ pound (2 sticks) unsalted butter, at room temperature

3 large cloves garlic, peeled

1½ cups packed flat-leaf parsley leaves

Fine sea salt and coarsely ground black pepper to taste

1 to 2 tablespoons extra-virgin olive oil

1. Place all the ingredients except the olive oil in a food processor or blender and pulse to make a smooth paste. With the motor running, drizzle in just enough olive oil to make a smooth but not too liquid sauce.

2. Spoon the sauce into clean jars, cap and refrigerate until needed. The sauce will keep for 2 to 5 weeks.

3. To serve, heat the sauce over medium heat until hot.

Salsa di Prezzemolo

Parsley Sauce

❦

When you need a quick hostess gift, make this elegant, eye-appealing parsley sauce. Delicious over grilled fish, scaloppine of veal, or pork, it is also the perfect cover for fettuccine, rice, or cooked vegetables such as zucchini and carrots or fresh summer corn. It will keep in the refrigerator for several weeks.

❦

Makes about 2 cups

Caponata

Eggplant Salad

❧

The word caponata *has no exact translation. It is sort of an eggplant appetizer salad, with an* agrodolce *(sweet-and-sour) taste. It is best to use small eggplants. This recipe makes a lot, but the caponata can be refrigerated for several weeks or frozen. Give a jar with a loaf of* Pane Rustico *(page 96).*

❧

Makes about 9½ cups

8 small eggplants, 4 to 5 inches long, cut into 1-inch chunks
Coarse salt
1½ cups water
1¼ thinly sliced celery (2 ribs)
About 1½ cups peanut oil
½ cup olive oil
4 medium onions, thinly sliced (3½ cups)
1 cup tomato paste
⅔ cup red wine vinegar
1 cup chopped pitted Sicilian olives in brine
½ cup capers in vinegar, drained
½ cup sugar
2 teaspoons unsweetened cocoa
Fine sea salt and freshly ground black pepper to taste

1. Place the eggplant in a colander, sprinkle with coarse salt, and let sweat in the sink or on a plate for 1 hour. Rinse and dry well.

2. In a small saucepan, bring the water to a boil. Add the celery and cook for 3 to 4 minutes. Drain the celery, reserving the water, and set aside.

3. In a large skillet, heat ¾ cup peanut oil to 375°F. Add half the eggplant and fry until softened and lightly browned, about 12 to 15 minutes. Remove to brown paper to drain. Repeat with the remaining eggplant, adding more peanut oil as necessary. Drain off the peanut oil.

4. In the same frying pan, heat the olive oil over medium-high heat. Add the onions and sauté until soft, about 10 minutes. Lower the heat to medium, add the tomato paste, reserved celery water, the vinegar, olives, capers, sugar, and cocoa, and mix well. Let simmer for about 5 minutes. Add the eggplant and celery, stir well, and let simmer for about 10 minutes. Add the salt and pepper.

5. Spoon the caponata into clean jars, cap, and refrigerate or freeze. (If freezing, be sure to allow room for expansion in the jars.) Serve at room temperature.

1 teaspoon active dry yeast

2 cups warm (110° to 115°F) water

4 to 4 1/2 cups unbleached all-purpose flour

1/4 teaspoon fine sea salt

1 tablespoon plus 1 teaspoon olive oil

1/4 pound prosciutto, diced

3 tablespoons fresh rosemary leaves

Sesame seeds for sprinkling

Coarse sea salt for sprinkling

1. In a large bowl, dissolve the yeast in 1/2 cup of the warm water. Cover the bowl and let the yeast proof for about 10 minutes, until foamy.

2. Stir the remaining 1 1/2 cups water into the yeast. Gradually add 4 cups flour along with the salt. Mix with your hands until a ball of dough is formed, adding flour as needed.

3. On a floured surface, knead the dough until smooth. Oil a large bowl with olive oil, add the dough, and turn to coat. Cover the bowl with plastic wrap and place in a warm place to rise for 1 hour, or until doubled in size.

4. Preheat the oven to 375°F. Lightly grease two cookie sheets. In a skillet, heat the oil and brown the prosciutto until it is just crisp. Remove the prosciutto to a dish.

5. Punch down the dough. On a floured surface, flatten the dough slightly with your hands. Sprinkle on the prosciutto and rosemary, and work them into the dough, until evenly distributed.

6. Divide the dough into 30 pieces about the size of large eggs. Roll each piece under the palms of your hands into a 12-inch-long rope and place the grissini on the cookie sheets, spacing them about 1 inch apart. Brush the tops of the grissini with water, then sprinkle with the sesame seeds and salt.

7. Bake for 25 to 30 minutes, or until nicely browned. Remove to wire racks to cool.

Grissini al Prosciutto e Rosmarino

Prosciutto and Rosemary Breadsticks

Tall, thin, crisp breadsticks towering in a country crock are perfect for an informal Italian buffet or small dinner party. Throughout Italy, diners munch on grissini while perusing the menu in ristoranti and trattorie. Most grissini are plain, but I have added crisp sautéed prosciutto and fresh rosemary to this version. These can be made ahead and frozen. Stand them up in a pretty vase and tie with a ribbon to give as a gift.

Makes 2 1/2 dozen

Farfalle di Due Colori

Two-Color Butterflies

❧

For a special-occasion first course, try this combination of plain and beet-flavored farfalle, "butterflies" or "bow ties." Making them requires some time, but the magenta- and golden-colored pasta can be dried and stored for up to a year. Presented in a pretty wide-mouthed jar, this pasta makes a special gift. Some of the beet color tends to leach out in the cooking process, so I add a touch of white vinegar to the pasta water to help minimize the color loss. Melted butter is all the sauce these farfalle need.

❧

Makes about 8 dozen

PLAIN PASTA

About 2 cups unbleached all-purpose flour

⅛ teaspoon fine sea salt

3 large eggs

1 teaspoon olive oil

BEET PASTA

2 to 2½ cups unbleached all-purpose flour

⅛ teaspoon fine sea salt

2½ tablespoons pureed, cooked beets (about 1 small)

2 large eggs

1 teaspoon olive oil

1. For the plain pasta, combine the flour and salt and mound on a work surface. Make a well in the center of the flour and add the eggs and olive oil. Using a fork, beat the eggs and oil, then begin incorporating the flour from the inside walls of the well. When the dough becomes too difficult to mix with the fork, use your hands to make a soft dough, adding flour if needed. Then knead the dough until it is smooth and no longer sticky. Place a bowl over the dough on a floured surface and let rest for 10 minutes.

2. To make the beet pasta, follow the same procedure, adding the beets to the egg mixture and mixing well before beginning to incorporate the flour. Cover the dough and let rest on a floured surface for 10 minutes.

3. Divide each dough into 8 balls about 1 inch in diameter. Work with 2 balls of each type at a time, keeping the rest covered. On a floured surface, line 4 balls of dough up in a row, alternating the colors. With a rolling pin, roll over the balls to flatten them into a sheet of dough about 7 inches long and 5 inches wide. Run the dough through a pasta machine set to the thinnest setting. Trim the ends of the sheet. Using a pastry wheel, cut the sheets crosswise into strips, then cut each strip into 2-inch lengths. Pinch the center of each piece to form a bow tie, and place on clean towels.

4. To store, let the bow ties dry, uncovered, on the towels for at least a day, or until they are brittle. Store in jars or plastic containers for up to a year.

5. To cook pasta to serve 6, bring 4 quarts of salted water to a boil in a large pot. Add 1 tablespoon white cider vinegar and 4 dozen bow ties. Cook until al dente, about 1 minute if fresh, 3 to 4 minutes if dried. Carefully drain in a colander. Toss with melted butter, sprinkle with freshly grated Parmigiano-Reggiano cheese, and a little freshly cracked black pepper, and serve.

1¹/₂ pounds ripe but firm Bing cherries with stems

1 cup sugar

1 vanilla bean, cut in half

2¹/₂ cups vodka

1. Wash and dry the cherries; do not remove the stems. With a nut pick or a sharp needle, prick each cherry in several places.

2. Place the cherries in two 20-ounce bottles or jars. Divide the sugar, vanilla bean, and vodka between the bottles. Cap the bottles and shake a few times to dissolve the sugar. Store in a cool dark place for 6 months before using, shaking the bottles from time to time.

3. To serve, pour the vodka over ice and add a few cherries for garnish.

Ciliegie in Vodka

Cherries in Vodka

❧

The Romans preserved cherries in honey. I preserve them in spirits to make the most attractive gift. I use wine-red Bing cherries for this refreshing vodka drink.

❧

Makes two 20-ounce bottles

Liquore di Arancia

Orange Liqueur

❧

Many Italian desserts, especially cakes, feature the intense flavor of a liqueur. I am partial to orange liqueur. Not only a delicious baking ingredient, it is a very soothing after-dinner drink. Give it in a handsome bottle as a hostess gift. The liqueur needs at least eight months to age and mellow. Substitute lemons for oranges to make lemon liqueur.

❧

Makes about 2 quarts

5 medium navel oranges, washed and dried

1 ³/₄ cups sugar

1 ¹/₂ quarts vodka

Zest of 1 lemon

One 6-inch cinnamon stick (or two 3-inch sticks)

12 whole cloves

2 allspice berries

1. With a wooden skewer, poke holes all over each orange. Place the oranges in a clean wide-mouth gallon-size jar and add the sugar and vodka. Cap the jar and shake well to dissolve the sugar. Add all the remaining ingredients and shake the jar again.

2. Store in a cool place, shaking the jar every few weeks, for at least 8 months or up to 1 year.

3. When ready to use, pour the liqueur into a cheesecloth-lined strainer set over a deep bowl. Squeeze each whole orange over the strainer. Discard the oranges, cinnamon stick, lemon zest, cloves, and allspice. Pour the liqueur into decorative bottles and cap them.

2 tablespoons vegetable oil

3 cups blanched whole almonds

3 tablespoons water

1 1/2 cups sugar

3 tablespoons unsalted butter

3 tablespoons fresh lemon juice

1. Brush a marble slab or cookie sheet with the oil. Place all the remaining ingredients in a heavy nonstick saucepan and bring to a boil over medium heat, stirring constantly with a wooden spoon. Cook, stirring, for about 15 minutes, or until the syrup has turned a deep caramel color and is very foamy; it should register 300°F on a candy thermometer.

2. Immediately pour the mixture out onto the oiled slab or cookie sheet, spreading it evenly with the spoon. Let cool completely.

3. Cut the croccante into rough 1-inch pieces with a heavy knife. Store in airtight jars.

Croccante

ALMOND CRUNCH

Croccante, which means cracklings, reminds me of peanut brittle, except that this sweet confection is made from almonds or hazelnuts. I usually buy it at street fairs and outdoor markets in Italy. Croccante is great party food. For gift giving, pile it into a fancy candy dish or decorative jar.

Makes about 3 dozen

I Fichi Secchi Ripieni

Stuffed Dried Figs

❧

In the rustic town of Grottaglie, in the region of Puglia, I ate the most delicious stuffed and roasted dried figs I had ever tasted. I saw them being baked in a panificio right along with the daily breads.

These figs are an unusual addition to the holiday table and make a unique Christmas gift from the kitchen.

❧

Dried Calimyrna figs
Whole almonds

1. Preheat the oven to 350°F. With a knife, cut down from the stem top of each fig just to, but not through, the bottom, so that the fig can be opened like a book.

2. Place an almond in the right side of one fig, then place an almond in the left side of another fig, and place one fig on top of the other, like a sandwich. Press on the figs lightly to seal them, and place on an ungreased baking sheet. Repeat with the remaining figs and almonds.

3. Bake, turning once for about 10 minutes, or until slightly browned. Let cool.

4. To give as gift, place the figs in a single layer in a gift box, cover with cellophane, and tie the box with a bow.

Chi è San Nicola?

Who Is Saint Nicholas?

San Nicola Pastara di Licia was the bishop of Myra in Asia Minor. Today he is known to children all over the world as Saint Nicholas, Father Christmas, or Santa Claus. He was a black man born in Turkey, and the veneration of the saint and his cult dates back to 1087, when some sixty-two sailors from Bari, in the region of Puglia, stole the saint's bones from Myra and took them back to their home. Although his traditional feast day is December 6, Italians celebrate on May 8, a more seasonably mild time of the year.

The saint's reputation for generosity and compassion centers around the legend of three daughters of a poor man, who were prostitutes. Hearing about this, San Nicola came to the house three times and tossed a bag of gold through the window, providing an adequate dowry for each of the daughters to enter into an honorable marriage. From this legend we have our modern-day Saint Nicholas, who comes bearing gifts.

In North America, on December 5, the feast of Saint Nicholas, stockings are hung by the mantel or door in anticipation of a visit from Saint Nicholas. I always took for granted the presents he left — the bright orange, pieces of torrone, and almonds; they seemed so commonplace. I was unaware of their symbolism until I went to Puglia, where oranges, torrone, and almonds are, among other things, gifts from the land.

I met up with his spirit in the Church of San Nicola in Bari, built in 1089, where the Saint's remains rest in the crypt of the church. In the somber atmosphere, one is reminded of the many miracles San Nicola performed, particularly by gold-and-silver-tooled depiction of the rescue of a boatful of people from a vicious storm at sea near Bari.

San Nicola is the patron saint of Bari, but devotion to him is widespread throughout Italy and much of Europe, with more than twelve hundred churches bearing his name in Italy alone.

Among the striking curiosities of the church in Bari, also seen in others in the regions of Abruzzo and Puglia, are the carved stone animals flanking either side of the entrance to the church. Cows guard the entrance, protecting all who worship from the devil's entry, but there are also ferocious falcons, silently roaring lions, swirling snakes entwining pillars, and birds of prey all ready to keep evil away.

Dolce Antica Calabrese

Calabrian Christmas Cake

❧

This unusual Christmas cake, made from yeast dough and filled with nuts, raisins, spices, and honey, has many names, ranging from pittenguise to dolce antica. Said to have originated in Calabria, the rosette-shaped cake must be made at least two months before it is eaten. This recipe will make four to five small round cakes that are the perfect size for gift giving. Start the process early in the day, and have all the ingredients at room temperature.

❧

Makes 4 to 5 small cakes

DOUGH

4 large eggs, at room temperature

¹/₂ teaspoon salt

¹/₂ cup white wine

¹/₂ cup vegetable oil

¹/₂ cup sugar

1 teaspoon active dry yeast

5 to 6 cups unbleached all-purpose flour

FILLING

4 ¹/₂ cups raisins

3 ¹/₂ cups walnut pieces

1 ³/₄ cup honey

1 teaspoon ground cinnamon

1 teaspoon ground cloves

About 2 tablespoons vegetable oil

4 to 5 tablespoons sugar

Parchment paper

1. In a large bowl, mix together the eggs, salt, wine, oil, sugar, and yeast. Cover and let stand for 10 minutes.

2. Add the flour 1 cup at a time, mixing with your hands until a soft ball of dough is formed. Knead the dough on a floured surface until it is smooth and no longer sticky, adding flour as necessary.

3. Place the dough in an oiled bowl, cover tightly with plastic wrap, and let rise in a warm place for 1 hour, or until doubled in size.

4. Line two cookie sheets with parchment paper. In a medium bowl, mix together the raisins, walnuts, 1 cup of the honey, cinnamon, and cloves. Set aside.

5. Punch down the dough and knead it for a few minutes on a floured surface. Take a piece of dough the size of a medium orange and roll it out on a floured surface, into a 9-inch circle. Place the circle on one of the cookie sheets and brush the dough lightly with vegetable oil. Sprinkle evenly with 1 tablespoon of the sugar.

6. Take a second piece of dough the size of a large orange and roll it into a 20 by 8-inch rectangle. Cut the rectangle crosswise into eight 2½-inch-wide strips. Spread about 2 tablespoons of the filling mixture evenly down the center of each strip. Starting at a short end, roll each strip up tightly like a jelly roll. Place them close together on top of the circle of dough, leaving a 1-inch border around the outside edge of the circle.

7. Brush the outside edge of the circle with water. Bring the edge of the circle up around the rolled strips, and tie the cake loosely with string. Continue with the remaining dough to make 3 or 4 more cakes. Cover and let the cakes rise for 4 hours, or overnight, in a warm place. They will rise only slightly.

8. Preheat the oven to 275°F. Brush each cake with a little vegetable oil, and drizzle 2 tablespoons of the remaining honey over the top of each cake. Bake the cakes for about 45 minutes, or until they are light golden in color. As they bake, baste the cakes occasionally with any drippings. Remove the cakes immediately to a cooling rack set on a piece of wax paper under it. Cool completely.

9. Wrap each cake in plastic wrap, then in aluminum foil, and store in airtight tins. After about a week, turn the cake tins upside down, then reverse the cakes again to distribute the honey collected on the bottom of the tins. These are best eaten at Christmas and should not be stored for long after the holiday.

10. Give as a gift in a decorative tin tied with a bow, along with the recipe.

Salsa di Frutta Secca

Dried Fruit Sauce

❦

Dried fruits make an intense sauce that is perfect with chicken, roast pork, and game. In this spicy rendition, mixed dried fruits are slowly simmered to produce a thick tangy sauce that is also a good topping for a plain cake.

❦

Makes 4 ½ cups

12-ounces mixed dried fruits

2 ounces dried apple slices

2 ripe pears, cored and diced

3 cups water

½ cup sugar

1 teaspoon ground cloves

1 teaspoon ground cinnamon

1 teaspoon ground allspice

1. Place the mixed fruit, apple slices, and pears in a saucepan. Add the water and bring to a boil over medium heat. Lower the heat and simmer, covered, for 10 minutes.

2. Add the sugar, cloves, cinnamon, and allspice and stir well. Cover and simmer for 15 minutes, or until the dried fruits are soft and the sauce has thickened. Remove from the heat and let cool. Refrigerate the sauce until ready to use.

3. To give as a gift, pour the sauce into decorative jars. Attach a copy of the recipe to each jar. To serve, reheat over low heat.

1 pound slivered blanched almonds

3 cups confectioners' sugar

2 large egg whites

2 tablespoons water

1 teaspoon almond extract

Cornstarch for dusting

1. Grind the almonds to a powder in a food processor or blender. Add the sugar and blend well. With the motor running, add the remaining ingredients, and process, until a smooth paste is formed. Transfer the paste to clean jars and refrigerate.

2. To give as gifts, add a decorative label to each jar and tie a ribbon around the jar.

To make molded marzipan fruits, vegetables, or free-form designs, roll small amounts of the paste on a work surface lightly dusted with cornstarch. Form the pieces into apples, lemon slices, watermelon slices, figs, tomatoes, or whatever else comes to mind. Let the pieces dry on wire racks for a day.

To paint, dissolve 1 package (1/220 ounce) powdered saffron in 2 tablespoons boiling water. Stir to blend. Using a brush, paint the surface of the shapes (this is your base coat), and let dry again on racks for a day.

Using food coloring or vegetable-based food dyes, paint the pieces using appropriate colors. Let dry. The pieces will last almost indefinitely.

Pasta Reale

Almond Paste

❧

When the Arabs arrived in Sicily in the ninth century, they introduced, among other things, the cultivation of sugarcane. One wonderful result of this was pasta reale (royal paste). Cloistered nuns made a sweet dough from the paste which was turned into elegant pastry confections. The dough was used as a filling for many types of desserts, and it was also molded by hand into realistic-looking fruits and vegetables. Today, the dough is sometimes pressed into plaster molds to make the shapes, which are then painted with vegetable dyes, elevating them into works of art. These pieces will last a long time and they are used as decorations for desserts, to give as gifts, or just to eat.

❧

Makes 1³⁄₄ pounds

Vaniglia Casalinga

Homemade Vanilla Extract

❧

Vanilla is a baking staple in Italy, where it is used to flavor cakes, cookies, pastry creams, puddings, and sweet breads. Making your own vanilla extract is both easy and economical. It begins with the vanilla bean, the seedpod of the orchid flower, and alcohol.

❧

Makes 1 cup

1 vanilla bean, coarsely chopped
1 cup brandy or dark rum

1. Put the vanilla bean in a clean jar and cover with the brandy or rum. Cap the jar and store in a cool, dark place for at least 6 weeks to let the flavor develop.

2. Strain the vanilla extract through a cheesecloth-lined strainer and into a decorative jar. Give as a gift with a recipe that uses vanilla.

3 cups sugar

1 vanilla bean

1. Pour the sugar into a bowl. With a small knife, split the vanilla bean lengthwise. Use the point of the knife to scrape the tiny seeds from the pod into the sugar. Stir to blend in the seeds. Cut the vanilla pod into 3 equal pieces.

2. Pour the sugar into three ½-pint jars. Push a piece of the vanilla pod down into the sugar in each jar. (Or put the sugar and pod into 1 large jar for your everyday use.) Cap the jars and shake once or twice. Store in a cool place. The sugar will be ready to use in about 2 weeks.

3. To give as a gift, tie a ribbon around a jar and give it with something from your kitchen made with vanilla sugar.

Zucchero Vaniglinato

Vanilla Sugar

I always have vanilla-flavored sugar on hand. It adds just the intensity of vanilla taste that I like to cakes, fruit desserts, and holiday breads. I have started taking it to friends in Italy, who think this is such a unique gift, as they always buy zucchero vaniglinato in small ready-to-use packets. Vanilla beans can be found in gourmet shops and through Mail-Order Sources (see page 331).

Makes 3 cups

A & J Distributors
236 Hanover Street
Boston, Massachusetts 02113
617–523–8490
Italian kitchen equipment and
pasta machines

Balducci's
424 Sixth Avenue
New York, New York 10011
800–247–2450
Italian food products

Bridge Kitchenware
214 East 52nd Street
New York, New York 10022
212–688–4220
Ravioli forms and other
kitchenware; catalog

Caffe D'Arte
719 South Myrtle Street
Seattle, Washington 98108
206–762–4381
Espresso, decaf espresso, and
fine blended gourmet coffees;
catalog

Crate & Barrel
140 Faneuil Hall Marketplace
Boston, Massachusetts 02109
800–323–5461
Italian cooking gadgets and
dishes

Dairy Fresh Candies
P.O. Box 7456
57 Salem Street
Boston, Massachusetts 02113
800–336–5536
Citron, almonds, baking
chocolate, Italian biscotti,
Alchermes extracts, and dried
fruits; catalog

Dean & DeLuca
560 Broadway
New York, New York 10012
212–431–1691
Porcini mushrooms, olives,
olive oil, pasta, and rice

Draeger's Supermarkets, Inc.
P.O. Box C
Menlo Park, California 94026
800–642–9463
Full line of imported olive oil,
cheeses, salame, olives, choco-
lates, baking supplies, dishes,
and cookware.

Fante's
1006 South 9th Street
Philadelphia, Pennsylvania 19147
800–878–5557
Italian cooking equipment,
gourmet espresso coffees,
cookbooks, and baking
equipment; catalog

Joe Pace and Son Grocer
42 Cross Street
Boston, Massachusetts 02113
617–227–9673
Prosciutto, salame, cheeses,
breads, pasta, and many other
imported Italian foods

John Volpi and Company, Inc.
5254 Daggett Avenue
St. Louis, Missouri 63110
800–288–3439
Full line of regional salame,
non-heat-treated prosciutto,
pancetta, and other cured
meats

Mail-Order Sources

King Arthur Flour Baker's
Catalogue
P.O. Box 1010
Norwich, Vermont 05055
800–827–6836
Unbleached flours, dried yeast,
baking supplies, and malt
extract

Le Marche Seeds International
P.O. Box 566
Dixon, California 95620
Italian seeds

Paprikas Weiss
1572 Second Avenue
New York, New York 10028
212–288–6117
Parchment paper, baking
chocolate, vanilla beans, candied citrus peel, and nuts

Penzeys, Ltd.
P.O. Box 1448
Waukesha, Wisconsin 53187
414–574–0277
Dried lemon and orange peel,
saffron, and a wide variety of
spices; catalog

Previn Incorporated
2044 Rittenhouse Square
Philadelphia, Pennsylvania 19103
215–985–1996
Baking and candy-making
equipment

Providence Cheese and
Provisions Company
Atwells Avenue
Federal Hill
Providence, Rhode Island 02902
401–421–5653
Italian cheeses

Shepard's Garden Seeds
30 Irene Street
Torrington, Connecticuit 06790
203–482–3638
Italian seeds

Sunburst Bottle Company
7001R Sunburst Way
Citrus Heights, California 95621
Herb and spice jars, vinegar
and oil bottles, cellophane bags

Sur la Table
84 Pine Street
Pike Place Farmer's Market
Seattle, Washington 98101
800–243–0852
A complete line of baking
equipment including pastry
bags, biscuit cutters, wedding
cake pans, rolling pins, and
cannoli forms

Williams-Sonoma
P.O. Box 7456
San Francisco, California 94120
415–421–4242
Specialty cooking equipment

Zabar's
2245 Broadway
New York, New York 10024
212–787–2000
Kitchenware and gourmet food
items; catalog

Anderson, Burton. *Treasures of the Italian Table*. New York: William Morrow, 1994.

Barolini, Helen. *Festa: Recipes and Recollections of Italian Holidays*. New York: Harcourt Brace Jovanovich, 1988.

Buttita, Antonio, and Antonio Cusumano. *Pane e Festa: Tradizioni in Sicilia*. Palermo: Edizione Guida, 1991.

David, Elizabeth. *Italian Food*. New York: Harper & Row, 1963.

Farmer, David H. *Oxford Dictionary of Saints*. Oxford: Clarendon Press, 1978.

Gracosa, Ilaria Gozzini. *A Taste of Ancient Rome*. Chicago: University of Chicago Press, 1992.

Lampedusa, Giuseppe Tomasi. *Il Gattopardo*. Giangiamcomo Feltrinelli, Editore, 1958.

Lanza, Anna Tasca. *The Heart of Sicily*. New York: Clarkson Potter, 1993.

Lissone, Mariani. *A Tavola Come una Volta*. 1992.

Malpezzi, Frances M., and William Clements. *Italian-American Folklore*. Little Rock, Arkansas: August House, 1992.

Mazzoni, Alberto, ed. *L'Arte Della Cucina di Don Felice Libera*. Bologna: Arnaldo Forni, Editore, 1984.

Pellegrini, Angelo. *The Unprejudiced Palate*. New York: Macmillan Company, 1948.

Prezzolini, Giuseppe. *Spaghetti Dinner*. New York: Abelard Schuman, 1955.

Riley, Gillian. *Renaissance Recipes*. California: Pomegranate Artbooks, 1993.

Sansoni, G. C. *Cucina, Enciclopedie Pratiche*. Florence, 1966.

Simeti, Mary Taylor. *Pomp and Sustenance: Twenty-Five Centuries of Sicilian Food*. New York: Alfred A. Knopf, 1989.

Visser, Margaret. *The Rituals of Dinner*. New York: Grove Weidenfeld, 1991.

Bibliography